UNDER AN AFRICAN SUN

MEMORIES OF A JOURNEY
HITCH-HIKING ACROSS AFRICA
IN THE 1970S

UNDER AN AFRICAN SUN

MEMORIES OF A JOURNEY HITCH-HIKING ACROSS AFRICA IN THE 1970S

DOUG ANDERSON

Under an African Sun:
Memories of a Journey Hitch-Hiking Across Africa in the 1970s
Doug Anderson

Published by Aspect Design 2010
Malvern, Worcestershire, United Kingdom
Reprinted 2011

Designed and Printed by Aspect Design
89 Newtown Road, Malvern, Worcs. WR14 1PD
United Kingdom
Tel: 01684 561567
E-mail: books@aspect-design.net
www.aspect-design.net

All Rights Reserved.
Copyright © 2010 Douglas Anderson

Douglas Anderson has asserted his moral right
to be identified as the author of this work.

The right of Douglas Anderson to be identified as the author
of this work has been asserted in accordance with
Section 77 of the Copyright, Designs and Patents Act 1988.

This book is sold subject to the condition that it shall not, by way of trade
or otherwise, be lent, resold, hired out or otherwise circulated without
the publisher's prior consent in any form of binding or cover other than
that in which it is published and without a similar condition including
this condition being imposed on the subsequent purchaser.

A copy of this book has been deposited with the British Library Board

Cover Design Copyright © 2010 Aspect Design
ISBN 978-1-905795-73-4

ACKNOWLEDGEMENTS

To the numerous parties who so kindly assisted me throughout my travels with information, lifts and accommodation spanning the full gambit from luxurious mansions in idyllic settings to rudimentary nomadic manyattas, each in their own way proving to be a veritable Ritz to this weary traveller.

A special thanks also goes to my sister, Sheila, for encouraging me to put pen to paper in the first place and then spending endless hours rectifying the numerous spelling and grammatical errors I had liberally sprinkled throughout the text.

CONTENTS

Introduction .. … … … … … … … … … … … … … … *13*
Chapter 1 Where, When and How … … … … … … … *15*
Chapter 2 Across The Pond … … … … … … … … … *19*
Chapter 3 Back to Blighty.. … … … … … … … … … *27*
Chapter 4 The Inbetween Year … … … … … … … … *38*
Chapter 5 Sahara and Beyond … … … … … … … … *43*
Chapter 6 Farewell to the Landy . … … … … … … … *57*
Chapter 7 The Hitching Starts Here … … … … … … *65*
Chapter 8 Alone Again … … … … … … … … … … *77*
Chapter 9 Behind the Scenes . … … … … … … … … *89*
Chapter 10 A Taste of a Medieval Age … … … … … … *99*
Chapter 11 A Hiccup with my Passport . … … … … … *113*
Chapter 12 Kilimanjaro … … … … … … … … … … *125*
Chapter 13 Serengeti … … … … … … … … … … … *135*

Chapter 14	Jambo	*143*
Chapter 15	Mosi-oa-Tunya (The Falls)	*153*
Chapter 16	Nyasaland	*163*
Chapter 17	Okavango-Crocodile Country	*175*
Chapter 18	The Kalahari	*187*
Chapter 19	Towards the Equator Again	*197*
Chapter 20	South Africa at Last	*207*

PHOTOGRAPHS AND MAPS

Map of route through Europe I *18*

Map of route through Europe II *26*

Pamukkale, the 'Cotton Castle' *28*

Rock Tombs near Fethiye *29*

Traditional Romanian wedding procession *32*

Check Point Charlie *36*

Map of route through Morocco, Algeria and Niger *42*

Travellers rendezvous at El Golea *50*

Land Rover in full flight *51*

Our Tuareg visitor *52*

Emergency repair to front spring *53*

A dip in the desert *55*

Map of route through Niger, Nigeria, Cameroun and Chad *56*

Oops! *60*

Map of route through Chad, Central African Republic, Congo and Rwanda	*64*
The Presidential Palace at Bangui C.A.R.	*67*
Ferry across the River Uele	*69*
A pre-prepared tree trunk being hauled to the bridge	*71*
A section of the road to Buta	*72*
With my Pygmy friend	*73*
Map of route through Uganda, Kenya, Ethiopia and Eritrea	*76*
Nomadic homes on the barren Lake Rudolph landscape	*80*
Monolithic Stelae at Axum	*85*
Map of route through Ethiopia	*88*
Priests carrying their Arcs of the Covenant at Timkat	*93*
Emperor Haile Selassie with President Pompidou	*94*
Detail of an outer wall of one of the eleven churches at Lalibela	*95*
Monolithic church hewn from the solid rock at Lalibela	*95*
Map of route through Yemen	*98*
Typical Yemenis armed with jambiyas and guns	*102*
A couple of locals enjoying the pleasures of Qat	*106*
The Imam's Palace at Wadi Dhahr	*109*
Map of route through Djibouti and Ethiopia	*112*
The salt encrusted water's edge at Lake Assal	*114*
Map of route through Kenya and Tanzania	*124*
Surrounded by Samburu warriors	*127*
Kibo peak on Mount Kilimanjaro	*130*
Glacial formations inside the crater on Kilimanjaro	*132*
Map of route through Tanzania I	*134*
Feeding Lisa the orphaned cheetah cub	*138*

Elephant damage to a Baobab tree	*140*
Map of route through Tanzania II	*142*
Memorial to Stanley and Livingstone meeting at Ujiji 1871	*150*
Map of route through Zambia	*152*
Kuomboka barges	*156*
At the Victoria Falls	*158*
Map of route through Zambia and Malawi	*162*
The view from the verandah over the tea plantation to Mount Mulanje	*166*
The crude illicit still near Chiromo	*167*
Flimsy bridge over a gorge on Mount Mulanje	*168*
Map of route through Botswana and Rhodesia	*174*
Punting through the Okavango Swamps in a mokoro	*177*
The rudimentary dwellings of Bushmen	*180*
Part of the mysterious Zimbabwe ruins	*184*
Map of route through Rhodesia, Botswana and South West Africa	*186*
An example of a vast 'upside down' Baobab tree	*188*
A butter maker in full swing	*194*
Map of route through Angola and South West Africa	*196*
Local Cuanyama girls in Southern Angola	*198*
The Fish River Canyon	*203*
Map of route through South Africa and Swaziland	*206*
Dutch style architecture at Tulbagh	*211*
Sturdy stone built home high up in remote Lesotho	*214*

INTRODUCTION

Having spent over seven years travelling in Europe and Africa many events occurred which became indelibly printed into my memory and over the ensuing thirty plus years numerous occasions have arisen where an appropriate anecdote has been reeled out often to be met with the response 'You should write a book.'

Throughout my journey I kept an A4 size diary and always felt that that was enough and never gave the matter serious consideration despite much egging on from family and friends alike, however finding myself housebound awaiting a minor operation and snowed in into the bargain, the idea of putting pen to paper reared its head and after some brief scribbling I was encouraged to see the project through.

The book follows the route through Europe and Africa which included regular unplanned but rewarding detours and recounts many of the experiences both good and not so good which occurred along the way.

Much has changed geographically in the ensuing years but throughout I have referred to places and countries by the name that existed at the time of my travels and being an old fashioned Luddite I have used the imperial format for measurements.

CHAPTER 1

WHERE, WHEN AND HOW

Getting arrested in the remote depths of Ethiopia, climbing Kilimanjaro and camping out with crocodile hunters in the Okavanga swamps were not on the agenda when the embryonic idea of seeing some of the world that lay beyond our shores was first planted in my mind.

It all began at a New Year party seeing out the iconic swinging sixties decade. In attendance were several students from the local teacher's training college who were regaling us with their exploits of their summer travels through Iraq, Iran, Afghanistan, Pakistan and India, and whilst I was enthralled I was also aware that at the age of twenty-three I had never ventured beyond Britain's shores and there and then a plan to remedy that situation was born. A new decade and a new challenge.

Since leaving school I had been working in the buying department of Kay and Company, one of the largest mail order businesses in the UK, which had its HQ in Worcester and was a major employer from the city and the surrounding area. A group of us from Malvern who all started around the same time had been progressing through the system and a steady long-term future was there for the taking.

I thoroughly enjoyed my job but was aware that upward progression was not going to happen overnight and had developed the first tinges of restlessness, wondering what other opportunities lay beyond the safety net of steady employment. That question seemed to be answered in that eureka moment at the New Year revelries – ditch the job and see the world.

The mantra was simple to say, but where, when and how all needed answering, I was effectively starting with the proverbial blank sheet of paper. A tour round Europe quickly became established as the where, ASAP as the when and the how vote went to the only respectable means of travel for any discerning young traveller, a VW camper van.

To ensure that there was no turning back I handed in my notice when we returned to work after the festive break and set about finding a suitable camper van. Issues such as where to go were put on the back burner adopting the cavalier attitude that without a specific route flexibility would be key and would allow me to take advantage of any unscheduled opportunities should they arise. In hindsight this was to prove the best decision I made and one that stood me in good stead over the next seven years.

Whilst the route was therefore taken care of, finding a VW camper van was a very different story. After scouring the pages of Exchange and Mart and making numerous futile phone calls I noticed one parked outside a house in Malvern and plucked up the courage to knock on the door and ask if by any chance they would like to sell it. The initial response was mixed, yes from the lady of the house and no from her husband, there was obviously some negotiating required but after an hour or so I left as the proud new owner of a 1963 'splitty' and ever since then have been a firm believer in the maxim that if you don't ask you don't get.

It was now early April and with that hurdle out of the way it was simply a matter of finalising when we left. I say we because by then Pete Hellis a colleague of mine had decided that a trip abroad would make a welcome break from servicing aircraft, a mechanical background that was to prove invaluable as we trekked our way across the continent.

Within a week of buying the camper we had given it the once over, bought our supplies, bid farewell to families and were heading down to London to say a few further goodbyes and have a last pint or two of proper beer before embarking on the Southampton to Le Havre ferry.

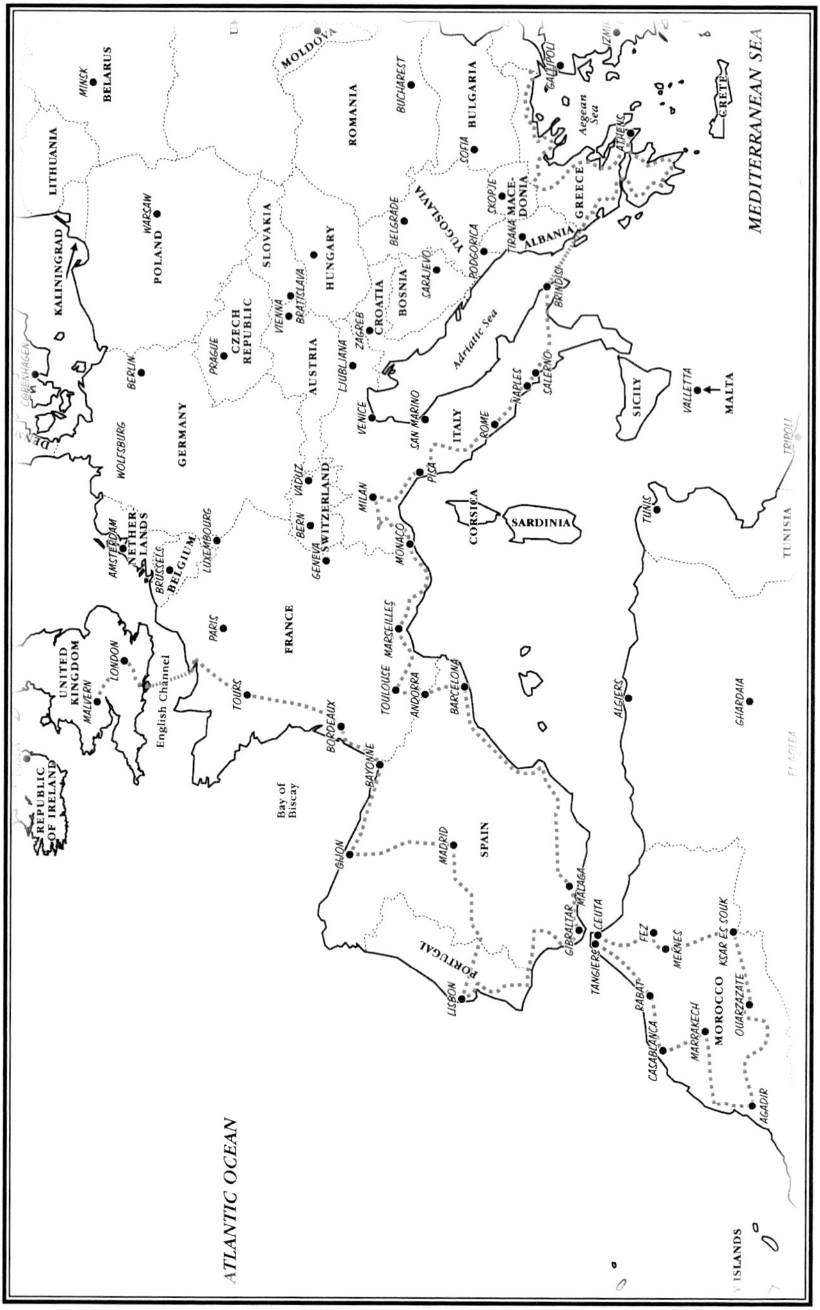
ATLANTIC OCEAN
MEDITERRANEAN SEA
REPUBLIC OF IRELAND
UNITED KINGDOM
MALVERN
LONDON
English Channel
Bay of Biscay
FRANCE
PARIS
TOURS
BORDEAUX
BAYONNE
TOULOUSE
ANDORRA
MARSEILLES
MONACO
BARCELONA
SPAIN
MADRID
GIJON
PORTUGAL
LISBON
GIBRALTAR
MALAGA
CEUTA
TANGIERS
RABAT
CASABLANCA
MARRAKECH
MOROCCO
AGADIR
OUARZAZATE
KSAR ES SOUK
MEKNES
FEZ
ALGIERS
GHARDAIA
TUNIS
TUNISIA
CORSICA
SARDINIA
SICILY
VALLETTA
MALTA
ITALY
ROME
NAPLES
SALERNO
PISA
SAN MARINO
VENICE
MILAN
Adriatic Sea
BRINDISI
ALBANIA
TIRANA
GREECE
ATHENS
Aegean Sea
CRETE
GALLIPOLI
MACE-DONIA
SKOPJE
BULGARIA
SOFIA
ROMANIA
BUCHAREST
MOLDOVA
YUGOSLAVIA
BELGRADE
PODGORICA
BOSNIA
SARAJEVO
CROATIA
ZAGREB
LJUBLJANA
HUNGARY
SLOVAKIA
BRATISLAVA
VIENNA
AUSTRIA
CZECH REPUBLIC
PRAGUE
POLAND
WARSAW
KALININGRAD
LITHUANIA
BELARUS
MINSK
GERMANY
BERLIN
WOLFSBURG
COPENHAGEN
NETHER-LANDS
AMSTERDAM
BELGIUM
BRUSSELS
LUXEMBOURG
SWITZERLAND
BERN
GENEVA
VADUZ

CHAPTER 2
ACROSS THE POND

The first decision of our journey was quickly upon us as we touched down onto French soil, should we turn left or right? It seemed to make sense to get the Spain and Portugal bit out of the way first, so right it was.

We headed off taking in our first tentative experience of driving on the 'wrong' side of the road but quickly adapted and were soon clicking up the kilometres as we headed south through Tours, Bordeaux and onto Bayonne. It was then over the Pyrenees and along the Bay of Biscay to Gijon then due south to Madrid. As we had missed out Paris, planning to visit it on the final leg of our sojourn, this was the first European capital city we visited and we were soon into the ritual of sightseeing which was to become a regular occurrence as we travelled through nineteen counties and principalities over the next seven months.

Heading west to Portugal gave us our first experience of culture change with the sight of ox drawn ploughs tilling the soil in a far more rural environment than we were used to, however with this came the charm and warmth of the local communities.

Having set up camp – or to be more specific parked the van – on the outskirts of a small village, we ventured in to sample the local tipple and despite our mutual lack of each other's language we somehow signed and cajoled our way through a proverbial evening of wine, women and song and in our naivety overdid the wine bit, but a memorable evening was etched into our minds.

Hugging the amazingly clear deep blue seas of the Atlantic we crossed back into Spain and made our way to Gibraltar which was tantalisingly close but in those days out of bounds, so the rock's famous Barbary Macaques didn't experience the pleasure of a visit from us.

From there it was up and along the first of the many 'Costas'. We travelled through Torremolinos to Malaga where an experience altered our direction of travel and indeed had a very lasting influence on what I would undertake over the coming years. It wasn't the viewing of a bullfight, which despite its pageantry and flamboyant colours left me cold, but an encounter with some fellow travellers many years our seniors who had started their journey several years earlier in South Africa.

We were invited into their spacious Mercedes camper which put our comparatively spartan accommodation to shame, and over a few hours and a few drinks we listened intently as their tales of the trip unfolded with countries I had never heard of tripping off their tongues. They convinced us that we should definitely not miss out on a trip to Morocco and the outcome was an about turn and back down the coast to Algeciras and a short ferry crossing to Spanish held Ceuta on the African mainland. From here it was a mere formality to cross over the border into Morocco and culture shock number two.

On the ferry we had met up with a young English speaking Moroccan who gave us the dos and don'ts of how to conduct ourselves whilst in his native country and he also invited us to visit him at his family home in Casablanca. Visits to Tangiers and the capital city of Rabat followed and a few days later we were being royally fed and watered in true traditional Moroccan style by Ali and his family, enjoying the cutlery free pleasures of eating couscous. Later we were taken out on the town and shown Casablanca by night secure in the knowledge that we were in the company of locals who would steer us clear of any of the multifarious pitfalls that could easily befall the unwary tourist.

The magical names of Moroccan towns and cities conjure up mystical images and Marrakech didn't disappoint with its vibrant souk teaming with water sellers accompanied by their pet monkeys, snake charmers and a smattering of ne'er-do-wells which kept us on our toes and ever vigilant. A truly fascinating place to wile away a few sun-kissed hours.

However as the saying goes, 'after the Lord Mayor's banquet etc.' and shortly after the high of being in Marrakech whilst on route to the coastal resort of Agadir, we encountered our first problem with the van. The clutch began to slip and the remedy entailed several visits to a friendly local garage where they allowed us to work on their premises, and gave us the use of a very large sized socket required to release the clutch. It was one of the few tools we didn't carry and one we should have purchased there and then but hindsight is a great thing, as time would prove.

With the engine out of the car and with Pete's mechanical know-how we undertook some additional work and eventually were ready for the off with the engine de-coked, a new oil seal fitted between engine and clutch and a replacement clutch plate in place.

The work had been spread out over a couple of weeks during which time we became domiciled on a campsite in Agadir along with an ever changing flow of fellow travellers in an assortment of VWs and 2CVs. Over the fortnight we became part of the scenery to the extent that our breakfast order of freshly cooked jam doughnuts was delivered directly to us by the friendly vendor at nine o'clock on the dot. Sadly Agadir had been at the centre of a terrible earthquake a few years earlier and still had a certain pervading whiff in the air when the wind was in the wrong direction but the serenity and glorious beach more than countered that.

The sabbatical over it was time to hit the road again and we ventured further south to the edge of the Sahara desert and a sign that bore the inscription 'Timbuktu 52 jour' depicting Taureg men astride camels. At this point we decided to head back to mainland Europe and not try our hand at dodging the sand dunes that lay ahead of us.

Our route took us through more magic sounding places, Ouarzazate, Ksar es Souk, Meknes and Fez all so different from anything we had encountered before and establishing Morocco as one of the highlights of our journey. That chance encounter back in Malaga a month earlier had been a godsend.

Unfortunately the same could not be said of all the help we were given on the mechanical front as we had no sooner got back to Spain when the first ominous signs of clutch slip returned, something that was to come back and haunt us time and again over the rest of the trip. Running repairs were once again carried out and the prognosis was that the crankshaft had slightly warped due to the extreme heat experienced in Morocco. This was causing wear on the oil seal which over a period of time allowed oil to seep onto the clutch with the resultant lack of adhesion i.e., lots of revs but little forward motion. Our finances did not run to having the engine stripped down and rebuilt so the simpler solution of carrying a spare clutch plate and accepting the inevitability of having to whip out the engine now and again was the chosen plan of action. Fellow VW enthusiasts will be aware that engine removal is a fairly easy task and several incidents later we were masters at it.

The rest of the 'Costas' followed as we wound our way along the coast and on through to Barcelona which has much to entice the traveller, among the highlights being Antoni Gaudi's Sagrada Familia unfinished church and at the other extreme a bar where we were able to watch Brazil beat Italy 4–1 to win the world cup.

Pete's background in aviation had a bearing on our next port of call as Toulouse was one of the centres of development of the mind blowing Concord aircraft and was therefore up on his agenda of places to see. To get there we first had to climb back over the mountains this time via the principality of Andorra. This tiny duty free enclave offered up some stunning scenery much in the mould of how I imagined the Alpine states of Austria and Switzerland would look.

We stayed overnight in Andorra and for our troubles were treated to the most fantastic thunder and lightning storm I had ever experienced. Once trapped inside the towering mountains the display seemed to be bounced from one peak to another unable to escape and the accompanying cacophony of sound even shook the van, yet we seemed safe tucked up in our sleeping bags peering through the windows at one of natures most dramatic displays.

We continued on northwards to Toulouse but were disappointed to be told that there was no possibility of viewing our *raison d'être* so the cameras were once again consigned to our bags and some years were to pass before I caught a glimpse of one of those magnificent flying machines that promised so much but was sadly doomed to fail.

Prior to leaving England we had arranged for our girlfriends Sue and Maggie to join us for a holiday within our holiday and in the middle of July they made their way out to Marseilles. Over the next fortnight we managed to cram in as many of the 'must see' tourist attractions as possible: posing in the casino at Monte Carlo, sunning ourselves at Cannes and Nice, viewing Pisa with its gravity defying leaning tower, and touring around arty Florence and, of course, Rome.

As many will be aware there is a surfeit of fine buildings steeped in history and more than enough ruins to fill a week of anyone's schedule in Rome alone and whatever one's religion or lack of it the Vatican City has to be seen, we even managed to sneak an illicit picture of Michelangelo's Pieta statue.

Having gorged ourselves on history and culture we continued south along the coast to Naples which sadly did not impress, though it had a very hard act to follow in Rome, then onto Pompeii where we climbed the volcanic Mount Vesuvius and walked through the eerie ruins of the ancient Roman city engulfed by the eruption in 79 AD.

Before we knew it the fortnight had flown by and having dropped the girls at the station in Salerno for their overland train trip back home we moved over to the Adriatic coast and the port of Brindisi. From here we caught the ferry over to Igoumenitsa and so began our second history lesson as we criss-crossed our way from the northern Greek mainland to the Peloponnese in the south, once more soaking up the ruins which abound from Olympia to the capital Athens.

We were quite fortunate that back in 1970 access to the Acropolis had not yet been stopped and we were able to climb up and inspect this awesome cluster of buildings at close range.

It wasn't only the ruins we soaked up as we toured around some spectacular scenery, the sun was also very inviting and some of the quiet beaches were just too good to ignore. Having found one such beach and decided to stay overnight I got a rude awakening from Pete shouting that there appeared to be someone in trouble out in the sea. Plunging into the water straight from my slumbers certainly focused the mind and sure enough there was someone in difficulty. Despite my five foot five inch frame the life-saving certificate skills I had been taught during my school days in Edinburgh came flooding back and with the help of the gentleman's daughter we got him safely back to the shore and after a short time he appeared to be pretty well back to normal if a little shaken.

They were most grateful and we were feted with wine and food and in the evening were invited to join them and some of their friends for a traditional Greek dinner. This turned out to be quite an evening as we later moved on to a party and finished up drinking and dancing till 3 o'clock in the morning, by which time the plates weren't the only things that were smashed.

One relatively recent geographical feature in Greece is the Corinth canal which was constructed in the late 1800s and completed in 1893. From the bridge over the canal connecting north and south it is difficult to try to conjure up the effort that went into shifting the rock and soil removed to create the near three hundred foot deep ravine which carves its way from east to west over its four mile length. How many lives were lost I have no idea but this man-made feature like those at Suez and Panama is a reminder of just what can be achieved where there is a will.

Leaving Athens we covered much of the northern mainland then followed the Aegean Sea coast eastwards and into Turkey.

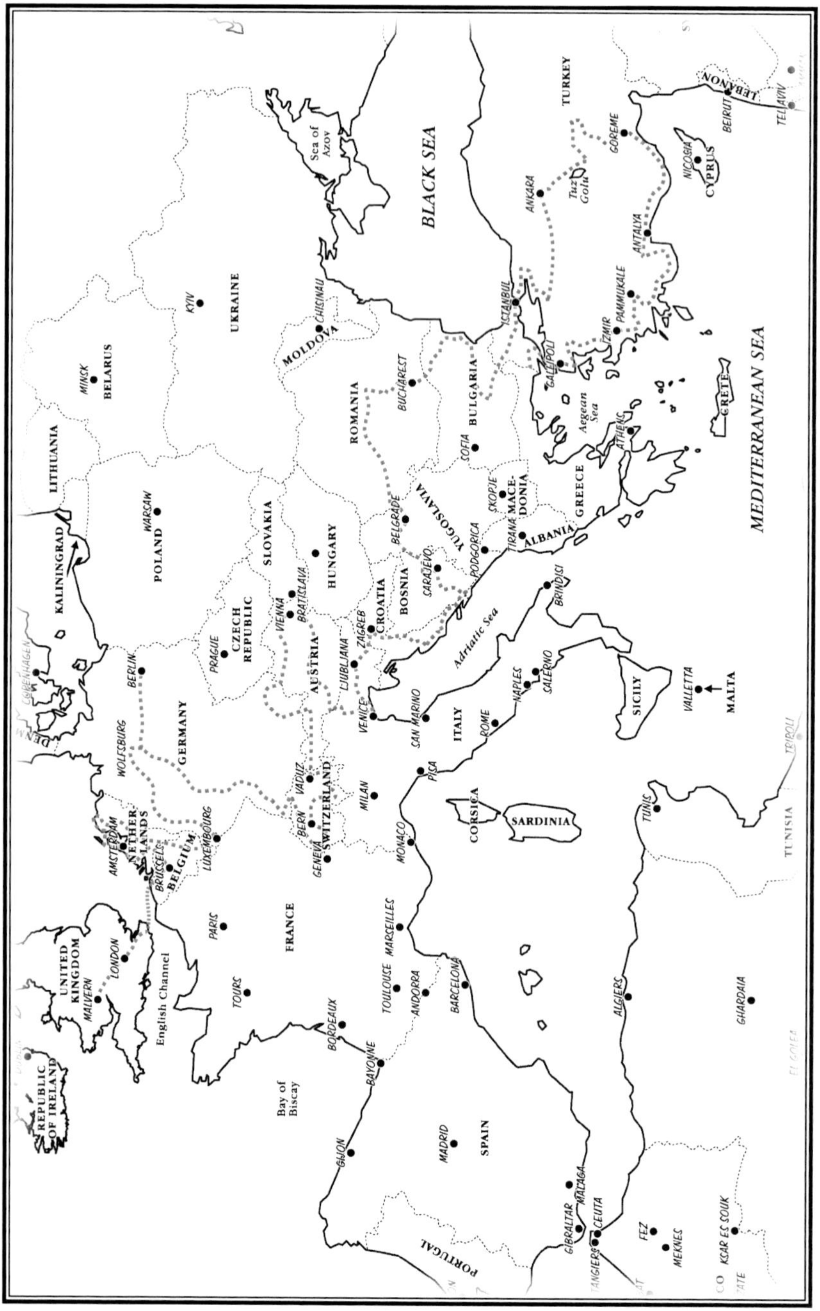
BLACK SEA
MEDITERRANEAN SEA
Sea of Azov
Adriatic Sea
Aegean Sea
English Channel
Bay of Biscay
Tuz Golu
TURKEY
LEBANON
BEIRUT
TEL AVIV
CYPRUS
NICOSIA
GOREME
ANKARA
ANTALYA
PAMMUKALE
IZMIR
ISTANBUL
GALLIPOLI
CRETE
ATHENS
GREECE
MACE-DONIA
SKOPJE
ALBANIA
TIRANA
BULGARIA
SOFIA
ROMANIA
BUCHAREST
MOLDOVA
CHISINAU
UKRAINE
KYIV
BELARUS
MINSK
LITHUANIA
KALININGRAD
POLAND
WARSAW
SLOVAKIA
HUNGARY
YUGOSLAVIA
BELGRADE
PODGORICA
SARAJEVO
BOSNIA
CROATIA
ZAGREB
BRATISLAVA
VIENNA
AUSTRIA
LJUBLIANA
CZECH REPUBLIC
PRAGUE
BERLIN
GERMANY
WOLFSBURG
COPENHAGEN
DENM
NETHER-LANDS
AMSTERDAM
BELGIUM
BRUSSELS
LUXEMBOURG
SWITZERLAND
VADUZ
BERN
GENEVA
MILAN
VENICE
SAN MARINO
PISA
ITALY
ROME
NAPLES
SALERNO
BRINDISI
SICILY
MALTA
VALLETTA
CORSICA
SARDINIA
MONACO
FRANCE
PARIS
TOURS
BORDEAUX
TOULOUSE
MARSEILLES
ANDORRA
UNITED KINGDOM
LONDON
MALVERN
REPUBLIC OF IRELAND
SPAIN
BARCELONA
BAYONNE
GIJON
MADRID
MALAGA
GIBRALTAR
CEUTA
TANGIERS
PORTUGAL
FEZ
MEKNES
KSAR ES SOUK
ALGIERS
GHARDAIA
TUNIS
TUNISIA
TRIPOLI

CHAPTER 3
BACK TO BLIGHTY

We didn't know what to expect in Turkey but it certainly didn't disappoint.

Shortly after leaving Alexandroupolis we crossed over from Greece and skirting the Sea of Marmara came to Gallipoli the sight of one of the many disastrous campaigns of the first world war, this one involving many of the Australian and New Zealand troops better known as the ANZACS. The fateful battle which raged between April 1915 and January 1916 cost countless lives on both sides and incidentally is immortalised in one of the greatest (anti) war songs ever penned, 'The Band Played Waltzing Matilda' by Eric Bogle.

We followed the road south largely hugging the coast, and slightly beyond Izmir headed inland to Pamukkale, a unique geological formation where the calcium rich thermal waters have cascaded over the rocks and over many thousands of years have built up a vast sequence of white terraces or travertines. In Turkish the word Pamukkale means cotton castle and that is a very apt description of this magnificent wonder of nature.

As if this natural wonder was not enough, nearby there is the site of the ancient Greek city of Hierapolis with many well-preserved ruins including the ancient baths, and a very fine amphitheatre. We had already given Ephesus a miss feeling we had seen more than our fair share of Greek and Roman ruins but once again were impressed by just what these earlier civilisations had achieved.

Leaving the breathtaking beauty of Pamukkale behind we took to a mountain road and headed towards the coast again via Mugla. The journey was somewhat slow being a very windy and not particularly well-constructed dirt road. Some five hours and ninety miles later, having traversed some very picturesque scenery on route we arrived at Mugla and continued over more dirt roads to a small coastal village. Here the local 'folk' band resplendent in their local costumes entertained us and a party situation developed and a good time was had by all, even if we didn't understand a word of what we were saying to each other.

More rough, dusty but scenic roads ensued as we wound our way along the coast to the town of Fethiye where the magnificent Lycian rock tombs are situated. These tombs, hewn out of the solid limestone rock face can date back to the period prior to the rule of Alexander the Great (fourth century BC) and are generally built with two Ionic-style columns, an arc and a pediment. The area behind the columns is carved out and opens up to the funeral chamber via a monumental door. Many hundred such tombs exist across the area and are a testimony to the skills of those early stonemasons and the high regard bestowed upon their dead and departed.

Pamukkale, the 'Cotton Castle'.

Rock Tombs near Fethiye.

We continued eastwards, now bound for Antalya, and just as the road conditions seemed to be improving, the car battery suddenly worked loose, shorted out and virtually caught fire and we were mightily relieved and somewhat amazed to find that after a bit of light 'frigging' the thing sparked back into life again and we were once more heading on our way with one potential disaster averted.

The coastal road was our companion until just before Adana where we headed north towards Ankara. Having reached the most distant point of our journey we were now in effect on the return leg, some five months after setting off.

Another of those 'beyond belief' moments occurred when we reached Goreme a spectacular landscape of fairy chimney rock formations sculpted purely by erosion which in turn have been hewn out to create troglodyte villages, dwellings and churches dating back to the dark ages and possibly as far back as the fourth century AD. Some of the buildings had understandably partly collapsed laying bare for all to see the elaborate interiors, but others were still inhabited or used for storage.

For the first time our evening arrangements were interrupted by the arrival of the local police who firmly suggested that we should move on to a nearby campsite to avoid the risk of being attacked by 'bandits', and as they volunteered to escort us there we felt it would have been churlish to refuse. So far the only attack we had had was from local kids who seem to swarm round the van wherever we parked, though their motive was largely driven by curiosity not malice.

Tuz Golu, the vast salt-water lake that spreads over five hundred and eighty square miles literally went on for endless miles as we forged ever more inland towards the Turkish capital city Ankara.

My recollections of Ankara are somewhat limited as on the approach we once again had the re-occurring clutch problem. Fortunately we found a garage with an outdoor inspection pit and as it was Saturday evening they allowed us the use of it on the Sunday. The day was frantically spent once more going through the well tried and tested routine. To say it was hot would be understating the obvious and the sight of two mad Brits clad only in swimming trunks beavering away in the midday sun must have brought a wry smile to many of the local inhabitants.

We also took the opportunity to do some other maintenance: attending to an intermittent faulty rear light and a fault on the rear brakes. Just as we were feeling a good days work had been achieved, calamity struck when we noticed some wear on the rear wheel bearing which without much persuasion from us disintegrated into several pieces. There was nothing further we could do until the garages opened the following day so what a few minutes earlier had been an upbeat mood quickly changed to one where much cursing and the words VW were closely linked.

A few somewhat expensive taxi rides in the morning saw us obtain the required part which was duly fitted and we set off once again leaving Ankara behind us unexplored.

Later in the day, whilst in a particularly remote part of the countryside we couldn't believe our ears when an ominous knocking sound started to come from the rear of the van and on inspection it was obvious that the main pulley was working loose and oil had once more seeped out. There was nothing else to do but once again remove the engine. Without the presence of any ramps or jacks a mound of earth was quickly built, onto which the van was reversed such that once the engine mountings were removed and the van pushed forward the engine was left precariously balanced on top of the said mound. Somewhat Heath Robinson – but it worked. The upshot of it all was that I made a trip into the nearest town to blag the use of the required socket (the one we should have bought back in Morocco!) while Pete stayed with the van and did some further mechanical work. Fortunately the whole escapade was resolved much easier than expected and with the engine back in place and the borrowed socket duly returned to its owner, we crossed our fingers and struck out once more for England.

The final port of call in Turkey was also one of the most vibrant and fascinating, the metropolis of Istanbul. This really is a city that everyone should visit: with its bustling market and minarets, none finer than those on the Blue Mosque. The edge was slightly taken off our visit as we returned to the van to find it had been broken into but amazingly nothing was missing and we could only surmise that we must have arrived back just in time. Linking the two of us to the British registered vehicle would not have required rocket science on behalf of any lookout worth his salt.

If Turkey had been excitingly different nothing could have prepared us for the austere, dour communist state that Bulgaria was in 1970. It became apparent fairly quickly that we were not really welcome, getting nothing but hassle from the local police, continually being moved on and when it came to shopping for the most basic of staple food you could spot the bread shop a mile away by the lengthy queue snaking down the road outside it.

It was also interesting to see the local take on the then current Vietnam War. Whilst we had been indoctrinated into believing that good old Uncle Sam was right, they had vast murals on the sides of buildings depicting fleeing Vietnamese children with bombs clearly marked USA falling on to them from the skies above. A sobering thought that so simply brought home how many in the world viewed us, including our hosts in Bulgaria.

Losing little time we crossed over into another communist state, Bulgaria's northern neighbour Romania and what a difference. It was still somewhat different from back home but people seemed so much friendlier if still relatively poor by our standards.

In no time we were in the capital city Bucharest which had many fine buildings for the traveller to admire, quite a bit of advertising and shops that resembled shops, in all a very pleasant experience, and things just got better and better from there on.

We climbed up into the Transylvanian mountains but as we progressed we met with mixed weather. After enduring a long, fairly wet day we veered off the main road and eventually found a suitable resting place by a small mountain stream and settled down for the night.

In the morning with the sun shining brightly we realised what an idyllic spot we had so accidentally stumbled upon surrounded by beautiful mountains which had been shrouded from our view by low cloud the previous evening. The stream offered the chance to catch up with some washing so a quiet day of domestic chores was pencilled in. However as the great Robert Burns put it 'The best laid schemes o' mice an' men gang aft agley'.

We had barely started sorting out what could last yet another week without being washed against what had well and truly passed its wash by date when a couple of young girls appeared looking very inquisitively at the sight of these two strangers in their little village and much to our surprise they approached us and greeted us in English. They were sisters who were on a weekend excursion to the village to visit relatives and had been learning English at school and were eager to practise their skills. They soon convinced us that rather than messing about washing we should join them and their family for a tour around the village (which we established was called Galas) and the surrounding area to which we agreed, with no idea of what the day held in store for us.

Traditional Romanian wedding procession.

The weather was glorious and the village setting was as previously mentioned idyllic. The morning was spent being ferried from house to house and introduced to friends and family then we were shown round their very own local museum. This was fascinating and somewhat unusual to find in such a small setting, whilst we expect a typical village to have a pub and a church this one had a museum and a church.

At one point there was a lot of very excited conversation flying around, none of which we could understand, but there was obviously something out of the ordinary afoot and it didn't take long before the girls put us in the picture. One of the families nearby had a daughter who was getting married that afternoon and everyone, including us, had been invited and what a memorable occasion it turned out to be.

The groom and his entourage were traditionally attired in loose fitting, white pleated tunic shirts worn over white trousers with dark waistcoats and bowler style hats. They also sported large colourful bags over their shoulders which draped down by their sides. The assembled group were paraded through the village to the bride's house on a highly decorated ox driven cart piled high with gifts and their worldly goods and once she had joined them the procession continued on to the church ceremony. This was followed by a fantastic party with a fine array of local food and wine begging to be consumed and as it would have been rude to refuse we played our part to the full and had one of the most memorable days of the whole journey.

As we were now on the cusp of October and had planned to be back home around the end of November we realised that with much still to see time was not on our side so on we pushed over the border into Yugoslavia. After ticking off yet another capital city – Belgrade – we headed over the mountains to Sarajevo. Being autumn the tree clad mountains were ablaze with those wonderful autumn hues of red and orange quite a contrast to the grey of the beaches and mountain backdrop of the Dalmatian coast.

We followed the Adriatic coast northwards then headed inland once again to Zagreb, Ljubljana and the beautiful glacial Lake Bled with its iconic castle marooned in the middle on top of a rocky outcrop.

We could never have imagined the horror that was to befall the country in later years when ethnic cleansing and genocide ripped it apart and created the many individual states that ultimately replaced it.

Our natural route should have been directly north into Austria but another of those 'must see' magical places was enticingly close by, so instead we headed west, over the border into Italy, and down to Venice, truly a place that everyone should see at least once in their lives. Steeped in history and with so many places of interest to take in, along with the unique network of canals, we could easily have spent more time there but the images of St. Mark's Square and of course the Rialto Bridge will remain forever.

To get back on track we drove directly north and crossed over into Austria and made our way east to Vienna. At this point we considered a visit over the border to Czechoslovakia, however, the uprisings of 1968 had left the country somewhat unstable and our Embassy strongly advised against it so instead we ventured across into the Bavarian region of Germany.

Whilst the buzzing centre of Munich and an evening spent in one of their many raucous Beer Cellars was highly enjoyable, the other axis of our emotions took over when we paid a visit to Dachau Concentration Camp, a horrible reminder of just what the human race is capable of.

Vienna had of course been well worth a visit but an element of 'capital city fatigue' was slowly setting in and the real beauty of Austria to my mind lay in the majestic setting of its Alpine region and it was there we were now heading.

The first few days whilst cold were still sunny and showed off the lush green mountains in all their glory and the gentle tinkling of the cow bells combined to create a beautifully tranquil canvas. As we wound our way ever upwards through the breathtaking scenery abounding around the mountain roads the first hints of winter started to appear with some snow flurries and a dip in the temperature to 'chilly'.

As we approached the Arlberg pass which would take us over into Liechtenstein and Switzerland it was late afternoon and we decided to set up camp for the evening and have a fresh start in the morning. The elements however had a different take on things and overnight the heavens opened and dumped several feet of fresh snow over the whole area and despite our best efforts to head in the appropriate direction we were sliding all over the place and, to put an abrupt end to any plans we had, the pass was closed.

Our finances by now were ebbing away and certainly didn't run to the cost of catching the car express through the tunnel so we slid our way around the mountain roads and found a suitable spot to spend the next twenty-four hours on the assumption that the road conditions would have improved by then. It was probably the most unpleasant day of our journey as we sat huddled up in the van intermittently turning on the heater aware that we did not wish to run down the battery, whilst watching the snow relentlessly piling up around us.

Somehow, with the help of nearly every bit of clothing we had being piled on layer by layer, we saw the rest of the day and that night out, and awoke to crystal clear blue skies, sunshine, and the most glorious panorama of snow clad mountains and virgin snow.

We dug our way out and slowly managed to return to the main road which in true alpine fashion had already had the attention of the snowploughs, and whilst far from perfect we were able to thread our way up and over the top. The relief was palpable and I momentarily forgot that stopping on ice-covered downward facing slopes can be a problem and there was a mighty sigh of relief when we came to a stop literally inches from the back of a parked car. We felt it best to make a hasty retreat and continued to cautiously slip and slide our way towards Vaduz, Liechtenstein's main town.

Vaduz was very, very classy which was not really surprising given its reputation as a tax haven for the rich and famous and having given it our approval we moved on to Switzerland.

The following couple of weeks were spent touring around the Alpine splendour offered up by the numerous passes and mountain hugging roads that interlink the many famous landmarks and cities of Switzerland and cemented our view that our Austrian/Swiss adventure was up among the top highlights of our seven month sojourn.

We were now very much on the last leg of our trip and having spent such a long time in the confines of the VW, and with winter and the ever shortening days upon us, home was beckoning, but before we raced our way to the lowlands of Belgium and Holland we still had a couple of 'appointments' to make.

Despite suffering from the aforementioned 'capital city fatigue' we wanted to visit Berlin with the intention of crossing over to the Eastern section.

To get there of course entailed crossing over East German territory via the autobahn and rather than have all the hassle involved with taking the vehicle we parked it up and hitched our way across. After about an hour of thumb waving we got a lift with a lorry driver and four hours later having waded through lots of red tape and bureaucracy we found ourselves among the vibrant western sector of the city with its flashing neon lights and all the trappings of a typical 'capitalist' city.

We spent the day having a good look round and visiting the infamous wall, then in the evening finished up in one of the many lively bars. We fell into conversation with some fellow Brits who were working there and were kindly offered a floor for the night which took care of our accommodation problems. With that resolved the serious matter of sampling the various German beers on offer started in earnest.

Despite supping a stein too many the night before we were still up bright and early, as today it was the turn of the Eastern sector to display its wares. We made our way to the famous Check Point Charlie and after the usual ritual of form filling were allowed through.

The weather was wet and miserable which in many ways was very apt as it summed up the general feel of the place, memories of Bulgaria came to mind. There were still many buildings in ruins and although some sections had obviously been developed the contrast to its western counterpart were overwhelming, and we could fully understand why some residents were willing to risk everything to cross over, the grass really was greener on the other side.

Check Point Charlie border crossing from West to East Berlin.

By 2.30 pm we had soaked up more than enough of the austere atmosphere the Eastern sector had to offer and started our return journey. Once back in West Berlin we got our thumbs into action and after a short delay got a lift back over East German territory and by 6.30 pm were reunited with our mobile home. It was now its turn for an outing!

The second of our 'appointments' was to reunite our VW with its birthplace, the vast Volkswagen factory at Wolfsburg, though if one was being pedantic our particular van would have been manufactured at Hanover to where production was switched in 1956. That said the cultural home of VW is Wolfsburg and with guided tours available to visitors that was where we were heading.

We had to kill some time at the factory before we were able to join the afternoon tour and subsequently passed a most informative and interesting few hours. Car bodies from above swooped down to be married up with chassis from below and with different models being produced down the same line one couldn't help wondering if a miss marriage ever took place, but somehow knowing German engineering we doubted it.

With our final goal achieved we set off through the industrial heartland of the Ruhr valley and then up to the wine rich Moselle region, before entering Luxembourg, and thence into Belgium.

Our final detour saw us heading to the northern extremities of Holland to cross over the Zuiderzee dyke, the sixty yard wide strip that runs for twenty miles and separates the North Sea from the inland waters and vast reclaimed Polder areas. Another example of man's engineering achievements.

The final days were occupied looking around Amsterdam, Antwerp and Brussels before our last destination, Zeebrugge from where on Thursday the 26th November we caught the 6.00 pm ferry to Dover arriving back in the UK at 10.00 pm. By the time we had driven back home to Malvern it was the middle of the night so our long suffering trusty four wheeled companion was given the pleasure of putting up with us for one more night.

CHAPTER 4

THE IN-BETWEEN YEAR

So, in 1971, I was now back home having seen the world and having had a thoroughly enjoyable time doing so, and with many reunions and the festive season out of the way it was time to knuckle down and get back into gainful employment.

The faithful old 'splitty' had found a new home but even that injection of cash wasn't going to last very long so the job hunt commenced.

I secured a position with the prestigious Royal Worcester Porcelain works in their export department and it didn't take very long to confirm the feeling I had already been nurturing that far from seeing the world I had barely scratched the surface. We were exporting to all the exotic corners of the globe and it made me reflect on my own situation.

Whilst I had certainly travelled many thousands of miles around Europe it struck me that in general it was much the same. Yes, the churches had different shaped spires, food varied slightly, some being spicier than others, one country's ruins were more impressive than another's and of course the geography changed but the two exceptions to this 'much the same' rule were the countries at the extremities of that journey, Morocco and Turkey. They had left much more impact because they were culturally different. Much as I wouldn't for the world have missed the Roman and Greek ruins, the stunning Alpine scenery or the numerous impromptu social gatherings where we got to sample the local food and drink, I couldn't help feeling that the really interesting places lay further a field.

This feeling grew stronger and stronger every time I encountered a fresh destination in my new role in exports and after only a couple of months I had convinced myself that rather that sending parcels to these far flung parts of the world I should somehow be sending myself. My second Eureka moment!

A truly world trip seemed the answer. It would obviously take longer than our jaunt round Europe so I started to put together some outline plans. Working on a six monthly cycle of travel and work I came up with a broad itinerary.

The first six months would be taken up travelling followed by six months of work to amass the necessary cash to fund the next six months of travel and so on.

Following this broad plan would see me travel through Africa, work, travel to Australia overland as much as possible via India etc., work, then traverse the American continent taking in both the South and North finishing up in Canada for a final spell of work to fund my return home. It all made sense to me but there was a lot of meat to be put on these bones before I was going anywhere.

I had always been active in the local 'folk' scene and indeed the guitar had been pressed into action on many an occasion throughout Europe where a good old sing song had often been an ice breaker and had fortunately also been well received. Roger Mortimer, one of the other regulars at our local club, heard about my plans and asked if he could join me so one of the obstacles was quickly resolved, a travel companion had been found.

We started to consider what we would need and the first priority was our mode of transport. Whilst I had built up a great affection for the VW camper brand we felt that the Sahara Desert and beyond called for something more substantial, and the words Land Rover and Africa seemed to be synonymous. An element of déjà vu crept in as we started the long search through car magazines etc. but we eventually tracked down a 1960 long wheelbase pick-up model along with a rear hard top and the conversion work commenced. A major plus in this direction was the fact that Roger's dad ran a large local garage and we were able to avail ourselves of the space to work and much more importantly the knowledge base to tap into when we hit a problem – and we did a lot of problem hitting.

A further consideration was the small matter of funds and although I enjoyed my work in exports, richer pickings were there to be had. 1971 was the year of gas conversion when the country was systematically being changed over to North Sea gas and my hometown of Malvern was going through this process. A chance conversation with a couple of the lads doing the work informed me that the company was looking to recruit more staff and despite the slightly anti-social hours, e.g. often travelling seventy or eighty miles for a prompt 7.00 am start on the Monday morning, the rewards were substantial. There was however, one small issue: I had spent all my working life in an office environment and would never class myself as a natural artisan, but I was informed that a full training course was part of the package and in no time at all I was let loose on the unsuspecting public, fettling cookers, fires and central heating systems as if I was a natural.

This new found gainful employment took care of the funding issue and with weekends spent sorting out the Land Rover the summer months fairly flew by and our target departure date of January 1972 drew ever closer.

Unlike the trip round Europe, where even back in 1970 movement from country to country was fairly straightforward, the African continent entailed much more bureaucracy. Visas and/or entry permits were required for most of the countries we planned to visit in the early months of our trip, as most had previously been under French influence. Fortunately the East African countries, our old colonial stamping ground, posed less of a problem for UK citizens.

To secure the required documentation entailed several trips to London and a tour of the relevant embassies and it goes without saying that nothing ever went smoothly. We often found ourselves queuing for ages only to be told that we required an additional document or signature to secure the holy grail that was the all important stamp in our passports, but with no other option open to us we had to smile politely, swallow hard and go along with them.

One problem however remained unresolved, as there were no Niger or Central African Republic embassies in London, the nearest ones being situated in Paris and we had little appetite for a specific trip over there just to get the necessary documentation. As we would be travelling through

France on our way down to Southern Spain and thence Morocco, we decided to leave things and sort out the necessary documentation when we arrived in Paris. With those notable exceptions we were now armed with a passport full of exotic stamps and signatures and one more task had been completed.

With our scheduled departure only a month or so away I had stopped attempting to blow people up and was concentrating on the last minute arrangements. With a bit of time on my hands I decided to make a visit to the Land Rover factory at Solihull, naively thinking that I could get them to check the vehicle over for us. We were after all using one of their vehicles to take on the Sahara Desert and all that Africa could throw at us.

On arrival at the factory it was politely pointed out that virtually everyone who made such a trip used one of their vehicles and that no assistance would be forthcoming. My pioneering ego was left well and truly deflated however they did invite me to have a tour of the premises and see the production line. With nothing else on my agenda I took up the offer, though secretly feeling very aggrieved.

During my walk around the plant I struck up several conversations explaining our plans and why I had made the visit. At the end of the production line I met one of the test drivers who's job entailed checking out each finished vehicle on a specially constructed circuit. As it was approaching lunchtime he kindly volunteered to run our vehicle around the track and give it the once over. Suddenly things started to look more positive, maybe the visit hadn't been in vain after all.

Any feelings of elation were very quickly quashed when he returned and quizzically, and with a tough of irony, asked just where we intended to go in the vehicle. To summarise, even briefly, the problems he believed we had would fill the next few paragraphs but all was not lost as each of the faults could be remedied. Suffice it to say that a few days later we had a fully sorted Land Rover along with a boot load of spares. Africa here we come!

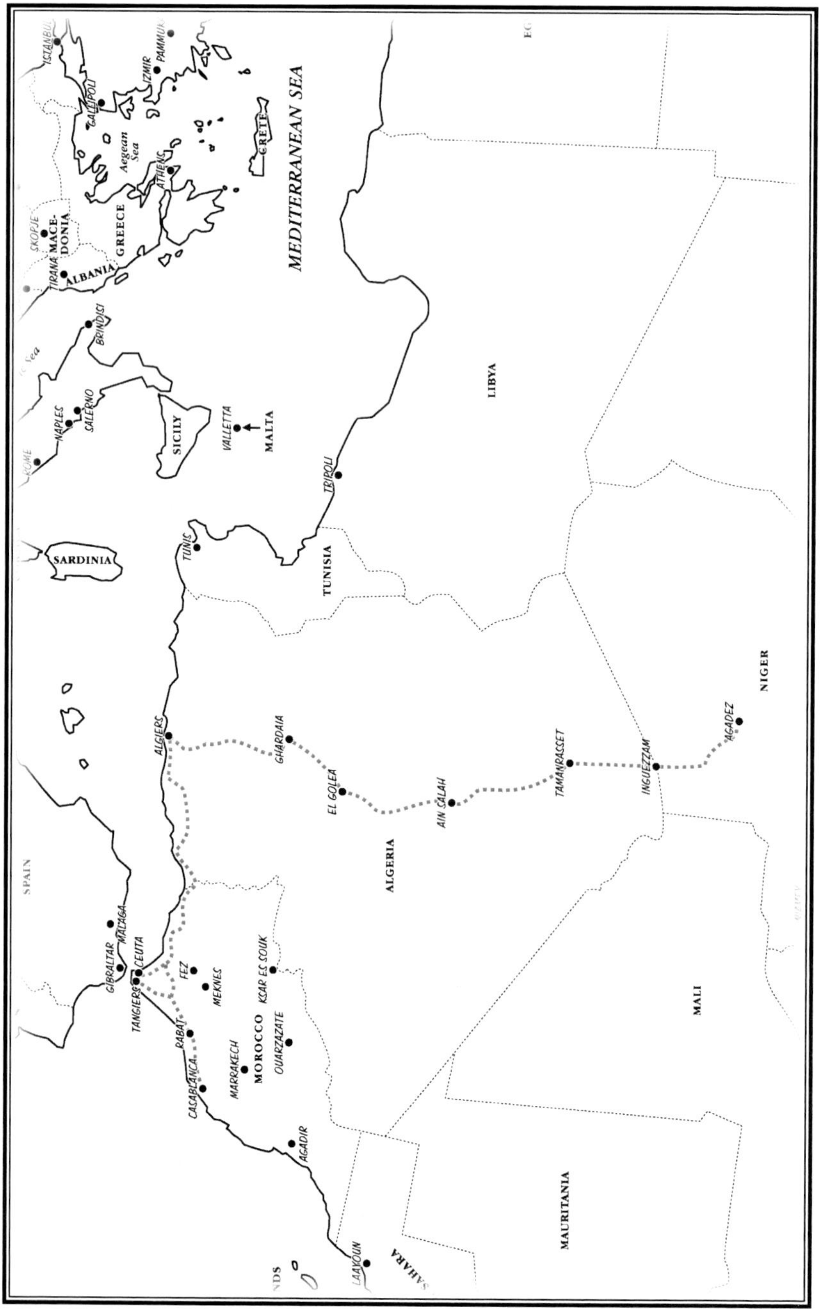

ISTANBUL
IZMIR
GALLIPOLI
Aegean Sea
CRETE
ATHENS
MEDITERRANEAN SEA
SKOPJE
MACE-DONIA
GREECE
TIRANA
ALBANIA
BRINDISI
ROME
NAPLES
SALERNO
SICILY
VALLETTA
MALTA
TRIPOLI
LIBYA
SARDINIA
TUNIS
TUNISIA
SPAIN
MALAGA
GIBRALTAR
CEUTA
TANGIERS
FEZ
MEKNES
KSAR ES SOUK
RABAT
MOROCCO
MARRAKECH
OUARZAZATE
CASABLANCA
AGADIR
ALGIERS
GHARDAIA
EL GOLEA
AIN SALAH
ALGERIA
TAMANRASSET
INGUEZZAM
AGADEZ
NIGER
MALI
MAURITANIA
LAAYOUN
SAHARA

CHAPTER 5
SAHARA AND BEYOND

With the dawning of the New Year our impending departure was drawing ever closer. Despite the expected set backs and a few unexpected ones we were pretty well on schedule and one of the final things still outstanding on our 'to do' list was to be inoculated against a string of foreign diseases and to stock up on other required medication in particular anti-malaria tablets which would become a staple part of our diet. Duly passed immune from yellow fever, cholera, and smallpox and tetanused up to our eyeballs we were ready to let the adventure commence.

The Land Rover now bore little resemblance to the vehicle we had purchased. The cab had been removed and replaced with the full-length hard top with luggage rack and an internal make over had been completed. It now sported the luxury of seats that converted to beds, a table which also doubled up as part of the bed and a Gas stove. We drew the line at running water and a sink deciding that we could bear the hardship of using a simple bowl for washing purposes. Storage space had been cleverly concealed in every spare nook and cranny in addition to the fitted cupboards. In all our entire creature comforts were well catered for, even if any self-respecting carpenter would have swiftly distanced himself from our handy work, it was home to us.

To accommodate the long distances we would be travelling between fuel stations, we had rigged up four carriers on the roof and two on the front. Each of these held a five gallon Jerry can and with the spare wheel mounted on the bonnet the finished article really looked the part and after its Solihull outing was raring to go, so go we did.

On Monday the 17th January 1972 we bid farewell to our respective families in Malvern and headed off to London for a further round of family goodbyes and a final hearty meal at my sister's flat where we spent our final night on British soil.

A bright start in the morning saw us up and away, with Dover our chosen crossing point as it offered the option of going by Hovercraft, a new experience for both of us, and once on board it seemed no time at all, despite a fairly choppy crossing, before we were ready to disembark at Boulogne.

I had missed out on visiting Paris last time round and knowing it had much to offer the sightseer we headed due south to soak up its charms. There was of course a much more pressing need for our visit as we still had to resolve the small matter of the vital visas which would allow us to cross through Niger and the Central African Republic.

With the aid of a travel agency and several Gendarmes we eventually arrived at Rue de la Longchamps and found the Niger embassy; however we were in for quite a shock.

Part of our 'interrogation' required us to outline our travel plans, and full of pioneering spirit we explained that we were embarking on a round the world trip with phase one taking us overland to South Africa. We had somewhat underestimated the contempt with which the white South African regime were held but were quickly made aware of it when we were unceremoniously kicked out of the Embassy and told in no uncertain terms that no visas would be issued.

All our planning suddenly seemed scuppered but one ray of light remained, as there was another Niger embassy in Algiers which would give us a second chance to obtain the vital permission. On the assumption that a revised destination of Kenya would prove acceptable to the authorities in Algiers and presuming that a 'not wanted' list wouldn't be circulating with our names on it we made our way to the Central African Republic's embassy.

Smarting from our rebuff and not wishing to have any more setbacks we changed tack and tried the aforementioned Kenya as our destination and were mightily relieved to find no recurrence of the problem. We were asked to leave our passports and call back the following day to collect them so with nowhere else to go and bereft of the most important document we possessed we set about exploring the famous sites of romantic Paris.

With the Eiffel Tower, Notre Dame and the Arc de Triomphe suitably inspected and the Champs-Élysées well trodden we returned to collect our passports and then set off for Southern Spain.

As Roger had not previously been in this part of Europe we detoured through northern Spain and Portugal using a different route from the one used last time and then on February 1st crossed over to Morocco (via Ceuta as before).

Having spoken so highly about Morocco it was little wonder that Roger wanted to see what it was all about and the idea of digesting another slice of Moroccan life met with no opposition from my end. Some ten days later we had completed our circuit and after following the northern mountainous coast road we crossed over into Algeria.

Our priority was to get to the Niger embassy and sort out our visas without which a major rethink of our route would be required along with the hassle of obtaining additional visas for several new countries such a rescheduling would necessitate.

Once in Algiers we tracked down the British Consulate. Prior to leaving we had set up a communication trail whereby messages could be sent to us via the Friday edition of the Daily Telegraph newspaper which we would buy, but already several copies had been missed, and our hopes that the Consulate library may have the illusive editions proved unfounded. It became obvious that this was not going to work out as planned.

We asked the consulate staff if they could direct us to the French Consulate which had responsibility for issuing visas on Niger's behalf. They obliged and we set off to track it down but little did we know how the day was going to unfold. Firstly the French informed us that they no longer carried out this task and told us that there was now a Niger Embassy in the city which dealt with this, however they had no idea where the said embassy was located and instead directed us to the Algerian Foreign Affairs Ministry. Eventually after much to-ing and fro-ing we arrived there and were told the embassy had located itself at the Hotel Albert, so off we went once more only to be told that it had recently relocated to the outskirts of the city. Despite finding the correct suburb and armed with the address written in the hotel staff's fair hand nobody, the police included, could help us find the elusive embassy, so we decided to go back to square one, the British Consulate.

We could hardly believe our ears when the receptionist after much enquiring told us that there was no Niger embassy in Algiers and once more directed us to their French counterparts. It was now mid-afternoon and to put it mildly a hint of frustration was starting to envelop us but with no better alternative back to the French we went. It was suggested that we might try the Swiss embassy, though the logic in this suggestion escaped me and just as we were about to tell them what we thought of that idea a young English speaking chap appeared on the scene and we were beckoned into his office.

He couldn't have been more helpful and after hearing our tale of woe set about some investigations of his own. He was able to confirm that the embassy did indeed exist, and after contacting the post office and the Hotel Albert a new phone number and address were supplied. Sadly it was now 5.00 pm and too late for anything to be sorted out so we set off to camp for the night, cursing, but clutching at the straw our new found friend had handed us.

An early start saw us on the search once more and though by no means as easily as we had been advised we did eventually find what appeared to be simply, house number twelve in an inconspicuous row of houses, no flag or plaque to herald its existence, but to our delight it was indeed the embassy. The formalities were completed and we were told to return at 4.00 pm and on the dot we arrived, and left shortly afterwards with grins like a pair of Cheshire cats, visas duly stamped in our passports.

With all the required documentation in place the real fun could now begin as we headed due south to see just what the Sahara Desert would throw up at us.

The initial drive south took us up and over some rugged mountain roads followed by a series of hills and plains leading us through a noticeably less fertile landscape and although we were still on a tarmac road we started to see our first sand dunes heralding a taste of what lay ahead. Forging ever southwards and encountering increasingly barren scenery we came across a sign that over the next few weeks would be critical 'Eau Potable'. In the desert conditions it goes without saying that water is not exactly abundant and where the drinking variety is available such signs are displayed, and despite carrying thirty-three gallons of the stuff it was always worth while topping up just in case any mishap should occur. Of equal importance was the fuel for the 'Landy' which again we topped up whenever possible.

One by-product of all this vigilance was the substantial load that resulted and this first manifested itself well before we went 'off piste'. At a routine stop we were giving the Rover a quick inspection and noticed that one of the rear shock absorber mountings was beginning to bend and crack and it was obvious that some swift remedial action was required. Understandably no one had thought of setting up a welding shop in our middle of nowhere location which left us little option than to plod on carefully towards the next town of Ghardaia.

The route was now crossing what could best be described as desert but not in the rolling sand dune image conjured up by the word. Here it was seemingly devoid of vegetation though somehow it managed to support a few tented enclaves of nomadic herdsmen along with their goats. As Ghardaia drew closer we found ourselves winding around and over a range of hills and dunes until as if out of nowhere we were upon it. The green palms and grasses were in marked contrast to the reddish brown soil that stretched endlessly beyond it supporting just the occasional tuft of coarse grass.

On the repair side of things we were advised to continue onto EL Golea where the tarmac road stops and the dessert tracks take over, as there were some entrepreneurial characters who had seen the opportunities that the location offered as a last stop before hitting the dunes and conversely the first stop after hitting them if travelling in a northerly direction. Either way the need for running repairs was enough for them to have set up shop.

Well before rendezvousing with this final port of civilisation we noticed that the distant sky had turned a peculiar colour and some twenty-five miles further on were confronted with the reason, our first sand storm. Further progress was pointless and having parked up in what we considered to be the most appropriate direction we hunkered down for the night as the sand laden winds whipped around us depositing a fine layer of dusty sand on everything.

Anyone with a mechanical background will be aware of the effectiveness of sand blasting as a means of cleaning up metals and the desert sand storms can have a similar effect. It was not uncommon among the indigenous drivers to see cars with large sections of bodywork void of paint, their panels gleaming in the virgin metal of their construction. Some had found a solution by smearing the most vulnerable areas with grease which acted as a magnet soaking up the sand and protecting the paintwork though it is debatable which of the two evils was easiest on the eye.

The next day with the sand storm over and everything dusted and shaken out to remove the part of the desert that had become domiciled within the vehicle, we moved on in the direction of El Golea. Some twenty-five miles further on we encountered the first real sand dunes rolling along on each side of the vaguely visible black strip we were still able to enjoy driving on. The picturesque panorama was set off with some roaming camels and at last the desert was visually starting to deliver the picture I had previously conjured up in my mind.

The road was like an ever-changing mirage with sand being whipped across it often leaving mounds and making it difficult to navigate over. It also had the eerie effect of making the rare sight of oncoming traffic appear to be floating, as the shifting sands hid their wheels from view.

With the heat of the midday sun increasing daily we thought it best not to push the old Landy too hard in those temperatures and instead confined our driving to early to mid-morning and mid to late afternoon. During our lunchtime break we had a quick check to see how our shock absorber issue was standing up to the gruelling conditions and to our horror found that one of the others had literally come out in sympathy as the top mounting had completely sheered away from the chassis, putting an immense strain on the already overworked springs. El Golea couldn't come quick enough as we were obviously struggling on the sandy tarmac and would have no chance once we hit the true desert terrain.

With much caution and a fair bit of good fortune we limped into town and tracked down a garage where the repairs could be done, but at a price. Sadly when you are stuck on the edge of the desert with broken suspension the options to haggle are limited to say the least and so we agreed to go ahead with the necessary work.

Though we had agreed everything, just when it could be done was more of a problem and we resigned ourselves to spending the next few days there. El Golea due to its position as the last town before the real desert takes over was quite a vibrant community and several other fellow trans-Saharan travellers were giving their vehicles a last once over and we decided to do likewise.

Apart from the suspension problem of which we were painfully aware a detailed inspection uncovered many more delights, mainly nuts and bolts that were slowly working loose. These were duly attended to though one particular problem gave us a lot more hassle. The steering box was hanging loose on three nuts the fourth having lodged itself in an awkward crevice. Tightening everything up was very straightforward but retrieving the errant nut proved frustratingly difficult but once completed it at least rectified the 'loose' feeling we had been experiencing from the steering.

With our garage appointment eventually fulfilled we struck out over the final few miles of tarmac but were brought to a rude awakening when things didn't feel quite right and it transpired that the newly welded mountings had in fact been braised together and unsurprisingly had fallen apart at the first pothole we hit. An about turn saw us back in El Golea once again and after much heated discussion a further appointment to sort the problem properly was agreed.

Without the shockers to take the strain the condition of the springs was frighteningly ominous and doubts about our ability to survive the trip ahead started to come to mind. Should we maybe just accept defeat, sell the Landy and quit when we were ahead? This train of thought grew alarmingly to the point that we sussed out what the local market for such vehicles was like and gave serious consideration to several offers. We even sold off some of the spares we were carrying to local dealers for a very good return but probably a drop in the ocean to what they would eventually sell them for to their 'no option other than buy at any cost' customers.

As previously mentioned the town was a mecca for like minded travellers and it seemed that everyone in the world was at it, but of course in reality only a handful of vehicles were setting out every few days. The range of chosen transport was in itself quite interesting and along with a couple of the sensible Land Rover options there were also those more adventurous in their VW campers and a couple of down right mad characters – two in a Citroen 2CV and another in a Renault 4. Interestingly our paths were to cross on several occasions over the following weeks.

Travellers rendezvous at El Golea.

It was whilst chatting to some folk who had travelled north to El Golea that we were advised that the best place to sell the Land Rover was in the sub-Saharan belt, Niger, Nigeria, etc. so we decided to take the plunge and go for it now that the repairs had been properly completed even if we had sold off many of our spares in the meantime.

Talking to those arriving from the south was a great source of information, and information was something that I was to find invaluable as my trip progressed.

We got advice on how to handle some of the pitfalls that lay ahead; tips on where and where not to go, general information about weather prospects and something that was well worth knowing, where the best deals were to be struck on the currency exchange front. Banks were often difficult to find and the appetite throughout the African continent for foreign currency was ferocious resulting in many favourable rates being attainable as long as you knew where to find them.

Listening to some of the accounts of the journeys from East Africa would have been enough to put many off. Dire weather and road conditions, rampant malaria and close encounters with the native inhabitants both two and four legged varieties abounded, but somehow I couldn't help feeling that many of these accounts had been enhanced to boost the teller's ego, surely it couldn't be that bad – or could it? We were about to find out.

Land Rover in full flight.

With the Landy in as good fettle as we could get it and with fingers firmly crossed we once again stuck out over the last few miles of tarmac and shortly afterwards got our first taste of what we would be encountering for the next thirteen hundred miles to Agadez. The road, as it was laughingly referred to, consisted of a strip of hard soil which had developed a corrugated surface due to the constant passage of the heavy vehicles which supply the few villages and towns that are sprinkled across the area. These mammoth multi wheel trucks were able to withstand the buffeting that bouncing over the corrugations causes and the trick was to get up sufficient speed to hit only the tops of the corrugations and avoid the dips in-between. The height from the lowest point of the dip to the top could be up to eighteen inches and getting up to the required optimum speed and conversely slowing down from it was a bone jarring experience with everything shaken about violently.

The other option was simply to drive along next to the road but here you were simply riding on the sand and as it was impossible to tell what depth it was, one ran the risk of quickly being consumed and stuck axle deep in the stuff with all the attendant digging etc. that resulted. It was debatable as to which of the two choices was the least of the two evils and invariably whichever one we chose seemed wrong, consequently we spent our days switching from one to the other and did our fair share of digging and cajoling the old girl out of many sand pits on the way.

Our pre-arranged driving schedule became more of a necessity as we drove ever deeper into the desert with the daytime temperatures hitting 115° Fahrenheit. Most days we would stop around 11 o'clock and rig up an awning which afforded us some shelter from the baking sun and during one such break in the middle of nowhere we saw a figure way off in the distance. Over the ensuing half hour or so the image grew larger and larger as it moved in our direction over the shimmering sands and eventually the clear outline of a native Tuareg in full blue regalia, mounted astride a camel hove into view. These 'Blue Men' of the desert as they are referred to are a very impressive and proud people and on reaching us he duly dismounted and made his way over to us. Needless to say there was no common language but it was clear that he was requesting some water, or to be more precise demanding water though not in an arrogant manner. His tall upright demeanour struck a fine image and slightly over awed by his presence we duly obliged for which he was obviously grateful. As he rode off into the endless vista of rolling sand I managed to snap a picture and that one shot of Tuareg, camel and sand epitomises the magic the desert has to offer.

The first town on our route south was Ain Salah some two hundred and fifty miles from El Golea and our first mission was to report to the Sous Prefecture's office to report our safe arrival. This procedure applies to all journeys made across the desert and involves checking out as one leaves one town and checking in at the next one, along with your estimated duration for that trip. It does provide some safeguard, alerting the authorities of a potential missing party should they not arrive within their submitted time window.

Our Tuareg visitor.

SAHARA AND BEYOND

Having cleared all the required paperwork we set off once more. The next leg of our journey was a mere four hundred and fifty mile jaunt down to Tamanrasset the final town within the Algerian section of the desert.

The image of a desert consisting of endless rolling sand dunes is slightly misleading and on this part of the route we crossed several hilly areas often following the meanderings of what appeared to be dried up river beds. Vegetation however was still extremely sparse, the odd scrubby tree being about the best it got but amazingly we also caught the rare sight of a bird here and there and even more amazing a few nomadic tribesmen with their goats and camels. Their homes appeared to be made from woven rushes and these were carried with them as they roamed around their barren homeland.

We continued to make steady progress despite being relentlessly shaken to pieces by the rough desert track. Approximately one hundred miles from 'Tam' we came across a large area of derelict buildings surrounded by barbed wire, and shortly afterwards had to make a diversion when we came to a sign declaring the area beyond was contaminated. It transpired that this area had been used by the French for nuclear testing. One unexpected spin off from this was that the diverted section of road was finished with Tarmac and for the next twenty miles we enjoyed the bliss of gliding along neither shaken nor stirred, but alas it was all over too soon.

As we rattled our way ever southwards catastrophe suddenly hit when the front nearside suspension collapsed. We had been fully aware of the poor condition of the rear springs but somehow they were managing to cope with the relentless battering the road dished out but here it was the front spring that had sheered off just beyond the bush which mounted it to the chassis. As springs were not in our arsenal of spares we could only attempt to bodge things up and hope a replacement could be secured when we reached

Emergency repair to front spring.

'Tam'. Using some twenty yards of nylon twine we tightly lashed the broken parts as close together as we could get them then followed the same procedure with our sixty feet of half inch thick tow rope. Amazingly it held together for the remaining fifty-five miles and two very relieved young men eventually arrived at Tamanrasset.

Having got there was one thing, going anywhere else was totally dependant on us sourcing a replacement spring. Our location was to say the least remote, seven hundred miles south of El Golea and six hundred miles north of Agadez, these being the two towns which bookend the serious part of this Saharan route. We were sitting ducks, there for the taking by anyone who had the required parts and we were duly ripped off royally, but did secure the all important spring and after a frustratingly long period spread over a couple of days the repair was completed. We now had a relatively good second hand spring which even bowed in the right direction but that in itself brought its own problem as it put much more strain on the opposite corner which now had a concave profile. It was apparent that some further work was required and the painful fleecing of our Dinars continued as we agreed to fork out for a further replacement to be fitted at the rear.

With the repairs completed we left the old Foreign Legion outpost around which Tamanrasset is situated and headed off for the border that would see us leave Algeria and cross over into Niger where the visa that had taken so much effort to secure would come into play.

The road was slightly better on this section and later flattened out as the dunes became the prominent feature of the landscape. Having cleared the Algerian passport control at In Geuzzam, the customs arrangements having been dealt with in 'Tam', we entered a long section of no-mans land. Throughout Algeria there had been piste markers every three miles but on this section none existed and the combination of a vast flat plain and the deepest sand we had encountered made this the hairiest part of the trip so far and it was with some relief that we eventually reached the Niger control point at Asamakka, only to become stuck a few hundred tantalising yards short of it.

Much digging and the use of the Land Rover's versatile gearbox saw us free just as the little Citroen 2CV which we had last seen in El Golea came effortlessly scampering past us. It was so light that they could simply lift it out of the sand if stuck and they had had a fairly trouble free journey. Irksome to see the mighty British Land Rover put to shame by a little French runabout!

Formalities completed and with midday creeping up on us, which in this region resulted in temperatures nearing 130° Fahrenheit, it was siesta time. Nearby there was a natural water supply and part of the sulphur-laden hot water had been diverted through a couple of large rectangular metal containers. These were just too inviting and in no time at all we were lying with the hot waters flowing past us as we relaxed in our new found baths.

The final three hundred miles of our Saharan adventure lay ahead of us, so refreshed, though radiating more than a hint of 'fragrance de sulphur', we once again set off to do battle with the dunes. At first the sandy conditions were as bad as any we had encountered requiring lots of work from the engine which in turn had to be rested frequently to allow it to cool down but as we moved south things improved and signs of vegetation returned along with nomadic groups of Tuaregs. Two weeks after leaving the relative safety of El Golea we arrived in Agadez, the worst was behind us and we had lived to tell the tale.

A dip in the desert.

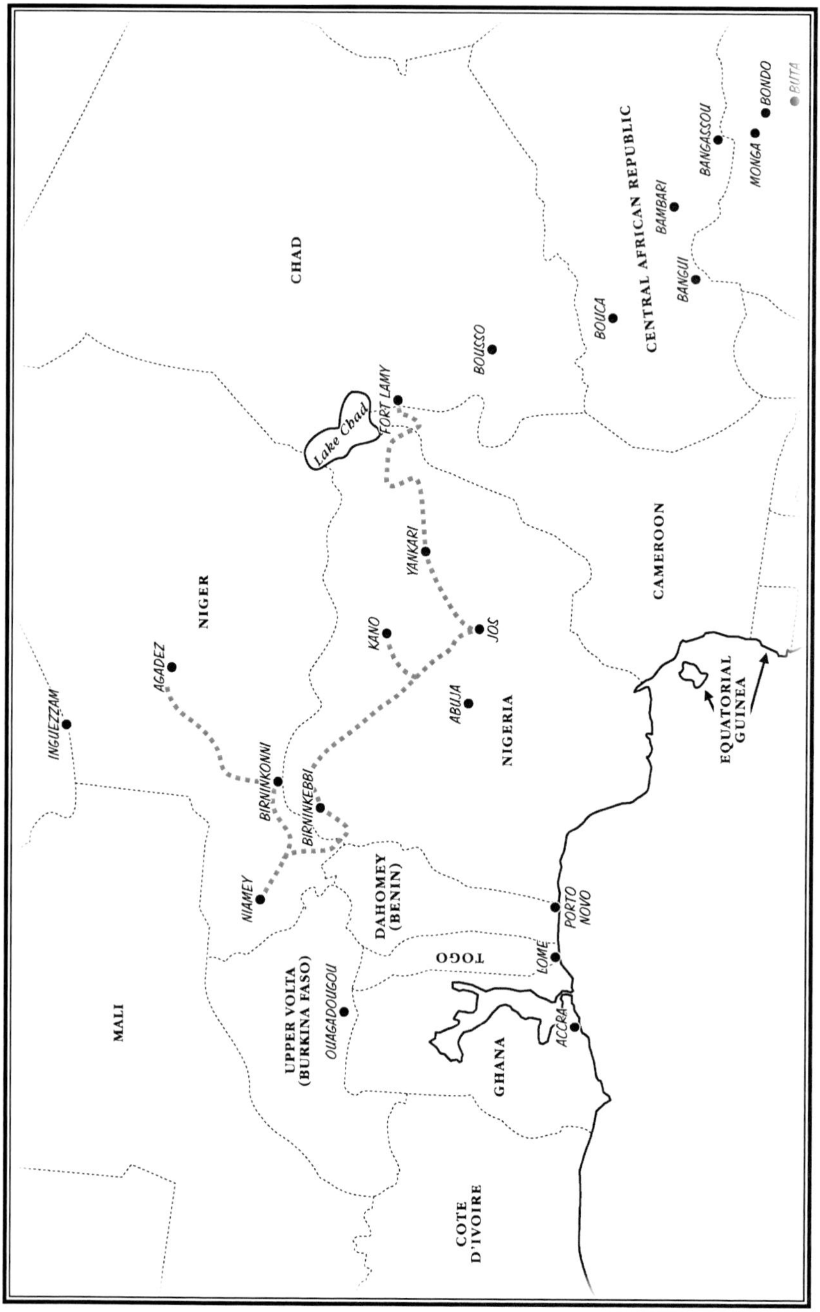
CHAD
CENTRAL AFRICAN REPUBLIC
BANGASSOU
BAMBARI
BANGUI
BOUCA
MONGA
BONDO
BUTA
BOUSSO
FORT LAMY
Lake Chad
NIGER
YANKARI
KANO
JOS
AGADEZ
ABUJA
NIGERIA
CAMEROON
EQUATORIAL GUINEA
INGUEZZAM
BIRNINKONNI
BIRNINKEBBI
NIAMEY
DAHOMEY (BENIN)
TOGO
LOME
PORTO NOVO
ACCRA
GHANA
UPPER VOLTA (BURKINA FASO)
OUAGADOUGOU
MALI
COTE D'IVOIRE

CHAPTER 6

FAREWELL TO THE LANDY

The campsite in Agadez was another of those meccas for travellers and many of the assembled crowd were folk we had met earlier or during our crossing and a real feeling of camaraderie drifted around, with tales or daring deeds abounding as we all exchanged the stories of our Saharan adventures.

This campsite also had the unexpected luxury of a swimming pool and whilst it may not have crept up to the stringent water quality rules we would enjoy back home any such thoughts were quickly forgotten, as the appeal of relaxing in it was too great to be ignored. Over the next few days life took on a very lazy veneer as we made life changing decisions such as how late to get up in the morning and how long to stay in the pool, but the serious business surrounding our future plans also had to be addressed.

Prior to making the crossing we had been told that the opportunities for selling our Land Rover would be far better in the sub-Saharan belt and as we were now there the matter needed to be resolved. Despite having replaced springs, etc. during the trip we didn't have a great deal of confidence in the old girl and as it had now fulfilled its main purpose of getting us through the desert we considered our options. For the rest of the trip down to South Africa we felt we could change to something smaller and more economical and having seen the heroics of the little 2CV it seemed the correct decision.

Before any new purchases could be considered we first had to find a new home for our current wheels and northern Nigeria being more populated appeared to be our best option. There was however one small problem. The validity of visas and entry permits varied from country to country some valid for a week or month some for a specific date and others as long as the passport was valid. The Nigerian one had a three month shelf life and on checking we realised that a combination of unexpected delays en route and a bit too much relaxing around the pool had taken up all but one day of it, and we needed slightly longer than that to get down to their border. Adopting a half full outlook we decided to press on anyway in the hope that they may still let us in.

On arriving at the border point at Birnin Konni we were greeted with a polite but firm refusal and directed to go to their embassy in the Niger capital Niamey and arrange to get a new permit. This entailed a five hundred mile round trip over pretty dire roads and we were cursing their inflexibility, after all we were only one day late and had crossed a desert.

Despite our pleading, they were obviously not going to budge and even a bit of financial inducement failed to change their minds so off to Niamey we headed. Not long after taking to the hard corrugated road we got a puncture. Wheel duly changed, we set off again only to pick up yet another puncture in no time. As the spare had now been used I set about the task of hitching into the next town complete with wheel and eventually returned, puncture repaired enabling us to get on our way. At the first opportunity we got the other one mended and were once more back to a full set. It appears that the local road maintenance team use a large metal rake that they haul over the corrugations, this 'sweeping' arrangement being designed to reduce the height of the corrugations, however the prongs shed shards of metal and punctures are a very common by-product of their efforts.

On reaching Niamey we thought it worth exploring the chances of selling the Landy there and set about sprucing it up. We were most fortunate to befriend a French couple who suggested we could park within their admittedly spacious grounds and with a ready supply of water on tap the metamorphosis commenced.

A good day and a half later, inside, outside, engine and all were showing the shining results of our hard work, however despite much endeavour and a few offers, no sale was forthcoming. Having well and truly outstayed our welcome at our French hosts we obtained the required paperwork, including a Chadian visa which we would need later, and duly made off back to Nigeria.

We took a different route and this time with everything in order we sailed past the border controls (there wasn't one on the Niger side) and headed eastward to the town of Kano. This was by far the biggest place we had visited since leaving Algiers and the area gave us the first introduction into African as against Arab culture. Generally the Sahara and above was inhabited by Arab groupings including many nomadic tribes folk but now we had crossed to the south the Bantu origins of the local inhabitants were the prominent feature.

Nigeria had of course been under British rule and as throughout the empire our forefathers had hung on to a bit of British life by creating their clubs, enclaves of 'Britishness' in the middle of their conquered lands from India to Africa and beyond. In colonial times these were very much a white only domain but with the passing of independence they had been opened up a little though in truth the old guard still held sway and only a handful of successful local business folk enjoyed the privilege of entering the inner sanctum.

The Kano club did however offer temporary membership to outsiders and had built up a reputation as a must visit destination for anyone doing a trans-African expedition. We duly signed up and were quickly soaking up the comforts it had to offer during the day whilst camping up nearby at night along with the ever changing flotilla of vehicles being used by the like minded travellers undertaking their adventures.

We once again hawked our Land Rover around to see if we could find a buyer and on the assumption that we would be down sizing we also used the vibrant market place to sell off some excessive baggage. Other bits and pieces found homes with our fellow travelling contingent but the big prize of selling the Landy eluded us, and pastures new beckoned.

The latest 'place to sell' tip was Chad and eventually we tore ourselves away from the comfort of the club and set of eastwards once more. During our two week stay we had become part of the scenery after giving an impromptu sing song one evening which resulted in us being offered a regular evening spot for which we even got paid. This in turn had opened many doors and led to us being feted by the committee members and partaking in much socialising, but all good things must come to an end.

Whilst camping at Kano we had become very friendly with another couple of lads, Ian and Steve who were also travelling by Land Rover to South Africa. Although they were aware that we were looking to sell ours and would therefore not be long-term companions we mutually agreed to travel together over to Chad. This provided a bit more peace of mind knowing we each had some back-up should any further ills befall us.

Oops!

On the way across the northern route we had chosen, via Jos, we detoured slightly and visited the Yankari game park which has within its boundaries the Wikki hot springs. We finished up spending the next five days in the company of some British VSOs who were working there. Days were taken up out on safari with the volunteers who were also the local gamekeepers, and included one encounter with a herd of Elephants that was too close for comfort, whilst nights were spent exchanging tales, singing and imbibing the odd beer or two.

A large area of the park was heavily forested with the tree canopy touching high above us blanking out much of the natural light from the damp dank atmosphere below, and with the long creepers dangling down from on high we expected Tarzan to suddenly appear swinging through the trees; it certainly conjured up the type of jungle scene you would expect to find in deepest Africa. To reach Chad we would be making a brief excursion into the northern tip of Cameroun and whilst on our way there we got our first taste of what a tropical storm could throw at us, relentless heavy rain, thunder and lightning and a ferocious dose of biting wind to round off the recipe. The rainy season was just round the corner and more of the same would be on the cards.

We crossed into Cameroun and were making the relatively short journey north to Chad when suddenly smoke started belching from beneath our bonnet. In what seemed like only a few seconds we had screeched to a halt and sprayed a liberal amount of the fire extinguisher's content all over the engine which fortunately had the required effect but why it had happened was a mystery. Once things had cooled down it turned out that the electrics had shorted out. Being a diesel engine meant we could operate without electrics once the engine was running so, having isolated the area where the fire had obviously been, we gingerly re-attached the battery, fired her up, then immediately disconnected the battery again and cautiously continued on over the border, albeit without anything that required powering by electricity.

The following day was spent meticulously checking out each circuit one by one until the fault was found, isolated and crudely rewired. With a generous application of the multi-purpose black tape to cover our handy work it looked quiet respectable and was fully functional, a good day's work achieved by all and a potential disaster alleviated.

The capital city of Chad, Fort Lamy (now called N'Djamena) lies on the Chari River which forms a natural boundary for the country, so as soon as we had survived the river crossing we were in the city on which we had now pinned all our hopes of selling the Landy.

The massive Lake Chad which also borders onto Niger, Nigeria and Cameroun lay a short distance to the north and we all decided that it would be worth a visit. Not wishing any further hassles to befall our vehicle it was decided to take Ian and Steve's. We set off north into the bundu which became ever more difficult to traverse finally resulting in us hacking a path way through the vegetation before finally admitting defeat, despite being only a few miles from our goal, and so we set about retracing our path back to the capital. We could only imagine that we had taken a wrong turning somewhere, as even the remote wilds around the lake must surely be more accessible than that.

Back in the relatively civilised surroundings of the city we once again set about cleaning up the Landy and ensuring all the obvious service issues were attended to, and then started our hunt for a prospective buyer.

First port of call was the local Land Rover garage which, though not interested in buying it from us, gave us several leads. Sadly none came to fruition but the old stiff upper lip and never say die mentality prevailed, and ten days and many false dawns later a chance meeting with some American evangelists got the ball rolling.

They were part of an assembly of members of the Baha'i religion, attending one of their rare coming-togethers, and initially they presumed I had called to 'join the faith'. However, I quickly put them right on that score and made a prompt exit but not before managing to arouse their interest in our vehicle.

Over the next few days many meetings occurred and much massaging of the facts and figures took place in order to facilitate a deal which was acceptable to all. Appropriate receipts were provided by us that allowed their budget for customs duty to be met. With all the red tape eventually completed we finally agreed a date to hand over the keys in exchange for a substantial wad of cash which virtually covered all the costs we had incurred to get there. This included the initial purchase, alteration, servicing and running costs of the vehicle plus all our food, etc. so it was like starting out afresh with our full budget intact.

Ian and Steve had moved on once they knew we had secured a sale and Roger had already decided to fly directly to South Africa where he had relations who could help us find employment. For my part only the Congo lay between me and the relatively good roads of East Africa where I had plans to buy some form of transport, possibly even a motorbike, to get me to our goal in the south.

One slight hitch occurred with Roger's plans, as his relatives were currently back in England so he decided to go back home and apply to emigrate directly to South Africa. The time this would take to arrange and the time it would take me to complete the overland journey we believed would be much the same and with his half of the spoils he made arrangements to get a flight home. As events transpired, he settled back into life in the UK a little too well and never did make the journey south.

Flights left on both Monday and Wednesday and Monday was the day agreed for the hand over of the keys. As normal, due to the heat at midday, business started early in the morning and as we had completed everything by 10 o'clock, it was then a mad dash to buy a ticket and get to the airport for the 1.45 pm flight.

Among the many possessions he returned with was the AA carnet which had acted as our surety against having to pay and reclaim customs duty each time we crossed a border. With it now duly stamped to the effect that the vehicle had been sold and all duties paid we could return it to the AA and reclaim our costs.

In all the rush of the morning it was no time before he was up in the skies winging his way homeward and only then did the reality of the situation hit home. I was now on my own in the middle of Africa and I questioned why I too wasn't on that plane.

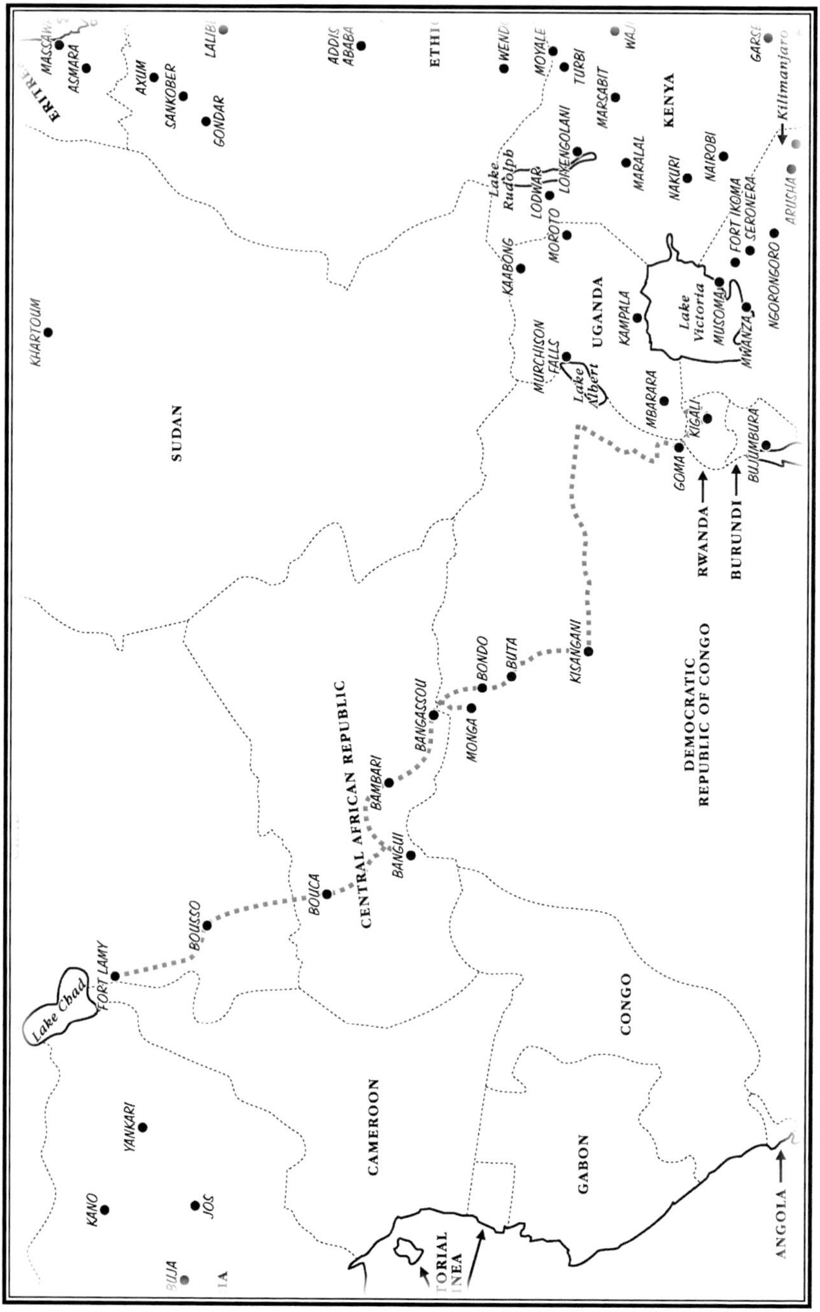
ASMARA
AXUM
SANKOBER
GONDAR
ADDIS ABABA
MOYALE
TURBI
KENYA
MARSABIT
Kilimanjaro
Lake Rudolph
LODWAR
MARALAL
NAKURI
NAIROBI
FORT IKOMA
SERONERA
ARUSHA
MOROTO
KAABONG
UGANDA
KAMPALA
Lake Victoria
MUSOMA
MWANZA
NGORONGORO
KHARTOUM
MURCHISON FALLS
Lake Albert
MBARARA
KIGALI
GOMA
BUJUMBURA
RWANDA
BURUNDI
SUDAN
KISANGANI
BUTA
BONDO
MONGA
BANGASSOU
CENTRAL AFRICAN REPUBLIC
BAMBARI
BANGUI
BOUCA
BOUSSO
FORT LAMY
Lake Chad
DEMOCRATIC REPUBLIC OF CONGO
CONGO
CAMEROON
GABON
YANKARI
KANO
JOS
ANGOLA

CHAPTER 7

THE HITCHING STARTS HERE

It was now nearly four months since we set off and the six-month schedule originally pencilled in for this African leg was looking optimistic to say the least.

Over the last week or so whilst trying to secure a sale I had met a real cross section of Chadian society and had got friendly with an English lad Brian who was working for the UN. He had been very helpful, allowing me and Roger to store stuff at his place while we sorted out what was, and what was not, going to be sold with the vehicle. The 'was nots' we had disposed of by hawking them around fellow travellers and the local market and I had whittled my worldly goods down to what could be fitted in my newly acquired kit bag.

Brian kindly suggested that I could stay at their place whilst making final preparations and on the 13th May I stepped out towards the city outskirts and the road south to the Central African Republic. I didn't step for very long, a mere twenty yards or so before I was lying in a heap having tripped, partly due to the sheer weight of my pack and mostly due to the fact that the umbrella I had attached broke loose and got tangled up in my legs. The notorious 13th omen continued even if it wasn't a Friday. Having spent a considerable part of the day by the roadside to no avail and aware that I wasn't going to cope with the size and weight of my pack I finished up back at Brian's and set about rearranging what I was carrying.

As we were now on the fringes of the wet season the umbrella had seemed a good idea though the sight of a back packer and a brolly was somewhat incongruous so that was one of the first things to go, and a few hours later with what I now considered to be only essentials I was prepared for an early start the following morning.

Take two. This time I managed to get a lift some sixty miles to a point where the road forked and our respective journeys went their separate ways and there I stayed for the rest of the day without sight of a single vehicle heading my way. What had I let myself in for? I certainly attracted the attention of the locals and as evening began to fall was most grateful for the offer of shelter in one of their homes. This was of mud construction somewhat more substantial than the reed and bamboo dwelling places of the folk further north and when the rain started to pour down it was as good as the Ritz to me.

Pretty well at first light I was back on the road and eventually got going courtesy of a Roman Catholic missionary who took me on towards Bousso and as most of the day had now passed I was invited to stay over with him and his fellow brothers.

The French I had absorbed during my school days was nonexistent and as Roger could get by for both of us, when and if required, it was now a hassle for me to be stuck in French speaking countries, and to this end I had started learning page after page of vocabulary from a phrase book, parrot fashion, but without grammar. I reasoned that it was better to be able to say, 'I go tomorrow,' or 'I go yesterday,' rather than say nothing at all. It was starting to work to a degree, the degree being that I had only got up the 'Gs' in the alphabet so conversation was limited for the time being.

After a very relaxing night and the chance to get rid of the countryside that had attached itself to me in the form of a fine coating of dust, I bade thankful farewells and took up my post on the road south. Sadly in keeping with earlier experiences I was still there at the end of the day as neither of the two vehicles that passed could accommodate me, however on the bright side I was now up to the 'Ns'.

The mission became my refuge for a second night and once again I was made to feel very welcome and surprisingly the question of religion, more specifically mine, was never raised.

THE HITCHING STARTS HERE

I had more luck second time round, getting a lift on down towards the border with a young Greek lad who had several businesses in the area. The Greeks here seem to have the same control of commerce that the Lebanese had back in Nigeria.

Prior to his arrival I had experienced a déjà vu moment when what should come down the road but our old Landy. My heart sank thinking of all the possible problems that might have manifested themselves by now, but my fears were unfounded, everything was going well, however they were not going in my direction. I was somewhat relieved to hear this as I would have hated to be on board if something had gone wrong.

The next few days followed much the same pattern of endless waiting for the odd vehicle, and even when successfully on board our progress was often curtailed when the rain barriers were deployed. This is a simple method of preventing excessive wear being caused to the dirt roads when wet, and despite the temperature reaching beyond 100° Fahrenheit between storms, it was not uncommon to be held back for half a day at the road blocks while things dried out. Suffice it to say, progress was slow.

The landscape was mainly flat but was now much more lush as we were approaching the equatorial belt having left the savannah grass and scrub to the north. Houses also seemed a bit more substantial though still mud in construction and were often adorned with crude decorations, crude in the 'basic' sense of the word not the 'pornographic' sense.

I crossed the border into CAR (Central African Republic) and headed for the capital Bangui getting ever deeper into jungle territory on the way. This was one of the poorest countries on the continent but in true corrupt fashion the rulers were lining their pockets.

The Presidential Palace at Bangui C.A.R.

This contrast was vividly apparent at the Presidential palace, a very modern, white, honeycomb design, complete with various fleets of cars, Mercedes included. I was in the throws of taking a picture of it, when a gun wielding guard came running across the compound to the gates where I was stood and at gunpoint made it clear that I was under arrest. The incident thankfully was quickly resolved when I was able to explain who I was, and what I was doing, to a more senior member of the guard and in a total volte-face I was then given a brief tour of the outside and allowed to take pictures at random.

The jungle drums had informed me that the Rock Hotel was a place used as a camping spot by many overlanders, and on arriving there it was like an old pals reunion with cars and faces that I had previously come across, some at Kano, some at Niamey and even an American couple in a very sad looking VW I had last seen in EL Golea. Needless to say the story telling went on well into the night.

Among the assembled crowd was Howie, an American, travelling by Land Rover who we had bumped into on several previous occasions. He too had been travelling with a companion but his colleague had decided to return home and an offer to travel along with him took all of a nanosecond to consider before giving my positive response. He had paired up with another English couple Dave and Sandra who were also in a Land Rover and we all quickly struck up a really good friendship and preparations were soon underway for our posse to head into the jungle that lay ahead.

The road to the Congo (Zaire) was at first tarmac but soon became the more common corrugated dirt surface with all the attendant rattling and shaking that goes with it. Howie didn't seem too happy with the way his vehicle was handling and pulled over to check things out just in time as the front wheel was now only held on by one of its five nuts and that was already half undone. The remedy was to remove one nut from the other three wheels and make regular check ups.

Our convoy continued to the river border crossing at Bangassou where we encountered our next round of fun and games. The ferry was free to use but was moored on the opposite bank and we were told that to start the engine they needed a battery. This posed no problem other than how to get it there, and thereby lay the catch. One of the conveniently situated locals would paddle the battery over in his dug out tree trunk, but for a price. We were at their mercy, but did successfully barter one

THE HITCHING STARTS HERE

off against another and with the fare agreed our battery was dispatched to the other side. Shortly afterwards the ferry was chugging us across the river and onto Congo soil.

Our suspicions about the whole set up were confirmed when Dave nosily looked around and saw two fairly new batteries attached to the modern diesel engine and ours nowhere to be seen. However, as discretion is the better part of valour and with our battery safely returned to us we took it on the chin and went on our way.

Hassles with customs were our next problem. In keeping with many crossings the official customs post can be many miles away from the actual border, in this case it was forty-five miles away at Monga, and as the road onwards from there was impassable it meant a considerable detour over a far from friendly mixture of mud and potholes before we were legally back where we had started.

We knew the rainy season would throw up many challenges and shortly a further road closure saw us altering our route and once more having the pleasure of paying the ferryman, this time to cross the Uele River. We had been told what the official tariff was but warned that they would probably double it, travellers like us being seen as easy pickings, however with the previous episode still fresh in our minds we were in no mood to be ripped off again.

Ferry across the River Uele.

This ferry consisted of five large dugout tree trunks lashed together and overlaid with planks, the complete arrangement being propelled manually by paddle power. On arrival, and true to form, the higher figure was demanded and when we pointed out that it was not correct they simply paddled off to the other side of the river. A period of brinksmanship followed as we parked across the landing area blocking the path of any other traffic while they sat at the other side. Eventually they gave in and took our offer and the scary passage over the quiet swiftly flowing water eventually got us safely to the other side.

We pushed on south through ever worsening roads and ever thickening vegetation towards Kisangani, previously known as Stanleyville which is situated on the river Congo. Our journey however came to an abrupt halt when late one afternoon we came across a couple of stranded vehicles next to a collapsed bridge. The term bridge sounds rather grand as it was in fact simply several thick tree trunks laid side by side, forming a ten foot wide crossing over the ravine below. A couple of the trees had collapsed into the ravine and no one was going anywhere until it was repaired, so we camped up next to the others and waited to see what would transpire.

Later that afternoon some officials from the road department carried out their inspection and plans for the repair were swung into motion. A large number of locals were recruited as labour, though where they came from I have no idea. The task was to forge a path into the dense jungle vegetation which bordered the muddy track we were on, find suitable replacement trees, fell them, cut them to the required length, square off what would become the top surface and finally drag them back to the road and manoeuvre them into position over the ravine. This obviously wasn't going to be a two-minute job and we resigned ourselves to a lengthy stopover.

The following day was June 1st, my birthday, and much to my surprise I was woken and presented with a hand made card from Dave and Sandra and saw a Happy Birthday message had been written in my diary by Howie. It's not everyone who can boast that despite being stranded in the middle of the Congo they still received their birthday post.

It proved to be a fascinating day seeing just how the local work force approached the job in hand. Firstly the right tree with an appropriate girth had to be located then, as one team set about felling it, another would start hacking a clearance through the dense undergrowth laying

A pre-prepared tree trunk being hauled to the bridge.

the hewn bamboo on the ground to act as a base over which the massive logs would be hauled. Once felled a party was assigned to the job of cutting it to size and levelling off the top surface whilst the next tree was located and the relevant teams got on with their respective duties. Choosing the right tree was deemed more important than choosing the nearest which meant much more work for all concerned.

When the first huge trunk had been prepared it was all hands to the deck and with a mixture of creepers and some rope, and a massive expenditure of energy from all concerned the bounty was slowly dragged along the pre-prepared pathway to the road and subsequently into position. All this was done to a shanty style accompaniment and the eerie sound of the combined groups chanting as they crashed through the undergrowth was something quite awesome.

Bridge construction continued over the next two days during which time more vehicles arrived to join in the party atmosphere that had developed among the assembled crowd which consisted of a real mixture of locals, truck drivers and overlanders all mucking in and helping each other out. We were even treated to a hairdressing lesson when one of the local women plaited another's hair in the tight complex designs sported by many Africans.

A section of the road to Buta.

The poor road conditions and our brush with this collapsed bridge made Howie and Dave wary about tackling the Kisangani route as an easier alternative was available, however a couple of the other vehicles still planned to go that way. The upshot was that I finished up joining forces with four lads in another Land Rover and the American couple in the sad looking VW who had also now arrived to join the waiting melee.

If we thought we had encountered poor conditions so far, the route south was to knock them all into a cocked hat. It was rough earth which had been turned into a quagmire with the mixture of rain and the passing of heavily laden cotton trucks and the undulating landscape meant we were either climbing or descending a series of hills with either direction causing its own set of problems. On one particular section where the mud was two feet deep we had a real struggle but with the use of bamboo and much digging and pushing we both somehow got through and eventually arrived in Kisangani.

One reason I wanted to go there was that after the debacle of our Daily Telegraph communication exploits I had started using the 'Poste Restante' facility whereby mail can be sent addressed to you care of a post office. This facility only tends to be available in larger cities and Kisangani was the destination I had given for the next mail to be sent to. Overall it worked very well and so it proved again and I was able to catch up with some of the news from back home.

THE HITCHING STARTS HERE

The two lads who owned the Land Rover, Jean-Pierre and Alain had a background in catering, Alain being a fully qualified chef. Part of the daily ritual was to source fresh food for our evening meal. This proved quite interesting when upcountry, and although some vegetables and fruit, mainly bananas, were available meat was a rarer commodity, though the odd leg of antelope was acquired. We couldn't quite bring ourselves to tackling monkey which was often presented whole, but having been smoke charred the resemblance to a small child was too much to stomach.

Road conditions remained pretty poor as we headed west towards Uganda through the heavily forested landscape and late afternoons were spent sussing out a suitable shelter in which to spend the night as the vehicles were too cramped to cater for us all.

During one of the frequent tropical storms we came to a shelter on the edge of a village and thankful to be out of the rain set up camp for the night which passed uneventfully until the early morning, and the arrival of some locals complete with wood, water and oil drums. They lit up their fires and we realised we must have camped in their cooking shelter, an illusion that was shortly shattered by the arrival of three large pigs. We had in fact taken up residency in the local abattoir.

On a more tranquil note we woke on another occasion to the wonderful harmonic gospel singing of the locals who had quietly skirted round without disturbing us as we lay sleeping in the porch of their church.

As we moved closer to Uganda we crossed through

With my Pygmy friend.

the area populated by Pygmies who enjoyed a protected status, the country being keen to preserve their culture and not at all keen to see them exploited by 'tourists'. I did however manage to get a picture taken next to one of them and as I am only five foot five it did show off their diminutive stature.

The nearer we got to the border region so the cultivation of the land increased. Coffee and banana plantations abounding and we eventually emerged from the thickly forested surrounds that had been the backdrop for much of my trip across the Congo onto a more open area of rolling grassland, the first signs that we were approaching East Africa.

In the distance we could see the snow capped peaks of the Ruwenzori Mountains or, as they are more romantically known, the 'Mountains of the Moon'. It seemed strange to see snow when we were virtually on the Equator but at 15,600 feet it probably wasn't so strange after all.

Having crossed the Equator, we followed the road pretty well due south taking in my second game park, the Albert Park, next to Lake Edward where we had a close encounter with some Hippos while camping out, but such are the dangers one exposes oneself to if daft enough to camp in the vicinity of the local wild life.

The final port of call in the Congo was Goma which lies on the edge of Lake Kivu and among the Vuringu range of volcanic mountains which includes the still active Nyiragongo. At night this creates a fantastic red glowing sky above it reflecting the molten lava from the cauldron within. This region is also the habitat of the mighty Mountain Gorillas which in more recent years have been the subject of many a wildlife documentary.

Rwanda now lay between us and Uganda where we would be splitting and going our separate ways, the vehicles and their occupants heading on south whilst I intended initially to head north.

With the border successfully negotiated the change in the countryside after the Congo was very noticeable with the picturesque mountains intensely cultivated.

The locals here broadly consist of two ethnic groups, the minority Tutsi and the majority Hutu. The former are from a Nilo-Hamitic background and are taller, sharing this trait with other tribes I would come across later in my travels, the Turkana and the famous Masia being amongst them. The Hutu on the other hand fall under the Bantu grouping. Many of the Tutsis had fled from problems in neighbouring

THE HITCHING STARTS HERE

Burundi and in years to come would be caught up in one of the worst cases of modern day genocide the world has known.

With Rwanda duly explored and their border controls negotiated we arrived at the Ugandan border only to encounter our next problem. It could possibly be put down to the thorough and exacting systems our British colonialism had instilled in them but whatever the reason they were determined to thoroughly check out all our documentation and stumbled on an inaccuracy with the carnet for Jean-Pierre and Alain's vehicle. They had at an earlier stage changed the engine but had not updated the paperwork. Needless to say, like myself they had already crossed numerous border controls without any major incident but they were unconditionally told to lodge a fee equivalent to sixty percent of the vehicle's value or none of us were going anywhere.

The delay was a hassle made worse as we had no local currency having blown our last Rwandan Francs on a celebratory beer and without crossing into Uganda we had no Ugandan Shillings so we were stuck in no man's land. Eventually the officials allowed one of us across to exchange funds and source some basic supplies but the impasse otherwise continued.

In the end a compromise was reached whereby they would allow us to cross without the vehicle, and if/when the documentation had been amended by officials in Kampala they would subsequently release it from an effective quarantine.

For me this was a result as I had already arranged to split from the group once in Uganda, for them however it meant packing overnight essentials etc. and leaving the rest of their belongings along with the vehicle at the border. The outcome was that Jean-Pierre undertook the task of sorting out the paperwork whilst the others remained with the Landy rather than leave it and all their worldly goods unattended.

So ended what had been a fascinating month of adventure with some really great companions and after a round of heartfelt thanks and best wishes I was once again on my own heading into pastures new.

76

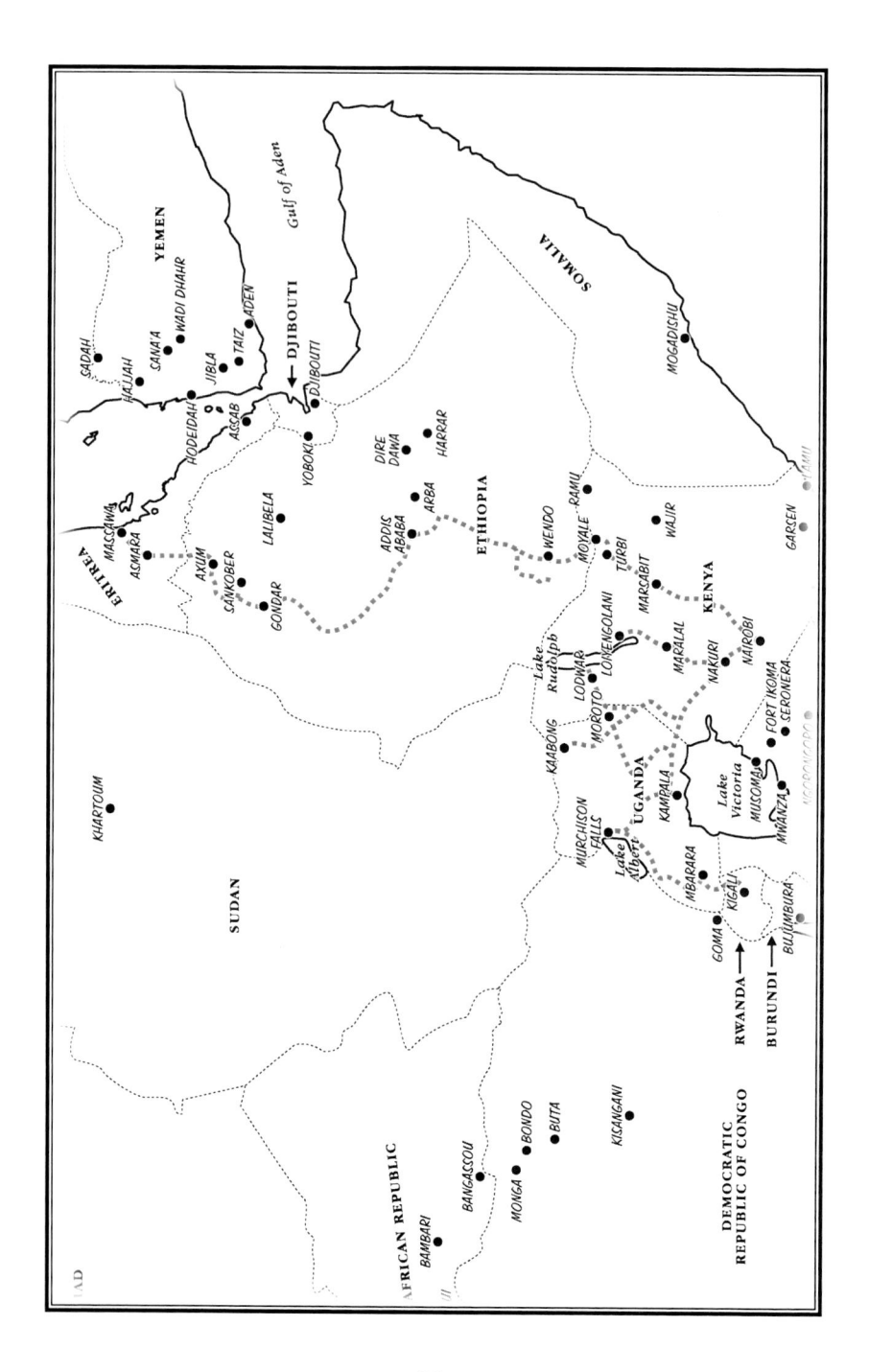

CHAPTER 8
ALONE AGAIN

Before heading for Kampala I had decided to travel up to the north west of the country to have a look at the Murchison Falls on the river Nile and this journey took me back up towards the Ruwenzori mountains which I was now viewing from the eastern elevation, though they were just as spectacular.

It took several days to reach the falls and on the way I had been invited to stay one evening at a Sikh temple where I enjoyed my first taste of Asian hospitality. Back home in Malvern we had not been a centre of immigration and very few had settled in the town. I had to admit my ignorance of the various religions practised by the ex-Indian and Pakistanis who had taken up residence in East Africa, and was intrigued to glean some background information not only about my hosts' beliefs but also about the Hindu, Buddhist and Moslem faiths.

The falls proved to be well worth a visit, though nothing like the mighty Victoria Falls found on the Zambian/Rhodesian (Zimbabwe) Border. The road had taken me through a landscape that was generally more cultivated than I'd previously experienced. Much of the crops grown were at subsistence level in small holdings or 'shambas' but I also came across an area of tea plantations and was able to visit one and learn all about what goes into producing the good old British cuppa.

Via a different route I moved on to Kampala and having spent a couple of weeks on my own I was developing a better idea of the ups and downs of travelling solo. The roads in Uganda were generally better, although as one moved away from the central belt around Lake Victoria they progressively deteriorated and in the far extremes started to resemble the mud tracks I'd become so used to throughout the CAR and the Congo. Traffic was more plentiful and hitching lifts didn't entail sitting for days on end just waiting for a vehicle to appear. I also found that in the more remote parts it was possible to arrange lifts with different government bodies including the police and local officials who were not averse to having a bit of company during their daily chores.

Remembering how we had slept out under a variety of shelters over the previous month, made me less worried about where I would be laying my head at night, and by politely requesting permission a wide range of abodes were home to my reveries.

I was also struck by the old boys' network. Often having acquired a lift, and frequently shelter for the night as well, I would be given the address of a friend or work colleague to visit at a later point in my travels, and even if it was only a matter of meeting them for a beer and draining them of all their local knowledge these contacts were a great source of information, and information was king.

In Kampala I checked out the British Embassy catching up with what was going on in the world outside my little bubble and here again struck up a friendship with one of the staff, Roger, an English lad who knew how to enjoy himself, and I was able to use his place as a base during my stay. The network went into action once more when I wanted to change the substantial amount of French Francs I was carrying in notes into the safer format of sterling travellers cheques. Having hawked round all the banks with little success Roger introduced me to a colleague at the Embassy who was able to have a word with the right person and the transaction was duly completed.

I was now giving some thought to my future plans and decided to postpone ideas of getting my own transport as hitching was definitely bringing me into contact with all sorts of characters and opening many doors on the way.

Kenya was the next country on the agenda, but my appetite had been whetted on hearing about the tribes people in the far north east of Uganda and so the first of many detours began.

One downside of hitching was the unwieldy sausage shaped kit bag I was carrying, and for the journey ahead Roger allowed me to leave some of my stuff at his place thus lightening the load and making things easier all round.

The initial roads up towards Karamojong country were fine but as I moved further north and the fertile lands grew increasingly barren so the roads deteriorated and being the rainy season getting around was fun to say the least. I did manage the final stint with some official from the ministry of works and eventually reached the town of Kaabong which was in a more mountainous setting, these mountains forming part of the western flank of the Rift Valley.

The Ugandan government under the relatively new leadership of Idi Amin was keen to stop the indigenous tribes folk wearing their traditional clothing, or lack of it, as it was in reality, but the Karamojong and the Pokot tribes from this northeastern region were a last bastion of the old ways. They were classed as ethnic agro-pastoral herdsmen and still moved their cattle around and lived in small 'manyattas' comprising of a thorn palisade enclosure within which were housed various buildings. The small huts constructed from wooden frames covered with skins or grasses, were mainly used by the females as the males slept outside weather permitting and were often away from the base with their herds. There were also pens for the animals.

Being another of the Nilo-Hamitic tribes they were tall and upright in stature. Their couture consisted of a single cloth robe or 'shuka' wrapped round their naked body then knotted over one shoulder in toga style for the men, and a basic goat skin skirt and modesty apron for the women, who in addition often sported a goat skin bodice wrapped around their shoulders and were mainly bare breasted. The men adorned the back of their heads with dried mud onto which colour was added and on special occasions bright feathers would also be used.

Mainly to protect their mud covered heads when sleeping each male carried a small wooden stool which doubled up as a pillow and to complete their outfit wooden clubs and metal tipped spears were also carried to ward off the enemy.

The enemy in question were the respective Karamojong and Pokot tribes of Uganda and the neighbouring Kenyan Turkana tribe who lived an identical life style and were of the same stock. Each were sworn rivals and cattle raiding skirmishes were commonplace. The slight advantage that the Turkana people enjoyed in their everyday existence was that being based over the border in Kenya no such outlawing of dress and traditions had been imposed on them.

Before leaving I was lucky to be told of a dance celebration that was taking place nearby. Whilst the somewhat monotonous jumping up and down on the spot that comprised much of the routine was basic, it was also quite mesmerising and trance-inducing, highlighted even more by the steady rhythmic chanting, clapping and stamping that accompanied it.

Many of the assembled crowd were dressed in their finery, the girls wearing colourful earrings, bracelets, armlets and massive necklaces cascading over their shoulders all intricately made from beads and/or silver and copper coloured metals, the larger necklaces indicating that the wearer was married. Several of the young warriors were sporting heavily scarred backs and upper arms creating a decorative crocodile skin look and signifying that they had killed someone on one of their aforementioned skirmishes. The scarring is created with an arrow head, making scores of small cuts into which an irritant plant sap is rubbed, a process that I would imagine is a tad more painful than the tattooing undertaken by many in our society. Other body decorations included distended ear lobes into which bone inserts were applied and large chin plugs, an extreme variant on the studs of today.

Nomadic homes on the barren Lake Rudolph landscape.

The excursion to the far-flung north proved well worth the effort and in total contrast to the modern lifestyle offered by Kampala and I decided to make a further detour over the unmanned border into Kenya, past Lodwar and up to the western side of Lake Rudolph (now Lake Turkana). I was able to hitch along with a group who were carrying out some studies into the fish population of the vast blue-green waters of the lake and thus spent a very interesting few days in this moon like landscape of barren volcanic rocks and sand. It was a most inhospitable region though still home to a small mainly nomadic few who also eked out a living from the lake's fish resources. It was then another long and often treacherous route back south into relative normality.

On my return to the capital city I was able to collect my remaining belongings and so moved eastwards into Kenya. Sadly I was not going to be the only one moving out, as on the same day that I left General Idi Amin announced that all Asians were being expelled from his country.

Time schedules were slipping badly and were about to be truly scuppered by my decision to head up to Ethiopia rather than immediately moving south, but before that I was intrigued to have a further look into how the Turkana people compared with their warring neighbours and thus embarked on another epic journey to their homelands, this time my destination was the town of Loiyengolani on the southeast side of Lake Rudolph.

The road was once again fairly quiet and I pushed further north through ranching country, not that I was really aware of that activity until given a lift by the wife of one of the local European farmers. Due to the poor nature of the soil vast swathes were required to accommodate the herds of cattle and sheep, fifteen acres per head of cattle and three for sheep and their farm was spread over forty five thousand acres. It transpired that this was only one of four farms they owned in addition to a part holding in a vast new venture down by the coast. To get around the various locations Gilford often used his small single engine Piper Cherokee aircraft and when he heard that I had never flown in my life the matter was quickly resolved and I was soon up with the birds having my virgin flight experience, something that will live with me for the rest of my life. As if that wasn't enough the following day he flew me up to Maralal and through a business contact arranged transport on up to my lakeside destination. And so two days later I was once more crossing the boulder strewn volcanic landscape on my way to make a second visit to this remote location.

A new lodge was under construction at Loiyengolani aimed at tapping into a niche market of the fishing community, Lake Rudolph as previously stated having rich reserves including world record size Nile Perch. Having met the parties involved in this venture another first took place as I was invited to join their small party on a fishing trip. This was serious business with the sea fishing rods, ratchet gearing and large lures all aimed at catching big trophies and with complete beginner's luck I managed to land four examples ranging from twenty eight to ninety two pound, quite a monster but a mere tiddler compared with the record two hundred and fifty pound specimen.

Just how this new venture would impact on the ways of the indigenous Elmolo and Turkana people only time would tell and I just hoped that they would be able to continue with their time warp traditional customs. Once more the trip into this far-flung corner of the country proved to be very interesting even though the costumes and customs were very similar to those I had already seen and a week or so later after many delays and some more horrendous road journeys I was in the capital city of Nairobi.

The usual trip to the Embassy resulted once more in an invitation to stay over at the home of one of the officials and a friendship that was to last over many visits to the city was born.

Both Doug and his wife Molly, who were considerably older than me, treated me like a son. One of their interests was folk music and they regularly attended a folk club in the city to which I was duly invited and I took no persuading before agreeing to join them. I was in my element singing along and thoroughly enjoying the atmosphere and that must have been apparent as Doug suggested that I should get up and do a spot. A couple of beers had supplied any Dutch courage required, so I agreed, and was soon up on stage giving it my all. You can imagine my surprise when after a much appreciated round of applause a loud voice from the back shouted, 'What the hell are you doing here?'

The voice belonged to Vic a colleague from back in Malvern who had been seconded to Nairobi by his company. Needless to say the night just got better and better. As if that was not enough of a coincidence another mutual friend, Janet, who was an air stewardess was due to visit Nairobi the next day and before the night was out Doug and Molly had kindly suggested that we should all meet up at their place and make a party of it and quite some party it turned out to be. The final cherry on the cake was that a few days later Janet was flying on one of her regular trips to America and had arranged to see another mutual friend, Angela, and so was able to pass on regards from the middle of Africa to Chicago. Somehow the old saying that it's a small world suddenly seemed so true.

Over time Nairobi was to become a regular haunt as I moved up and down the country on various sorties to see the pink flamingos at Lake Nakuru, the stunning mountain scenery around the Aberdares and Mount Kenya with its Secret Valley game lodge (a more affordable alternative to Tree Tops) and much more that the Rift Valley had to offer. It was then time to leave the relative comfort of central Kenya and hit out to the remote north and across to Ethiopia but not before I had invested in a backpack and ditched my unwieldy kit bag.

The journey north was a lot more difficult than I had imagined with lifts few and far between and truly atrocious road conditions especially once north of Turbi. This final sixty miles took a total of four days to cover in an ex-army Bedford truck which for most of the journey was being towed behind a piece of four wheel drive heavy plant machinery. Even this got bogged down on several occasions in the thick mud which the black cotton soil had been turned into as a result of the seasonal rains but eventually we reached our goal and I cleared yet another border post at Moyale and now had Addis Ababa in my sights.

As I moved through southern Ethiopia the mountain scenery and frequent detours to visit many of its beautiful lakes made up for the rough road conditions. The first thing to hit me once in the country was the stark difference between it and its southern neighbours. There was a form of national dress worn by all. For the ladies this comprised of a white cotton dress decorated with a colourful border accompanied by a white cotton shawl (Netela), whilst the men wore white or khaki coloured cotton jodhpurs style trousers, white shirts and sported a heavier white cotton wrap (Gabi) draped over their shoulders. Their religion was also more evident, but as they had adopted Christianity, the Coptic branch, well before we in the west took it up that was not really surprising.

The whole country was much more steeped in history. If popular myth was to be believed, it could trace its ruling lineage back to the days of King Solomon and the Queen of Sheba, who's son became the first ruler, and from there onwards right up to the then incumbent Emperor Haile Selassie.

Addis Ababa was an interesting mixture with the grandeur of the Hilton hotel almost rubbing shoulders with the squalor of the shanty town of homes many of which could easily have been mistaken for nothing more than a pile of rubbish, because that was what most were constructed from. Old bits of tin, rugs, matting and cardboard all pieced together to offer some basic shelter from the elements.

I would be returning to Addis later but for now I had the northern town of Asmara as my next goal.

The two centres were connected by two main roads which generally follow the west and eastern flanks of the massive mountain range that runs down the backbone of the country. My chosen route on the way north was the west one which climbed and twisted its way past several prominent monasteries and skirted round Lake Tana where I went off track to see the spectacular Blue Nile Falls.

Just north of Lake Tana lies the ancient city and previous capital of Gondar. Also know as the Camelot of Ethiopia it boasts many old castles and finely decorated churches, none finer than Debre Berhan Selassie. Every inch of the inner walls of the church is covered in paintings of saints and the ceiling plays host to no less than a hundred and twelve angelic faces; it could be regarded as a little busy in its content but certainly awesome nevertheless. Emperor Fasilides founded the city in 1635 and each successive Emperor took it upon themselves to build their own castle, and this practice continued over the next two centuries thus the inordinate number of fine ruins concentrated in this one city.

My cultural journey continued north with the Simien Mountains towering up on my right as I followed the road onwards to Axum another very important town in the expansive history of this country.

In discussion with several people I'd chatted to during my trekking the raw beauty of these mountains had come up time and again and I decided to leave the beaten track and make a trip up to the small village of Sankober. This is the first resting place on a four day round trip up Ras Dashan which at 15,157 feet is the tallest peak in Ethiopia. This was an 'on foot' expedition, which, over a series of ever climbing undulations took in some fantastic views of the gorges and mountain peaks, but took out of me a lot more than I had expected, so I fitted in a lazy day of relaxation before making my return journey.

It is one of the areas where the wild Walia Ibex can be seen. These sure-footed, long curling horned mountain goats are now protected

ALONE AGAIN

Monolithic Stelae at Axum.

and have adapted to their perilous sheer sided domain and somehow scramble over it with frightening ease. I remembered seeing a natural history documentary about them several years earlier but never thought I would be up there mingling with them in their home terrain.

Reunited with the main road I moved on to Axum. This ancient city was the capital of the eponymous kingdom of Axum that flourished as a major trading centre as far back as 400 BC.

One of the main features of the old ruins are the numerous stelae, some broken, but many still standing as erected between 200–500 AD. They are believed to be funeral monuments to the ancient rulers who would have been buried beneath them and these monolithic granite structures can stand up to eighty feet in height.

They are all south facing and intricately carved to resemble buildings, with windows, rows of log-ends dividing each storey and false doors at the base. The apex is in a semi circular shape that symbolises the heavens. There is however another theory that simply puts them down to being phallic symbols. I'll leave the reader to choose which legend they attach to them.

These stelae predate the coming of Christianity to Ethiopia but Axum's other major attraction is very much wrapped up in that belief.

The Ethiopian Orthodox Church believes that the son of Solomon and the Queen of Sheba, their first ruler, brought with him the biblical Ark of the Covenant housing the tablets onto which the ten commandments had been inscribed. The said Ark is claimed to be housed in a chapel next to the very sacred Church of Our Lady Mary of Zion in Axum, but no one is allowed to enter to view it, except a handful of the religious hierarchy, this however does not prevent many believers making a pilgrimage to this holy site. Call me a sceptic but I can't help feeling that it has a touch of 'the emperor's new clothes' syndrome about it.

From Axum it was a short jaunt up to Asmara. The city, perched some 8,000 foot on the edge of the Rift Valley escarpment, was in more recent times under Italian influence and much of the architecture reflects this including an Art Deco cinema and a fine Roman Catholic cathedral, not the most common site in this Orthodox Christian country.

The past several weeks had been crammed with culture and sightseeing and with Christmas fast approaching and being on my own I was keen to locate a quiet haven where I could pass the festive season away from everything, and the Red Sea town of Massawa was suggested as just one such place, so I made the short journey east to the seaside to enjoy a relaxing break.

On arrival I couldn't believe my eyes, as the whole town appeared to be full of white tourists and my quest for a tranquil location appeared to have been shattered. All however was not as it seemed. The assembled crowds were in fact an MGM film crew who were on location making the imaginatively named 'Shaft in Africa' another follow up to what had been the highly successful movie 'Shaft'.

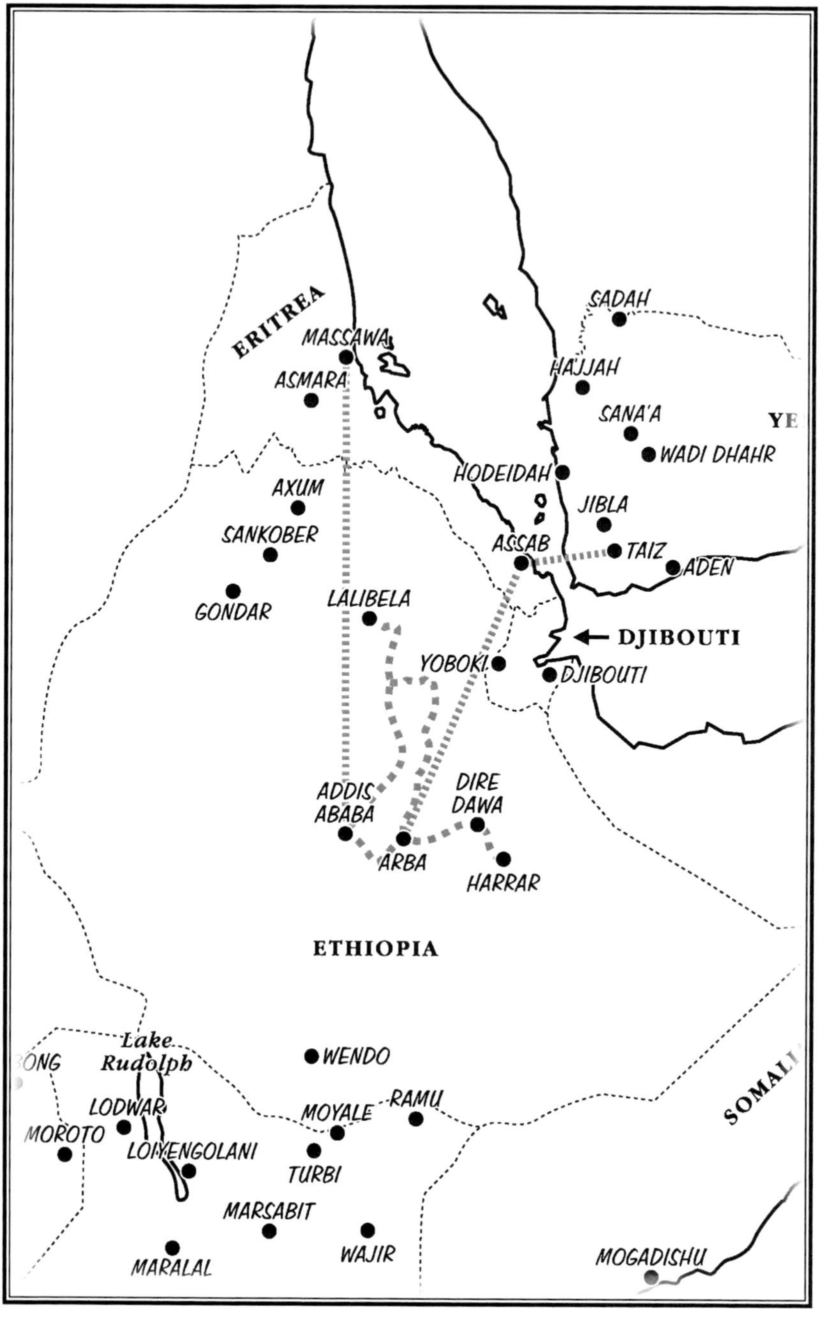
ERITREA
MASSAWA
ASMARA
SADAH
HAJJAH
SANA'A
YE
WADI DHAHR
HODEIDAH
JIBLA
AXUM
SANKOBER
GONDAR
ASSAB
TAIZ
ADEN
LALIBELA
DJIBOUTI
YOBOKI
DJIBOUTI
ADDIS ABABA
DIRE DAWA
ARBA
HARRAR
ETHIOPIA
Lake Rudolph
ONG
WENDO
LODWAR
MOYALE
RAMU
MOROTO
LOIYENGOLANI
TURBI
SOMALI
MARSABIT
WAJIR
MARALAL
MOGADISHU

CHAPTER 9
BEHIND THE SCENES

Having got over the shock of seeing what I'd taken to be a tourist invasion morph into a movie crew I was interested to find out a bit more about how it all worked. I have to confess that I am not a movie buff and had never before been close to anything like this, so it was all new and I was keen to take it all in.

I got introduced to a couple of chaps, Jim and Dave, who were in charge of the second unit an expression which meant little to me until they explained how the crews worked. The film crews are split into two divisions. The first or main crew works with the 'Stars' and cover all the close up work, the second unit is responsible for all the additional filming from crowd scenes, panoramic shots of the countryside, distant pictures of trains or planes and shots where the main actor's double can be used, e.g., if being filmed from behind. It can also be called on to supply a second camera angle in certain situations such as a fight sequence or where a complex stunt is being performed, especially if there is only one chance to get it in the can.

Although I was interested in what they were up to, they in turn were interested in what I was doing, and as they had been washed off set due to the heavy rain we made our way to a local bar and exchanged tales of our exploits. They asked where I was staying and when I explained that I had just arrived when I met them, the offer of a suitably sized floor space in their hotel room was extended along with the chance to have a shower and freshen up.

In the evening we all went off to the Red Sea Hotel, the local equivalent of the Hilton, where the bulk of the actors and crew were staying, however Jim and Dave had opted for a more low key hotel where they could enjoy the local ambience. It also meant that more of their expense allowance could be diverted to cover their drinks bills which if that day was anything to go by must have been quite considerable.

Before turning in for the night I was invited to join them the next day to see what went on behind the scenes.

We awoke early in the morning to the sound of torrential rain that persisted for most of the day preventing Jim and company from continuing with their proposed location shots. Continuity is a big factor in the film business with several sequences often shot one after another, though they may appear at different times in the finished film, so making sure the correct outfit is worn for a particular scene is important, equally so when filming is spread over a day or two. Ensuring costumes and props are identical sounds simple enough but can be quite a challenge. There are some movie buffs who take it on themselves to examine films looking for just such inconsistencies.

With their unit non-active I was taken to the main studio where a scene was being prepared which would see the lead couple in an 'interesting' clinch in the cabin of their yacht. The preparation and dummy runs were fascinating but understandably when it got to the real thing all but essential crew were expelled from the set.

The following day the sun was out but it turned out not to be the only thing that was out. One of the scenes the unit was in the middle of filming involved six baddies on horseback being taken out one by one by our hero. Unfortunately the first two had already been killed in earlier filming and the desert area being used for this sequence of stunts had, over forty-eight hours of rain, been transformed into a sea of green which looked even worse when viewed from the low camera angle required. Before any more killing could go on the whole area had to be raked over.

I found the filming really interesting and felt for Miguel, the sole stunt man, who had started off as one of the six horsemen and having been thrown from his horse then had to dress in one of the other costumes and go through the painful procedure again, and again, and again until all six had been disposed off. Possibly a bigger budget movie would simply employ six stunt men but this one had poor old Miguel parting from his mount in a variety of spectacular ways, but he came out of it unscathed.

During the day I had tried to make myself useful as a bit of an odd job man which had not gone unnoticed, and in the evening a proposal was put to me to join their unit in just such a capacity whilst they remained at Massawa. It sounded like money for old rope to me and I threw myself wholeheartedly into my new role.

It was great fun and I was being paid for it, how much better could it get. The rain had played havoc with the film schedules and lots of hours were required to catch up but Christmas day was declared a holiday.

The American forces had a large presence in the area, now Eritrea, helping the Ethiopian army fight the then terrorist threat, and as MGM was an American company, arrangements had been made for all the crew to have lunch at the American Club.

We all assembled and enjoyed a fine meal after which some of the crew decided that a spot of water skiing would be the ideal way to pass a Christmas afternoon and I was asked if I would like to go along. I explained that I had never tried it but would give it a go and with some tuition, lots of spills, and much hilarity I got the hang of things. Richard Rowntree, Shaft himself, had also joined us and a great afternoon skimming over the Red Sea soon flew by.

My duties were gradually increased to cover the catering arrangements for all our crew whilst out on location and with a wide range of customs and palates to accommodate, vegetarians, etc. included, this in itself was a small logistics nightmare.

Filming was coming to a close in Massawa and the whole outfit was moving on to Addis and much to my pleasant surprise I was asked to continue with them and courtesy of a chartered aeroplane was soon back in the capital.

Several days filming took place covering the arrival of Shaft's aircraft, crowd sequences in and around the city and several general location shots. The main crew was stationed at the Hilton and whilst I couldn't stretch to that I was able to stay in a small hotel this time round, rather than a park shelter which had been my previous resting place. One of the taxi drivers who was based at the Hilton was seconded to our unit to ferry us around in his Pontiac. As there were spells when we were waiting around kicking our heels we spent a lot of time chatting and Kebede filled me in on many aspects about the Ethiopian way of life and we struck up quite a rapport.

The next location was out in the country at Harrar, a fantastic old city with a strong Arab influence and full of character. To get there I was put in charge of a couple of vehicles which would be transporting much of the unit's equipment and this allowed me to take in the scenery on the way through the Awash river basin and up the steep twisting route in the mountains from Dire Dawa to the plateau above and our destination. The journey had been a lot slower than expected due to problems with one of the vehicles and in all we had been on the road for fourteen hours so didn't need rocking to sleep.

With filming completed in the fascinating old town it was back to Addis for some final shots and a reunion with my taxi driver friend Kebede. The whole crew would be flying out on Sunday 14th January heading for Madrid where the European section of the film was to be shot, even though it would be portrayed as Paris when it hit the screens, and a very tempting offer was put to me. As they would all be going on a charter flight I was invited to join them and finish off the rest of the film in Spain, however, tempting as it was, I just had a feeling that once I got back to Europe I might not return, so reluctantly declined.

Before we knew it Sunday had arrived and Kebede and I went to the airport to bid our farewells, and a most memorable month long adventure which all started on a rainy afternoon in Massawa came to a close with me once again asking why I hadn't taken up the offer of a seat on that plane.

As the aircraft disappeared out of site Kebede asked me what I was going to do now they had left and the old reality of being alone yet again sank in, but not for long.

One of Kebede's nieces was getting married in the afternoon and I was swiftly invited to attend and among all the celebrations I soon cast off any negative thoughts I had; it does appear that as one door closes another one opens.

Like any wedding celebration, food and drink played its part. The national dish of Injera and Wot was naturally on the menu and the highlight of the meal was one inch cubes of raw, yes raw meat, though which animal had provided them I have no idea. This was washed down

Priests carrying their Arcs of the Covenant at Timkat.

with a choice of Tala, the local beer, or Tej, a honey based spirit which was deceptively easy to knock back in copious amounts not realising that the smooth sweet liquor was harbouring an alarming amount of alcohol.

When talking to Kebede about his country he pointed out that one of their biggest religious festivals, Timkat, which is Ethiopia's Epiphany, was about to be celebrated and he suggested I waited to see it before moving on. A couple of days later we were in a very special position to see the whole ceremony unfold.

Many people are baptised by fully immersing themselves in the waters and all the churches parade through the towns sporting their own versions of the Ark of the Covenant, each wrapped in rich colourful cloth and borne on the head of the priest. They collect together for the ceremony at the holy water and after the baptisms are over the Arks are paraded back to their respective churches. The whole festival was a blaze of colour and it seemed as if the whole of Ethiopia was taking part.

Our special viewing position came about through Kebede's brother who worked at the Emperor's palace and was able to fiddle us tickets for the main enclosure next to the open-air holy baths around which this Addis Ababa ceremony was being held. We had pole position and were only a few feet away from Haile Selassie and the French President Pompidou who was on a state visit at the time.

Emperor Haile Selassie with President Pompidou.

With all the festivities behind us it was time to get back to the serious business of travelling, and as we had flown down to Addis from Massawa I had missed out on my proposed south bound route which harboured one of Ethiopia's gems, Lalibela and that became my next goal.

The main road out of Addis was pretty busy and getting to the Lalibela junction was fairly straightforward however getting from there up to the mountain top village itself was a totally different proposition. The road was little more than a dirt track, narrow, steep and covered in hairpin corners and few vehicles ventured up it. Eventually however a fully laden lorry did appear and along with a couple of dozen locals I was able to cross the driver's palm with the required amount of shekels to allow us the pleasure of precariously perching on top of the load and getting covered in a layer of fine dust into the bargain, but beggars can't be choosers and two days later we did eventually reach the town which the mountains held as their prisoner.

There were a few hairy moments on route as the lorry often couldn't negotiate the tight hairpins in one go, and had to undertake a series of forward and reverse movements in order to get round. The forward bits were fine but the reversing was scary to put it politely as the overhang at the rear of the vehicle would often be protruding beyond the mountain's edge of the track and great faith was placed in the skills of our benefactor.

The site of Lalibela is one of Ethiopia's most sacred places and the rock-hewn churches date back to the twelfth and thirteenth century. It is astonishing to think that back then without any of the tools at our disposal today, they managed to fashion the churches out of the solid rock. As if clearing a church high trench and sculpting the outline of the buildings was not hard enough the resultant block of rock was then 'scooped' out to create the inner churches complete with altar, supporting pillars and windows. The outer walls were then decorated in much the same designs as those used on the stelae at Axum, and the finished articles must surely rate amongst the modern wonders of the world.

BEHIND THE SCENES

A few other intrepid visitors had also made the pilgrimage and after several days in the village the rare opportunity of a return journey was secured, but half way down the local police took a dim view of the assorted cargo of goods and humans and we were ordered off the vehicle. One lad and myself decided that rather than hang around waiting to see when some suitable transport may appear, we would simply walk the remaining forty odd miles. Refreshed after a night spent under the stars and adopting the principle that the shortest distance between two points

Detail of an outer wall of one of the eleven churches.

Monolithic church hewn from the solid rock at Lalibela.

is a straight line we took to the slopes and went for it, eventually reaching the main road some eight weary hours later.

Rather than simply retrace my steps back to Addis I decided to head off into the edge of the Danakil Desert. I reached a rare junction in the road where a new route was being constructed and considered that if I could follow it to the far end at Arba I could save myself many miles. All seemed to be going well after several lifts took me from one camp onto the next, slow but positive progress.

It was now midday on a Saturday and only then was I informed that all the workers had left as this was their weekend off and it appeared that I was going to be stuck out in the middle of nowhere at least until Monday. I resigned myself to the bleak surroundings which were going to be my home for the following day or two and started to use the time catching up with correspondence and the like. Later that afternoon I heard the sound of an engine and I perked up, only to find that it belonged to a light aircraft.

The Swiss pilot and his companion worked for the German company Trapp who were constructing the road, and the passenger had been flown in to repair some machinery. The pilot spoke excellent English and during our chat he talked about the Yemen where his company was also involved, in a joint venture with Tarmac, building a road under some aid scheme or another. The more he spoke the more fascinated I became. He summed it up as being in a time warp back in medieval times and as it had only recently started to allow foreigners in, the country was unspoilt by any tourist orientated development.

The head of the Trapp company was due to be flying over to their Yemen site the following week and he suggested that there may be a chance of getting a lift with them. Into the bargain the return journey could also be arranged as they charter a weekly flight which ferries supplies between Djibouti and the Yemen and as required, seats were made available on the charter for work personnel who were flying to or from Europe. Djibouti being an ex-French enclave had direct flights to Paris.

Surely this would be the mother of all 'hitches' but there were a few issues to be overcome. First and foremost would Dr. Trapp allow me to fly with them and secondly could I get back to Addis, arrange visas etc. and be back at the main camp in time to take advantage of this salivatingly tempting offer. Whatever the outcome it was too good a potential opportunity to ignore but time was not on my side.

The small training aircraft they had arrived in was a replacement for their regular Piper Aztec which was being serviced back in Addis where Carl the pilot was returning the following day. It was agreed that if we could manage to take off from the camp, with me and my luggage on board, he would also fly me back to Addis. To aid our chances of take off rather than use the somewhat bumpy official airstrip we would use the new road which, although not yet sporting its asphalt top, had a good surface and also provided a longer area to get up to the required speed.

Somehow we all managed to squeeze in and with total disregard to any safety issues I crossed everything hoping we would manage to get off the ground and a few anxious moments later we were airborne. The flight down to the main camp near Arba took us over pretty flat uninteresting scenery and eventually we managed a successful landing and phase one of my new mission was complete.

On arrival Carl disappeared and shortly came back with the next piece of good news, the boss had agreed to take me along on the proviso that I got all my paperwork in order. What a change of fortune the day had thrown up, one minute marooned in the middle of nowhere next preparing for the trip of a lifetime within my trip of a lifetime.

The following day with only Carl and myself in the plane the journey to Addis was far more comfortable and relaxing, and so I was set to do battle with the Embassies as soon as they opened for their week's business.

In addition to obtaining an entry visa for Yemen I also had to arrange an exit visa for Ethiopia. Despite my early start it took most of the day to sort everything out and in so doing I had lost vital travelling time as I still had to somehow get back to the main camp ready for the off.

Having successfully got to the junction of the new road frustration set in as I waited and waited for an all important lift and I started to get the horrible feeling that all the kind help and running around over the past few days would be in vain, but in the late afternoon a much relieved me found myself sitting on a load of machinery on the back of a pick-up truck getting thoroughly covered in thick dust but happy in the knowledge that I would be there in time for the flight in the morning.

And so after days of running around like a headless chicken I found myself relaxing in the comfort of a private plane heading for Arabia.

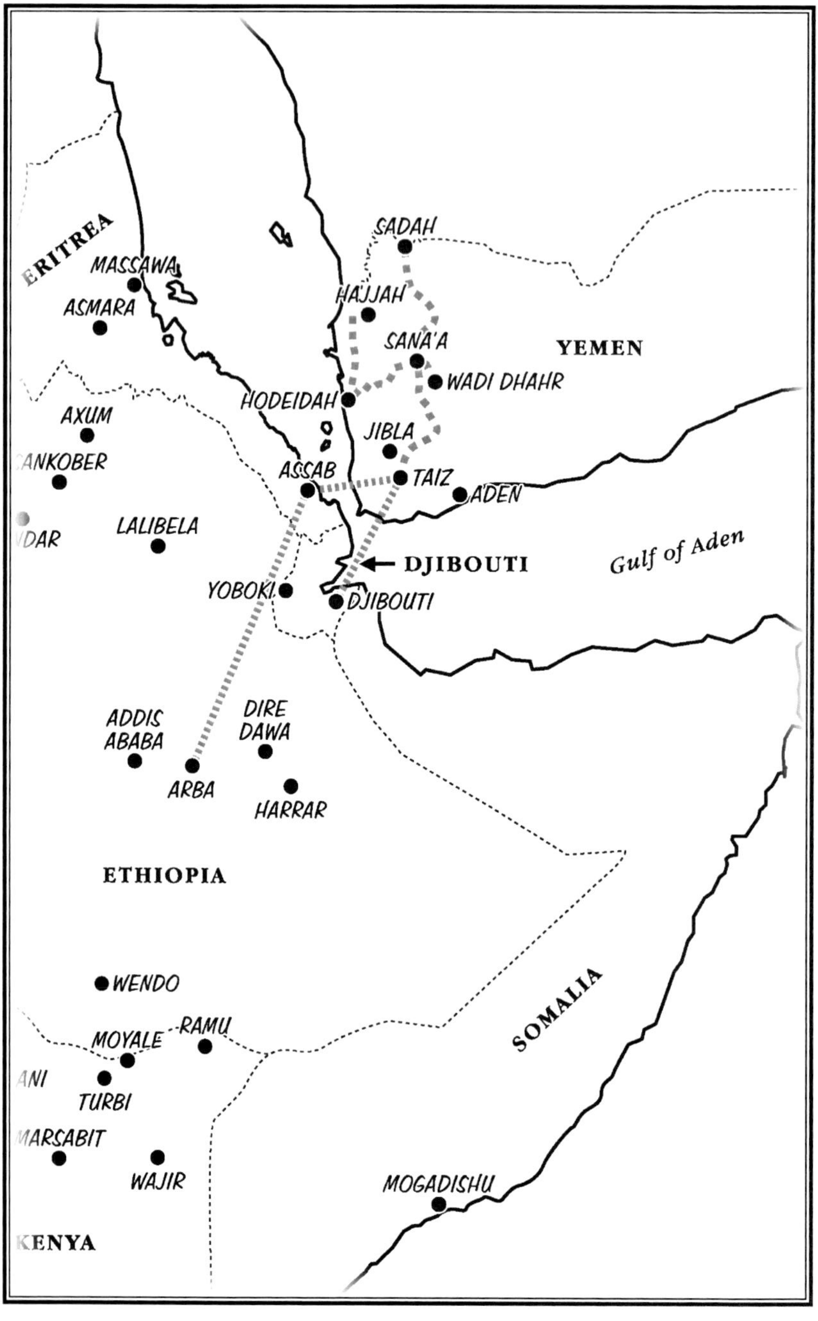
ERITREA
MASSAWA
ASMARA
AXUM
ANKOBER
DAR
LALIBELA
SADAH
HAJJAH
SANA'A
YEMEN
WADI DHAHR
HODEIDAH
JIBLA
ASSAB
TAIZ
ADEN
DJIBOUTI
Gulf of Aden
YOBOKI
DJIBOUTI
ADDIS ABABA
DIRE DAWA
ARBA
HARRAR
ETHIOPIA
WENDO
RAMU
MOYALE
ANI
TURBI
SOMALIA
MARSABIT
WAJIR
MOGADISHU
KENYA

CHAPTER 10

A TASTE OF A MEDIEVAL AGE

The flight took us over the mainly flat landscape bordering on the southern edge of the Danakil Desert and after about one and a half hours we touched down in the coastal town of Assab. With all the necessary paperwork and permits checked we were then airborne once again crossing the Red Sea, over the flat sandy coastal land belt of the Tihama before rising up into the mountains to our destination, Yemen's second city, Taiz.

Here we were met by representatives of the joint venture construction programme and whilst Dr. Trapp and his colleagues went off with their German entourage myself and Carl headed into Taiz in the company of one of the British team.

First impressions were very much as I had conjured up from Carl's description during our original meeting. The word medieval sprung to mind. This was obviously not by any means a culturally poor country being able to trace its history way back to 2000 BC, but one got the feeling that its once highly developed society had somehow stood still for centuries and had been overtaken by the rest of the so called civilised world.

This southwestern tip of Arabia consisted of two parts North and South Yemen. In the south Britain had occupied the port of Aden back in 1839 and established a colony there, a situation that remained up until 1967 when it gained independence after a bitter struggle. The north which had been part of the Ottoman Empire up until early in the twentieth century had remained under the feudal style governance of the Imam and the local network of Sheiks and had been a very closed society. It only slowly opened its doors to outsiders after the overthrow of the Imam in the revolution of 1962 when the Republic was created. Previous attempted revolutions in 1948, 1955 and 1958 had been ruthlessly quashed with the demise of their leaders by public beheading, a practice that was still continuing during my visit.

Many aid programmes had been established to help this poor country move forward and the World Health Organisation, the United Nations and many foreign government ventures were all visible on the ground.

The infrastructure was benefiting from several road building projects and in addition to our joint Anglo-German one, both the Russians and Chinese were also constructing new road links. During my stay in Yemen I also came across many more diverse programmes involved with agriculture, water, education and health often involving volunteer groups from around the globe. It seemed that everyone wanted to be involved and I couldn't help cynically wondering just how much was philanthropic and how much was to do with the runny black stuff that comes out of the ground in this region of the world.

The joint venture group were involved with building a new road between Taiz in the south and the capital city of Sana'a located in the centre of the country. They had established a series of camps along the route which were currently housing the ex pat work force and families along with all their machinery and equipment, but the plan was to bequeath them to the country when they left. Whoever got access to them was in for some relative luxury as these mini villages had been well constructed and well equipped, even sporting swimming pools. An earlier such American project had become home to Ambassadors, W.H.O. personnel and the like.

One spin off for lucky old me was that I was invited to drop in and avail myself of their hospitality whilst on my travels and this in turn more often than not took care of the next step of my journey as there was a reasonable flow of construction traffic of one sort or another ploughing its way up and down the country.

A TASTE OF A MEDIEVAL AGE

The town of Taiz consisted of typical Yemeni buildings, perched on a hill with narrow streets running between them, often too narrow for vehicles to pass and this pattern proved to be the case in all the old parts of the towns I visited. The buildings, often four or five stories high were stone built though some appeared to be stone on the first couple of levels then brick on the upper floors. The roofs were flat and the outer walls often colourfully decorated. Inside rooms were mainly whitewashed plaster with the living area strewn with bright carpets and cushions. They also had a basic form of sanitation but the less said about that the better. In all far and away more substantial than the average dwelling found in African towns, but a far cry from the creature comforts of a typical European dwelling.

The local's attire was also different, with the women mainly clad in black from head to foot and veiled in true Moslem tradition. The men wore a skirt style wrap and jackets which they appeared to keep on at all times, indeed it was not uncommon to see workers hard at their task but still wearing their jackets.

A very important part of the men's outfit is the Jambiya. This is the curved dagger worn by virtually all men over the age of fourteen and is not only a fearsome weapon but also a status symbol. They vary in quality depending on what materials are used and the decoration of the sheath.

The primary quality issue surrounds the handle, with the very expensive ones being made from rhino horn whilst lower down the price scale either bone or wood is used. The double-edged, wide, eight inch long blade is made from steel and the dagger is housed in a sheath, mostly made from wood which is then decorated with leather, silver and even precious stones depending on one's budget. The whole unit is worn on an often colourful two to three inch wide belt over the middle of the lower abdomen.

In addition to the Jambiya, the men, especially out in the more rural parts, often carry rifles with fully laden ammunition belts criss-crossing their chests and shootings were not uncommon, several occurring during my stay.

Having soaked up the atmosphere of my first encounter with Yemeni life in Taiz, I ventured out into the surrounding mountains to Jibla where the intensity of their agriculture was astonishing. Despite the very steep slopes, the mountain sides were totally covered in small terraces, some

Typical Yemenis armed with jambiyas and guns.

only a few feet wide, which were being readied for the oncoming wet season when, I was informed, the barren looking brown vista changes to a green hue with the terraces performing their duty of harnessing the precious water supplies to the maximum.

Next I set off north towards Sana'a and as promised was made very welcome at the various camps along the route. The mountainous scenery on the road north again housed the intense terracing which was a feature throughout the country.

The road took us past the wreck of a DC3 aircraft, which despite having happened quite some time back had not been cleared away and was still much as it was when the crash happened. I couldn't help thinking that in Africa the whole thing would have been cannibalised with the metal used to make homes, here however the solid stone structures created by the highly skilful masons rendered such scavenging unnecessary.

The capital city of Sana'a sits at around 7,500 feet and vies with Damascus for the claim to being the oldest known city in the world. In keeping with all the Yemeni towns it is built on a hill with the usual narrow streets and stone built flat roofed houses, the old city being enclosed by its ancient walls. The newer section outside the walls was starting to show signs of more modern times with new buildings, albeit still following the old architectural styles, and even a couple of sets of traffic lights, the only ones I encountered in the whole country.

The use of their camels in their working lives was clearly on show at a small seed oil production plant. In reality this was the yard outside somebody's house where oil was being produced from seeds by grinding them up in a giant vat. The grinding effort was supplied by a most unfortunate blinkered camel that simply spent its day walking round and round the vat in a circle powering a large wooden pestle that was attached to a harness on its back.

I had come across another example of camel power on the way up to Sana'a whilst stopped in a rural area, where a crude but effective form of irrigation was being deployed. From the head of a deep well, irrigation channels had been built spreading out in several directions over the cultivated area. The task of drawing the water up from the depths of the well was assigned to a camel which simply walked up and down a strip of land with a rope attaching itself to the pail which was raised and lowered as it plodded its way to and from the well head. On reaching the top of the well the pail then hit against a simple mechanism that tipped the contents into the required channel. Very simple and straightforward but effective and yet not something I had come across in Africa, another example of how much more developed this rural countryside was compared to its neighbours across the water.

The opportunity cropped up to take a trip down to the coastal belt which runs the length of the country sandwiched between the mountains and the Red Sea, and we set off through the twisting mountain road before dropping down to the much more humid atmosphere of the Tihama coast.

The people who live here have more of an African look to them and have a different dress code, with the traditional full black covering for ladies replaced with more colourful lighter wear and they all sported a wide brimmed, conical shaped straw hat worn perched on the top of the head, not pulled down about their ears. For the men a straw Fez style hat was *de rigueur*. Even the houses were more in keeping with those I'd seen in many parts of rural Africa, single level and grass in construction.

Roland, with whom I'd gone down, was one of the engineers on the joint venture and his prime reason for the trip was to collect his car which was being imported through the port of Hodeidah. He was dreading the bureaucracy which lay ahead, but not half as much as he was dreading meeting the local governor who was one of the most powerful Sheiks in the country. On a previous visit he had been sidelined by the Sheik into providing his professional opinion on some plans for a new hotel complex that the Sheik wanted to develop.

The twist seemed to be that his plan was to build it at virtually no expense to himself by calling in favours, and where necessary applying the required amount of pressure to obtain these favours, from those he felt could help. Unfortunately Roland's fears came to fruition as the man himself had to stamp the import documents. We were beckoned into his office and effectively put under house arrest so that Roland could attend a meeting the following day to discuss the ground works of the project, and despite pointing out that he was seconded on government business we were 'invited' to stay overnight at the Sheik's behest.

These guys really do wield some power and it is not surprising that to achieve the office some people will go to great lengths. The Sheiks fall broadly into three categories, those who inherit the position due to their birth line, those who are religious leaders and some who manage to simply buy their position, it made me realise the similarities to a certain house in our own parliamentary system.

The following day we were instructed to attend a meeting along with the other partners in his project, all high ranking local dignitaries and businessmen and somehow I was also drawn in.

During my travels I had slowly been whittling down the contents of my backpack, and my wardrobe was basic to say the least, a couple of shirts, a pair of denim shorts all of which could be washed overnight and ready to wear in the morning, a pair of desert boots and one pair of cord trousers which constituted my Sunday best. I felt it only right to make the effort to smarten up for the meeting but needless to say looked like a pauper by comparison to the assembled gents many in their long white flowing robes.

The assembled crowd sat around on deep colourful cushions and the discussions commenced. The technicalities were way above my head but I passed the time taking in what I could and also taking in the cult of qat chewing.

Qat is a mild narcotic which I had come across in parts of East Africa and Ethiopia under different names but here it is very much part of everyday life, with the local markets full of vendors openly plying their stash. Previously I had seen people simply chewing away at the leaves but in Yemen it was much more of a ritual.

The leaves were slowly chewed extracting the required juices with the remaining cud slowly built up and retained in the mouth. Over a period of several hours the residue would take the form of a large ball held in their distended cheek as if they had a golf ball in their mouth. Eventually when the residue was too much to retain it was politely discarded and the process started all over again.

Throughout the episode chilled water, often with cinnamon or cloves added to flavour it, would be sipped to clear their throat of any stray fibres and such qat parties often lasted several hours as was the case in this instance. As if the delights of qat were not enough they could also avail themselves of the pleasures offered by a very ornately decorated hookah pipe or hubble-bubble pipe, gurgling away gently which was slowly passed around the assembled crowd.

Eventually with his duties finally fulfilled Roland and I were 'released' and headed back up the mountain road to the capital once again.

The region to the north of Sana'a was regarded as bandit country and special permission was required to visit it which in a perverse way made it more interesting and so with the requisite paper in hand I set off for the most northerly town of Sadah close to the Saudi border.

A couple of locals enjoying the pleasures of Qat.

A TASTE OF A MEDIEVAL AGE

Here again a road construction project was in place, this one courtesy of Mr Mao's Chinese who had already built the Hodeida road I had taken earlier. Part of the road was finished with a good asphalt surface but when that disappeared it deteriorated to a pothole covered track and progress slowed down accordingly.

About half way along the route I came to one of the Chinese camps and as the perimeter wall afforded some shelter and shade from the fierce heat I rested up waiting for my next transport opportunity to come by. I had been settled for an hour of so with no vehicles in sight when one of the Chinese workers, clad in the standard blue coloured jacket and trousers worn by them all, beckoned me to come inside.

English was not their forte and equally so Chinese was not mine but with the aid of maps, sign language and much pointing they got the idea of what I was up to and where I was heading. At one point a lot of noisy discussion broke out among them and the result manifested itself some twenty minutes later in the form of a veritable banquet of Chinese food. I was also given a litre bottle of genuine Chinese beer to swill it all down with. There was much hilarity among the workers when I asked for chopsticks instead of the cutlery they had kindly supplied, and with the traditional eating utensils in hand I set about doing justice to the food laid out before me.

The contrast in the camp compared to the luxury of the European ones was like chalk and cheese. Here the perimeter wall and many of the storage buildings were constructed using old oil drums filled with sand and rock and even the accommodation blocks were simple wooden affairs with long home-made tables and benches to eat from, reminiscent of my school dinner days.

After the meal was over the sign language went into overdrive and I established that I was being offered a lift part of the way up the road and gratefully accepted. I suppose some of the detail got lost in translation but the upshot was that I was perched high in the cockpit of a large crane being sent north on a low loader at what could kindly be put as a leisurely pace.

My next lift, which took me through to Sadah, couldn't have been more different as a Land Rover full of gun toting individuals pulled up. They were actually Saudi mercenaries who had been down in the south of the country helping in a skirmish against communist infiltrators from South Yemen (Aden). Saudi, along with the northern part of the country, had always backed the royalist Imam in the previous revolts and groups of individuals were still available to help out for the right cause and no doubt the right money. Progress with them was swift despite the rough terrain and whilst it had taken five hours to cover twenty miles in the Chinese crane the remaining fifty miles were gobbled up in a mere four hours.

Sadah, not unexpectedly, followed the layout of all the non coastal towns, perched on a hill with the buildings close together again enclosed in a six foot high wide perimeter wall with look out posts dotted along its length. The buildings here were virtually all made from sun dried mud brick and the whole town had a ruddy sandy colour to it.

Visitors, or more accurately European visitors, were not a regular site here and many of the women fled or quickly covered their faces and I was quickly surrounded by lots of excited children. This posed a problem as I was pick pocketed while trying to exchange some Yemeni Riyals, their normal currency, for a Maria Theresa Thaler the old Austrian coinage that was adopted throughout much of the Arab world and was still actively used in this remote northern region.

Though the miscreant disappeared into the sea of bodies I was quickly led off to the local police station and after relating the tale was presented with two sheets of paper covered in Arabic script and directed to another office. I couldn't believe it when I was ceremoniously presented with the amount of money that had been taken from me, and then found out that the second document was a complimentary pass to allow me to stay at the government rest house that evening, quite an unexpected outcome.

Whilst at the police station I noticed a couple of young lads wearing shackles round their ankles connected by chain which obviously restricted their movement somewhat and let it be known to all around that they were trouble, and shortly afterwards I came across another similarly clad chap in the town. Justice does have its rough side out here where an eye for an eye culture seems to be tolerated.

I had another couple of places I wanted to visit before catching my flight back to Djibouti and once safely back in Sana'a I made the short trip east out to Wadi Dhahr, an oasis village where the old Imam had a country home. It was the home I had come to see. Perched on the top of a single eighty foot high rock stood the typically Yemeni designed stone built structure which covered the entire surface of the outcrop measuring eighty by two hundred feet, another astonishing feat of the local builder's craft.

A TASTE OF A MEDIEVAL AGE

To get to my remaining port of call I had to first retrace my steps back down to the coastal plain and the port of Hodeida, then follow the coastal road north. This again was a fairly remote region and vehicles were few and far between and with the combination of high humidity and high temperatures it wasn't the most pleasant of journeys. Whilst vehicles weren't abundant I did see a few four legged means of transport making their way across the skyline and was taken by one particular chap who was curled up around the saddle fast asleep while his trusted camel plodded onwards regardless. He obviously had a lot of faith in his mount's sense of direction.

Hajjah, my destination, is a small village set at the top of a perilous mountain road that twists and turns its way up from the coastal plain below. I was able to join a typical highly decorated lorry for the ascent, which was reminiscent of the climb up to Lalibela in Ethiopia, many forward and reverse manoeuvres being required to negotiate the sharp hairpin bends. In some ways I was pleased that by the time we were making our ascent darkness had fallen so I wasn't so aware of the potential danger a simple driving error could evoke.

Once in the town I was almost immediately approached by an armed official, but there was no cause for alarm, he was only interested in guiding me to their government hostel whereupon I was accommodated by the local Sheik.

The rugged mountain scenery surrounding the town was spectacular and well worth all the hassle, heat and humidity I'd endured to get there. Once more the steep sided mountains played host to the multitude of small terraces in this case cultivating the ubiquitous qat which had replace the previous cash crop of coffee.

The Imam's Palace at Wadi Dhahr.

The return journey down the mountain gave up further evidence of the earlier revolutionary conflict with several damaged tanks and other military hardware strewn across the mountainside. The bulk of this was Russian which the south supporting Egyptians had used though by the look of things not very effectively.

And so with my taste of the medieval experience complete I made my way back to Taiz and with the necessary arrangements completed hopped on board the charter flight to make the short crossing over the Bab el Mandeb straits to African soil once again.

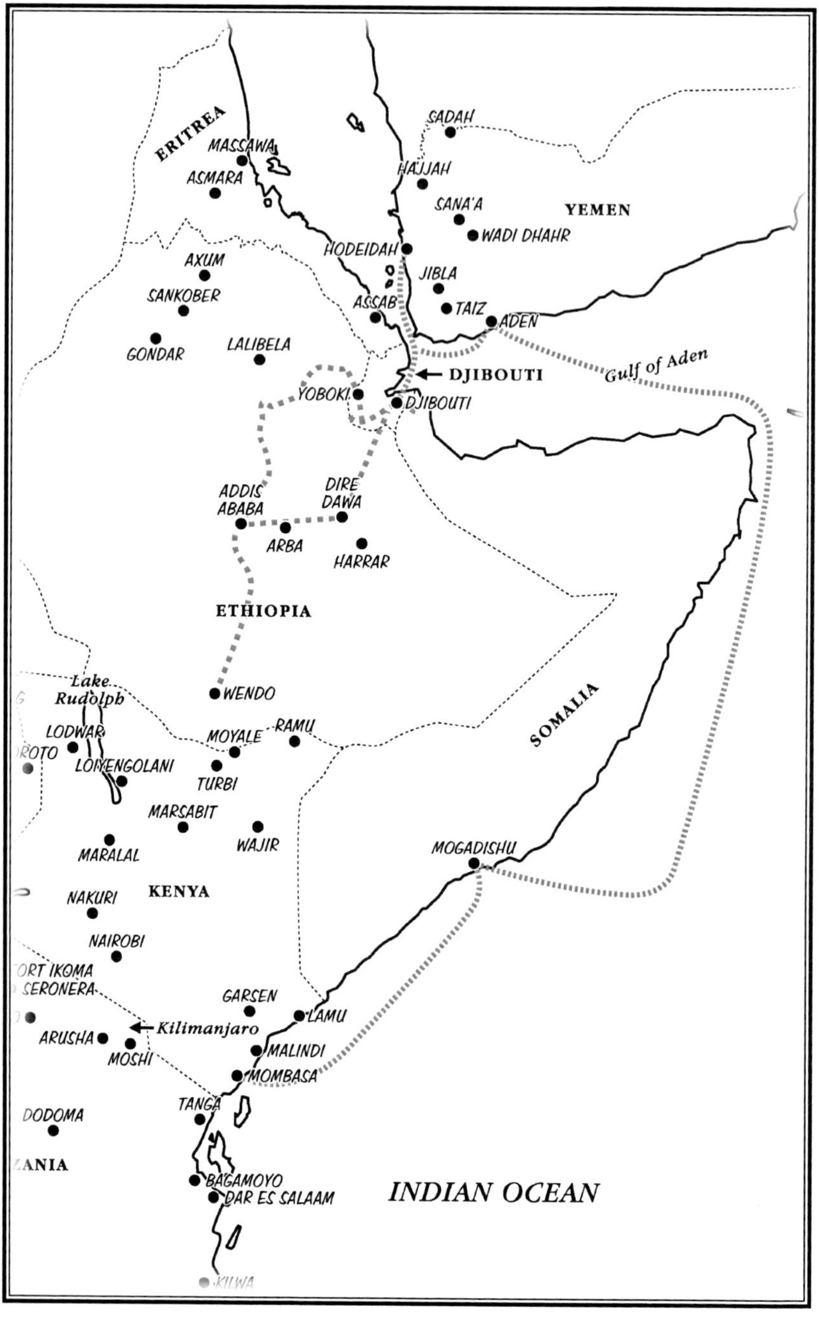
ERITREA
MASSAWA
ASMARA
SADAH
HAJJAH
SANA'A
YEMEN
WADI DHAHR
HODEIDAH
AXUM
SANKOBER
JIBLA
ASSAB
TAIZ
ADEN
GONDAR
LALIBELA
DJIBOUTI
Gulf of Aden
YOBOKI
DJIBOUTI
ADDIS ABABA
DIRE DAWA
ARBA
HARRAR
ETHIOPIA
Lake Rudolph
WENDO
SOMALIA
LODWAR
RAMU
MOYALE
LOIYENGOLANI
TURBI
MARSABIT
WAJIR
MARALAL
MOGADISHU
NAKURI
KENYA
NAIROBI
SERONERA
GARSEN
LAMU
Kilimanjaro
ARUSHA
MOSHI
MALINDI
MOMBASA
TANGA
DODOMA
BAGAMOYO
DAR ES SALAAM
INDIAN OCEAN
KILWA

CHAPTER 11

A HICCUP WITH MY PASSPORT

The first thing that hit me as the plane's doors were opened at Djibouti airport was the hot humid wind that was swirling round, akin to standing in front of a fan heater. It seemed that within seconds I was dripping wet from the clammy climate that is a feature of this small enclave of France clinging to the edge of the Red Sea in the horn of Africa.

To give it it's correct name the 'Territoire Francais des Afars et des Issas' was the former French Somaliland and was more generally referred to as Djibouti, the name of its only major city. The Afars and Issas were the two tribes who occupied the region and between whom some bitter rivalry still existed which in the rural areas often boiled over into bloodletting battles normally sparked off by one side or the other raiding their enemy's camel and goat herds.

Djibouti enjoyed quite a good economy backed directly by France and having the status of a duty free country most sea journeys were broken off here to take advantage of the bounty on offer. The French connection was everywhere to be seen, much of the administration and police personnel were French and Djibouti also played host to one of the last active outposts of the legendary Foreign Legion.

My priority was to obtain a new passport as I was rapidly running out of space and already had several entry stamps that overlapped.

Unfortunately there was no British representation in Djibouti, however, an Embassy did exist in neighbouring Somalia, through which I intended to travel on route to Kenya, so all was not lost.

Before heading south I was interested in visiting Lake Assal, the lowest point on the African continent some five hundred and fifteen feet below sea level and, with the exception of Antarctica, the most saline place on earth, even beating the infamous Dead Sea, though the latter is considerably lower at twelve hundred feet below.

Being a crater lake, with no rivers running into or out of it, the high temperatures, which can reach 125° Fahrenheit in the summer, favour evaporation. This has resulted in a large saltpan being created around part of the lake edge and in turn this valuable commodity is mined and forms an important revenue stream for the local Afars.

To get to the water's edge I had to walk across the sea of salt, which gleaming in the hot sunshine was like walking on a snowfield but without the cold. The intensity of the evaporation was evident by plunging my arm into the water then withdrawing it and seeing a layer of white salt forming immediately before my eyes, not a place to take a dip even though the air temperature made the water look very inviting.

With the unforgiving mixture of heat and humidity which even made sleeping outside uncomfortable, I was keen to get moving on, and having secured a visa for Somalia I made my way down to the nearby border crossing.

I cleared the Djibouti controls and walked through a short section of no man's land over to the Somali checkpoint. I presented my passport and was somewhat taken aback when they refused me entry. I pointed out that I had a valid visa that I had just obtained a day or so before, but still my entry was barred. With polite reasoning getting me nowhere I started to remonstrate and a heated discussion ensued, however it was quickly brought to a halt by

The salt encrusted water's edge at Lake Assal.

me when the arms they were wearing were suddenly pointing in my direction. Swallowing very hard, I smiled, apologised, and retreated to the safety of Djibouti soil whereupon I let them know in my best Anglo Saxon what I thought of them all and where I felt they could stick their country. This of course resolved nothing but it did give me an inordinate amount of satisfaction.

The escapade with the border guards left me with what had now become a major passport problem. The last space of any size had been taken up by the invalid visa, leaving nowhere available for even an Ethiopian stamp which would at least have meant I could return to Addis Ababa and sort things out at our Embassy there. I was at a loss to know what to do and was land locked with Ethiopia to the north and west and Somalia to the south. To the eastern flank lay the Gulf of Aden and I started to consider the possibility of getting down to Kenya by boat as there was a reasonable flow of merchant traffic up and down the East African coast.

I spent several days running around between the port and the various shipping agents and on one occasion thought I may have struck gold when a P&O ship docked and the captain turned out to be a fellow Scot. Unfortunately company rules forbade the carrying of passengers and I was soon resuming my hunt for a Kenya bound vessel, but not before I had been invited aboard to drown my sorrows over a couple of beers. Just being on board the relative comfort afforded by the ship's air conditioning was a welcome relief and when an offer to stay for lunch was extended I was more than grateful to accept. As the day wore on I was given a tour of the vessel and engine room and finished up having dinner and being given the comfort of an air-conditioned room for the night. This was sheer luxury as I had been sleeping out in a sheltered spot I'd located but the evening humidity and the presence of a vast variety of insects made sleeping none too pleasant, and at least I wouldn't have to check my boots in the morning to see what might have crawled in and set up home overnight.

During one of my numerous sorties into the town I met some French lads who were connected with the Foreign Legion and they informed me that there was an unofficial route out of Djibouti used by smugglers taking their duty free merchandise over the border to Ethiopia. It seemed that whilst the Legion were there and helped in the control of incoming traffic, mainly human, they had a fairly relaxed view to anything moving out and it was suggested that this may be a solution to my predicament. At least I would be in a country with an Embassy so I switched my attention away from the sea route and headed inland into the remote desert border region.

The last little outpost of Yoboki, in the flat desolate bolder strewn wastes, was reached courtesy of a lift with one of the Legion's officers and it transpired that a certain amount of illicit traffic did indeed flow over into Ethiopia, though by it's very nature securing a lift with it wasn't straightforward. Despite this and with some 'assistance' from the local garrison, arrangements were made and a few days later our motley crew was assembled for the off.

As daylight faded I climbed on board the back of a fully laden Land Rover along with several other assorted bodies, many regaled with arms of one sort or another, and set off along the dried up river bed that was the chosen route of our illegal journey west. Darkness was soon upon us and as we picked our way across the rough potholed track the eerie silence was broken at one point by the distant sound of an engine and shortly afterwards the faint glimmer of lights hove into view. With no alternative route available we turned off the lights and bounced our way to a sheltered area and waited to see just what was approaching. It was certainly a nerve tingling moment but eventually the other vehicle passed, no doubt on a similar mission to ours, and we were soon once more picking our way among the boulders as we snaked our way ever onwards.

Eventually some four hours later the first signs of the main Addis to Assab road flickered into sight with the lights of the odd vehicle picked out in the night sky. Again our lights were turned off and with only the help of the limited moonlight we cautiously wove our way closer to the main road. Once this milestone was reached it was relatively plain sailing for the next fifteen miles up to a small village where we all disembarked. The bounty was quickly unloaded and secreted away in a couple of houses. With the midnight hour nearly upon us I was offered a roof over my head and was soon tucked up in my sleeping bag pondering my next move.

I could see potential problems on the horizon at our Embassy, due to the fact that I had no current entry visa, however, having already crossed from Kenya into Ethiopia before, I was aware of the geography of that border region. There was a considerable distance between the two

A HICCUP WITH MY PASSPORT

respective border control points and by skirting round the Ethiopian one I could then arrive at the Kenyan control where only a small stamp was required which I could still accommodate within my existing passport. With all this achieved I would be legally in Kenya where I could arrange for a new passport to be issued in Nairobi. It seemed a good plan to me and in the morning I set about putting it into fruition.

Initially the journey saw me back once more in the capital from where it was a straightforward route due south. We were in the throws of the rainy season and once the asphalt surface disappeared the dirt roads deteriorated the further south I headed as the route followed from one Rift Valley Lake onto another. I was making reasonable progress and reached the town of Wendo where the road splits and the final two hundred and twenty miles of dirt track takes over down to the border.

As we arrived in the town we were subjected to a random passport check and fully aware of my illegal status I told them that I had left my passport with friends back in Addis whilst taking this trip around the southern lakes. Unsurprisingly they were not convinced and I was invited to accompany them to the local police station.

I found myself among an assortment of others who had been similarly detained, in the office of the local police chief and he was obviously not a happy bunny. Things were somewhat chaotic and I was asked to empty the contents of my pack onto his table. My passport and travellers cheques were in a blue plastic folder which eventually emerged onto the desk. I explained that it contained my cheques and briefly opened it and as my passport was underneath them it wasn't immediately apparent. With a stroke of divine intervention the telephone rang and it was obvious that as a result he had more important things to attend to and gestured me to pack my stuff away and with a silent sigh of relief I hurriedly complied.

If I thought I'd got away with it I was sadly mistaken as after a heated conversation in his local dialect with one of his menials it turned out that I was under arrest and would be escorted back to Addis Ababa to obtain my illusive passport and present it to an official at the police H.Q.

The return journey to Addis was an interesting one spread over a couple of days and whilst I was spared the indignation of being handcuffed the poor officer assigned to accompany me was more like a shadow and was obviously terrified that I was going to do a runner at some point. We used local buses to cover the route and stayed in small hotels where he would politely lock me in my room overnight, he had however nothing to fear as I was enjoying the hospitality of the state and had worked out my strategy for my impending meeting.

On arrival in Addis I came clean to my shadow that I had in fact been carrying my passport with me, but aware of my illegal status had been wary about how this would have been received out in the middle of nowhere. I suggested that he took me to the appointed H.Q. where I would plead my case, and whilst he was obviously a little perplexed at having been duped he agreed and with his duties fulfilled I was handed over to the appropriate security personnel.

The initial meeting quickly established that I needed to be referred to the Ministry for Immigration and a meeting with no less than the vice-minister was arranged. This would be make or break and after being escorted to the said Ministry I hung around for ages but it did give me time to perfect my story and eventually I was summoned to his office.

Relations between Ethiopia and Somalia were at very low ebb and I capitalised on the ridiculous unexplained treatment I had received at the hands of the Somali border guards, showing the relevant visa and explaining the resulting predicament regarding my full passport. I adjusted a couple of facts in particular regarding my arrival into the country, informing them that I had crossed over as part of a Danakil camel train, in order to avoid causing any undue trouble to my true benefactors. I was given a surprisingly positive hearing but informed that any decision would rest in the hands of the Minister and that could take a day or so.

Not wishing to be behind bars in the mean time I explained that I had a friend in Addis with whom I could stay and by way of a surety I offered to lodge my passport and travellers cheques with them and was pleasantly surprised when this arrangement was accepted. So it was that Kebede got an unexpected visit having presumed that I would be in some far flung southern country by now.

I had been given a further appointment to find out the outcome of my case and anxiously arrived as requested and after the obligatory couple of hours wait was ushered in. My heart fell when he explained that their action should be to send me to court and after any punishment had been completed, deport me back to where I came from, Djibouti. As I was trying to comprehend the magnitude of what was being said, he then went on to explain that in this instance they were going to adopt a more lenient position and see if a compromise could be reached. Leaving

A HICCUP WITH MY PASSPORT

my cheques with them they would allow me to take my passport to the British Embassy and presuming all went well there I would then be deported. I tried to persuade them to allow me to exit to Kenya but that hit a stone wall, so it seemed it was going to be Djibouti or nowhere.

Whilst not ticking all the boxes this was to say the least a result and without wasting any time I made my way round to the Embassy, filled in the necessary forms and duly got presented with a nice new empty passport. It was however bound to my old passport by means of a knotted ribbon and an official seal on the erroneous assumption that the old one contained my current visa, a small detail I had failed to mention. Armed with my new documentation I returned to collect my surety and was faced with my next bombshell; they wanted me to fly out as soon as possible. Though I could understand their wish to get rid of me, the cost of flying was enormous especially compared to the train service which twice weekly crossed from Addis to Djibouti and after much pleading an agreement was reached which involved me presenting myself, together with a letter I was given, to the guards at the border.

With train tickets purchased and the Addis authorities notified of my departure I boarded the train for a long hot journey back to the weather hellhole of Djibouti along with the most eclectic mixture of passengers and animals. It seemed that many of the folk on board were travelling with all their worldly goods including goats and chickens so the cacophony of sound was deafening and the tightly packed compartments of the rather dated train made me wonder why I hadn't complied with their initial demands and flown out.

Progress was slow as we stopped at every hamlet on the way whereupon another round of pandemonium would break out, as bodies pushed and shoved to get on or off whilst a melee of colourfully clad vendors strove to sell their wares to all and sundry. An additional delay was incurred when the engine developed a heating problem and the engine wasn't the only thing overheating as the heaving masses in the fetid stationary carriages added to the already stiflingly ambient temperature.

The journey consisted of two parts. The first train went as far as Dire Dawa where it was all change to another train for the remaining leg into Djibouti, and as if I needed anything else to go wrong, our train arrived too late to meet the onward connection and my all important rendezvous with the border guards. Had it been a simple matter of kicking my heels for an hour or so till the next one came along that would have been fine but the next one wasn't going to be along for three days so I made my way to the local police station to check in. The officer in charge duly phoned my contact at the Ministry and I can only imagine what his reaction was, but with no other option available to me I resolved to once again being detained at their pleasure and was given the use of one of their prison cells as my accommodation.

In reality my detention was not at all onerous as the policeman in charge decided that rather than me being stuck at the station all day I may as well join him on his rounds. This proved to be very eventful if slightly morbid as we took in a variety of crimes out in the surrounding rural countryside including cattle theft, murder and a case involving an unfortunate young girl who had had a run in with a crocodile and needless to say had come off worst, requiring the police to ferry her to the nearest hospital where at least we were informed that her prognosis was positive.

The few days quickly flew by and at last I was once again sweating it out on the final leg of the train journey and on reaching the border was greeted by the guards as if I was a VIP, probably just relieved to eventually see the back of me, and so I arrived back in Djibouti and back to square one but at least I now had a new passport in my possession.

I was now persona non grata in the surrounding countries and the sea route offered the only affordable option out. So began another round of visiting shipping agents and the docks and eventually my efforts were rewarded when I secured a mutually acceptable deal for a small cabin on a coastal boat which covered a round trip from Kenya to Yemen and back moving a variety of cargoes between the different centres.

The trip was scheduled to take ten days and our first port of call was back to Hodeidah in Yemen. For the duration of the trip I would be classed as a crewmember which simplified immigration control, as crew were issued with shore passes, so I was able to have a quick look around one of my old haunts once again. On docking we were inundated by local entrepreneurs who work a black market mainly in booze and it appears that the crewmembers work a sideline buying duty free goods in Djibouti then selling them on at a tidy profit with a blind eye being turned by the master of the ship to this extra-curriculum activity.

With both official and unofficial cargos duly discharged and loaded we were ready to move on round to Aden, but not before today's mechanical problem was resolved. The vessel appears to require constant fettling and today it was the generators that were the cause for concern. There were three on board one of which had already gone down and now another had packed up. The prospect of having no power didn't bear thinking of so the necessary repairs were undertaken and our scheduled journey time started to slip.

Already on that first crossing I had proven that I wasn't in possession of sea legs finding the natural movement of the boat on the swell somewhat stomach churning, but I presumed I'd get used to it as the journey progressed. Boy did I get that wrong!

On leaving Aden after another mechanical delay, this time concerning the water pump, we continued along the eponymous Gulf then rounded the horn of Africa into the Indian Ocean and it was as if someone had flicked on a giant wave switch. The relative calm I'd experienced so far was immediately replaced by heaving swollen seas and strong southwesterly winds, this being the monsoon season.

For the next three days I was riveted to my bed and even the thought of food was enough to make me feel ill. The small cabin I was occupying was situated just above the level of the natural water line and all that was visible through my small round porthole was the ever changing scene of sky one second whilst above the sea line and water the next as we dipped below it. Fortunately things did slowly improve as we ploughed further south but time had been lost and even more delays hit us when we eventually reached Mogadishu.

As the port is in shallow waters all cargo is transferred on and off shore via a flotilla of small barges, but before any business could start the paperwork had to be cleared and we arrived just after the relevant offices had closed. Worst still, the next day was a local holiday so we were left being tossed up and down anchored half a mile off shore.

Holiday over, the serious job of sorting out the new and old cargos got underway, quite an art in itself, as the swelling seas made transferring goods from one vessel to another a hairy experience and more than one bit of cargo finished up as flotsam in the ocean.

Whilst the crew were battling with the elements my crew status allowed me to get on shore and so ironically I found myself walking freely around the capital city of the very country that three months earlier had refused me entry and so started off my passport escapades.

Once all goods had been duly assigned we set off for the final push down to Mombasa. Over the following days conditions continued to improve and I eventually acclimatised to my surroundings and was able to get up and about and socialise with the other crewmembers. Whilst chatting I established the full benefits their wheeling and dealing operation can accrue. It all starts in Kenya where they purchase local carvings which are sold to contacts in Djibouti. The proceeds are then used to buy duty free booze that is offloaded in Yemen in exchange for sterling and with additional business often carried out in Aden they arrive back home where the sterling is favourably exchanged back into local currency. With a combination of mark ups and currency exchange a six-fold profit can be made on their initial investment, nice work for those who get it.

Although the seas had calmed somewhat another factor came into play which revived my feelings of nausea. A large part of the cargo we had been carrying throughout was whale meat. This would normally pose no problem over the scheduled timetable, however, due to the numerous delays it was on the turn. Unfortunately my cabin was in close proximity to it and as each day passed so the stench grew stronger and though I could escape above deck during the day, nights became a nightmare.

The combination of mechanical problems, atrocious weather and holidays had seen my ten day trip become a three week marathon but I had survived which was more than could be said for the Peugeot car which had been strapped down as deck cargo and was now looking in a pretty sorry state, the crashing waves having taken their toll on it's bodywork.

So at last on 1st July we docked at Mombasa and I was once again on terra firma, raring to see what delights the rest of Africa would offer up.

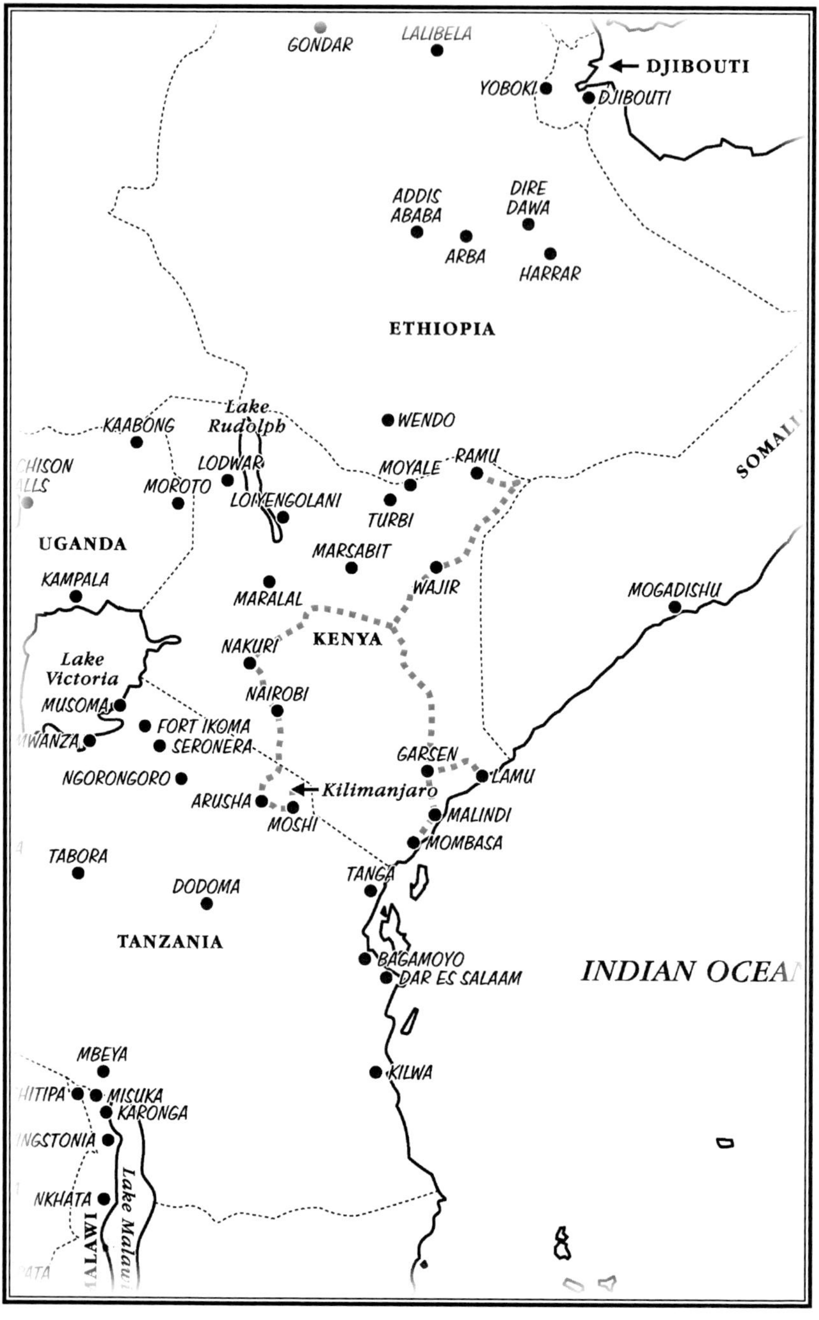

GONDAR
LALIBELA
DJIBOUTI
YOBOKI
DJIBOUTI
ADDIS ABABA
DIRE DAWA
ARBA
HARRAR
ETHIOPIA
Lake Rudolph
WENDO
KAABONG
LODWAR
MOYALE
RAMU
MOROTO
LOIYENGOLANI
TURBI
SOMALI
UGANDA
MARSABIT
KAMPALA
WAJIR
MARALAL
MOGADISHU
KENYA
NAKURI
Lake Victoria
NAIROBI
MUSOMA
FORT IKOMA
SERONERA
GARSEN
LAMU
NGORONGORO
Kilimanjaro
ARUSHA
MOSHI
MALINDI
MOMBASA
TABORA
TANGA
DODOMA
TANZANIA
BAGAMOYO
DAR ES SALAAM
INDIAN OCEAN
MBEYA
KILWA
MISUKA
KARONGA
NKHATA
MALAWI
Lake Malawi

CHAPTER 12
KILIMANJARO

Mombasa is one of Kenya's better known coastal resorts and plays host to a number of fine hotels along it's sandy beaches which in turn give access to the warm waters of the Indian Ocean.

There was lots of coral just off the shore line and even a simple bit of snorkelling was most rewarding with a multitude of colourful tropical fish on display along with some less friendly specimens such as the highly poisonous puffer fish. This slow swimming fish can ingest vast amounts of water quickly and blow itself up to several times its normal size and coupled with its deadly toxin for which no antidote was known it was definitely best avoided.

Fine as the hotels and beaches were I was as interested in visiting the old part of the town, and the ties to its Arab background were immediately obvious with its narrow streets reminiscent of those I'd so often seen in Yemen.

Another even better example of the Arab influence on this coastal belt lay further north on the island of Lamu. The road there took me past the slightly smaller, less well known resort of Malindi and on to the tiny town of Garsen. From there the road branched off through small cashew nut plantations and deteriorated into swampy black glutinous soil on its final sixty-five mile run across the Tana River flood plains towards Lamu.

To reach the island the final leg of the journey was by motorised ferry. The trip took us past several dhows, not so colourfully decorated as those I'd come across in the Arab peninsula but still cutting a fine profile with their large single sail propelling them across the water.

Some thirty minutes later we reached our destination and I made my way into the town centre where an old fort dominated the square, though this was now acting as a prison. Around the centre it was much as expected with typical Arab style flat roofed buildings all closely packed together, many sporting intricately carved wooden doors. Vehicular access was non-existent in this part of the town and indeed cars were a rarity on the complete island, and most of the exploring I did over the next few days was on 'shanks's pony'.

Though the centre of the town was very Arab influenced, around it there were the wooden framed, mud and coral, grass-roofed homes of the African residents and away from the town itself this was the norm.

As evening fell I secured a place on the flat roof of one of the small hotels, this being much cooler than the rooms, and with the benefit of a full moon cascading its light across the shimmering ocean below and silhouetting the anchored dhows, paradise was the word that came to mind. Indeed paradise could well be used to sum up the whole island with its long white sandy beaches and coconut palms giving a very tranquil feel about the whole place.

From Lamu I decided to continue north right up to the far northeast corner of the country following its border with Somalia, and the proximity to that country was well evidenced in the local community who were largely of Somali origin and led a pretty nomadic life style.

Homes here were in a domed shape, constructed from curved branches that formed the frame, tied together with leather thongs, over which woven palm leaf matting was placed as roofing. One indication of how our societies differ was manifested in an official government sign I came across which proclaimed 'Burial of the dead is strictly forbidden', though as it was out in the middle of nowhere I'm not sure that anyone would have been any the wiser if such activities were in fact being practised.

From this far flung corner of the country I made my way back south using a different route which took me once more towards the central highland mountains and on my travels I came across a larger than normal gathering of Samburu tribes people. The Samburu are a sister tribe to the better known Masai and share their looks, nomadic life style

Surrounded by Samburu warriors.

and predominantly red colour for their clothing. The ochre dye is also used to decorate the plaited hair of many of the young warriors.

The group were turned out in all their finery with the girls wearing numerous colourful bead necklaces cascading down to their shoulders and it turned out that they were assembled ready to attend a festival at the Nakuru state home of President Kenyatta.

They and a group of Turkana dancers were to perform for the President and having shown my interest in their folk culture I was invited along and so rubbed shoulders with the second head of state I'd encountered during my trip. Sadly but understandably no photography was allowed so I wasn't able to add him to my collection, but for a few hours I enjoyed the palatial comforts of his residence before it was all over and I was back down to earth, literally, with my ground sheet keeping the damp and the assorted creepy crawlies at bay as I once more laid my sleeping bag out under the African sky for the night.

Over a collective period of many months combining my first and now this second visit to Kenya I had managed to see pretty well every corner of it from the majestic grandeur of the central mountains to the coral edged coast line and the remote northern extremities next to Somalia and over by Lake Rudolph and so it was time to bid it farewell and head south over the border into Tanzania.

In a very strange twist of fate my friend Beryl, who had hosted the New Year's Eve party from which my urge to travel had originated back at the end of 1969, had completed her training and taken up a teaching post at a school in Arusha. The town, nestling at the foot of Mt Meru, is one of the larger towns in northern Tanzania and is very popular with visitors due to its relative proximity to two of the countries best known attractions, Kilimanjaro and the vast Serengeti national park.

Beryl had settled in and become well established in the town's social side of life by the time I arrived, and needless to say we had much to catch up with as a lot of water had passed under the bridge since we last saw each other. As I'd witnessed on numerous occasions information and contacts are priceless and Beryl had soon introduced me to colleagues of hers who were to open many a door that would normally have remained closed or at best hidden.

Having already been to the lowest point of the continent at Lake Assal I had shown an interest in climbing Kilimanjaro, Africa's highest point standing at 19,340 feet. I am no mountaineer but was aware that no special skills were required; the deciding factor between success and failure lying in one's ability to cope with the altitude and that would only become apparent when on the mountain.

As luck would have it I had decided to take a trip along to the town of Moshi which lies at the foot of Kili, and was picked up by an English chap who had been teaching in the area, and was shortly due to return to UK, but not before climbing Kili. He had already been up once and this time wanted to climb down into the Reusch crater around the ash pit and collect samples of the sulphur that is found around the volcanic fumaroles, and he asked if I would like to join him. With his past knowledge it seemed an opportunity too good to miss and in no time a date was set for the coming weekend, giving me a couple of days to sort out my preparations for one of the trips of my lifetime.

There was a series of small huts situated on the mountain which we could use as basic shelter and the plan was to make a five day round trip, three days to get up and explore the ash cone and two for the descent. We had worked out what food and water rations we would carry and in no time at all the departure morning had arrived.

Before setting off to the base control point we popped into the tourist office to obtain our hut reservations and were inundated with offers from guides and porters. As Mike had already been up the mountain before and we had ensured we were not carrying more than twenty-five pounds in our packs neither of these were required. It was then a bus ride to cover the fifteen miles to the Marangu trailhead from where the hike commenced.

By the time we eventually got going on the lower path and started our first ten mile stint it was 1.45 pm and we had hardly covered any distance when we were stopped and questioned as to why we had no guides or porters and despite our explanation a heated discussion ensued. The parties concerned were obviously touting for business but we stuck to our stance that neither were needed and forged on regardless.

The lower slopes are home to the Chagga people and as we made our way up we were surrounded by children trying to sell us floral halo shaped headbands which we later found out replicated those given by the guides to successful climbers on reaching the summit. The colour and splendour of these adornments diminished as we climbed further up with the last offerings being little more than woven grasses.

Our later than scheduled departure saw us climbing during the hot sun of the afternoon through banana groves and then into the cooler forest where the dwellings ceased. We followed the path through the peaceful wooded slopes for the next four or five miles then emerged onto an open plain supporting grassy vegetation. This took us on a further mile before once again we encountered a short wooded section prior to reaching our first goal the Bismarck or Mandara hut that stands at 9,000 feet. It was now around 6.00 pm.

The huts on the mountain were basic with wooden bunk beds but they offered shelter from the elements and were never geared to cater for our creature comforts. Once dark, around 7.00 pm, any light was courtesy of torches by which we conjured up our gourmet evening meal of soup, cheese and bread, swilled down with coffee, before turning in for an early night. One bit of kit I had been able to avail myself of from Mike was a down-filled sleeping bag and it was to prove a godsend over the next couple of nights as temperatures progressively dropped as altitude was gained.

We were awake not long after the rising sun and got ourselves slowly sorted for an 8.00 am start. I had never flown above the cloud line before so had never experienced the view which met us as we left the hut. There below stretched the never ending sea of white cloud surrounding our seemingly isolated harbour, with only a few other peaks poking through across the horizon.

The first half hour saw us climbing through steeply forested slopes which among the myriad of vegetation boasted giant heathers rising twenty to thirty feet into the canopy above. Once through this we emerged onto an open plain which gave us a clear view of the three peaks of Kilimanjaro, Kibo being the highest with its smaller sister Mawenzi to its side, a saddle of mountain separating the two, and Shira. The latter two are extinct but the main peak Kibo is dormant and could erupt again.

The next seven miles over the plain saw us negotiating a series of nine river ravines then around 1.00 pm we reached hut number two, Peter's or Horombo, depending on whether one gives it the old or new Swahili name, situated at 12,335 feet. We were able to spend a lazy afternoon and took full advantage of a nearby mountain stream to clean up and replenish our water supplies.

Fellow climbers used the huts, and this second one also plays home to descending parties whilst the first and third are mainly only used during the ascent. Whilst we were making our own way up, we came across our antithesis when a party of four Americans arrived complete with their entourage. This comprised a cook, two guides and seven porters and whilst we got stuck into our soup and tinned fish, they were feted

Kibo peak on Mount Kilimanjaro.

with a much more extensive fayre served on table cloths with matching serviettes, though I couldn't help feeling they had somewhat missed the point.

Day three started with a difference when we were greeted by a couple of policemen, who it turned out were on their way to recover the body of a missing climber whose remains had been discovered in the glaciers above. A sharp reminder, that despite the relative ease of the climb, the mountain needs to be shown due respect.

Once again we were on the move by 8.00 am and steadily climbed over heathery bush up to the saddle which separates the two main peaks and it was then a further four miles to the final Kibo hut named after the peak below which it stands. The last mile or so of this ascent took us up a deceptively tiring gradient but this was merely a training exercise for the final three mile push up the last 3,000 feet to the summit which awaited us in the early morning.

Our 1.30 pm arrival at Kibo gave us time to acclimatise during the afternoon though fortunately neither Mike or myself had shown any side effects from the thinning oxygen found in the atmosphere at the 15,520 feet where we were now located.

I didn't sleep very well probably mulling over the final push and was quite pleased when our early morning reveille hour arrived at 1.00 am. I was climbing in my tennis shoes, which were not the most waterproof of footwear, and had brought along plastic bags to fit over my socks to prevent any moisture seeping through to my feet, and today was going to prove if this ploy would indeed work.

With all available clothing layered on we set out at 1.30 am and with the aid of the partial moonlight slowly picked our way onwards to the bottom of the final scree slope where we arrived at 3.00 am. In the early hours of the morning the freezing temperatures act as an adhesive on the loose stones binding them slightly together but it was still very easy to find oneself taking two steps forward and one step back. Slowly we got the hang of things and zig-zagged our way to the summit shortly before the first hints of daylight crept over the horizon.

We sat for about twenty minutes awaiting the rising sun and I had never felt so cold in all my life, shivering involuntarily and while the plastic bags had done an admirable job of keeping out the damp they had done nothing to help keep my feet warm. At last the sun started to creep into its new day and at that moment the film in my camera ran out. I had a mad rush to locate the replacement and an epic few minutes while the blocks of ice that had replaced the ten digits at the end of my arms undertook the intricate business of reloading.

Despite the cold, the sunrise was worth all the discomfort, the glorious red orb casting its glow over the sea of clouds that was again spread out like a tablecloth below us. Once into the sky it didn't take too long for its warming effects to start permeating through our bodies, making us feel human again, and having taken in the ambience of being perched on the top of Africa, the next stage of today's adventure got underway.

Mike had come prepared with compass and bearings and so we set off down the inner wall of the outer crater dropping two hundred and fifty feet to the snow-covered floor below. Massive glacial ice blocks surrounded us as we crossed over to the inner crater and the central ash pit. It took us a cautious half hour to reach our final goal, the Reusch crater protected by a one hundred and fifty foot scree wall.

Once into the crater Mike collected his required sulphur samples from the fumaroles and after a not too close inspection of the deep four hundred yard wide ash pit we about turned and made our way back to Gillman's point on Kibo's outer edge then started the long return journey.

Glacial formations inside the crater on Kilimanjaro.

The scree slope which in the early morning hours had been vaguely stuck together had now been exposed to the effects of the morning sun. Trying to get a sure footing was none too easy but with a combination of skiing over the surface and bumping along on our backsides we reached the plain below and crashed on down to Peter's hut for our final night on the mountain.

The mountain stream was a welcome sight and after freshening up we had a slap up meal using up our remaining supplies, an eclectic mix of spaghetti, mince, rice and corned beef followed by a wonderful night's sleep relaxed in the knowledge that our goal had been achieved.

The final day covered the twenty-two miles down to the bottom, retracing the path we had come up on, and at 2.15 in the afternoon we were back down, and after a welcome bus ride were in the comfort of Mike's house, feet up, enjoying a cold beer or two. All the discomfort and stiff limbs were soon forgotten, and replaced with all the memories of a truly great adventure which were indelibly printed on my mind.

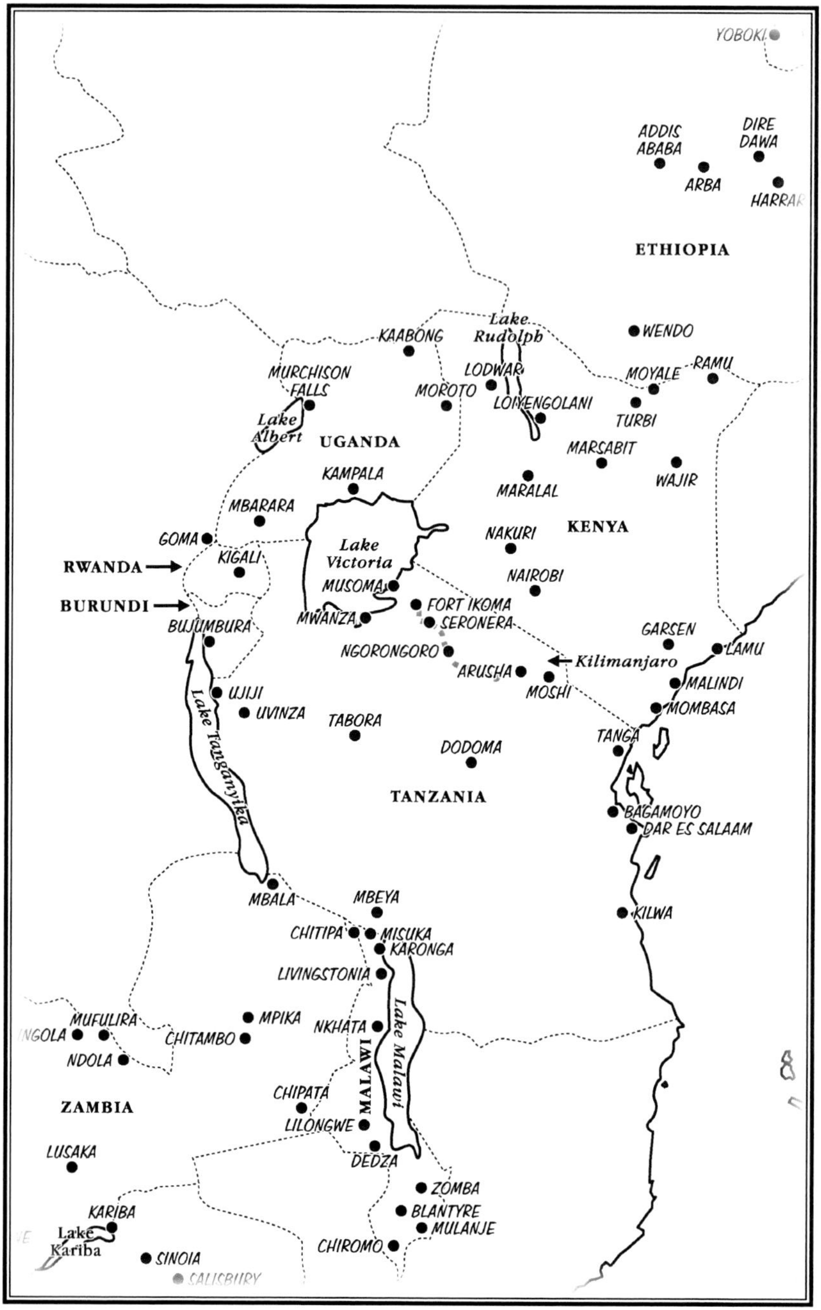
YOBOKI
ADDIS ABABA
DIRE DAWA
ARBA
HARRAR
ETHIOPIA
Lake Rudolph
WENDO
KAABONG
MURCHISON FALLS
LODWAR
MOYALE
RAMU
MOROTO
LOIYENGOLANI
TURBI
Lake Albert
UGANDA
MARSABIT
KAMPALA
WAJIR
MARALAL
MBARARA
KENYA
NAKURI
GOMA
Lake Victoria
RWANDA
KIGALI
NAIROBI
MUSOMA
BURUNDI
FORT IKOMA
MWANZA
SERONERA
BUJUMBURA
GARSEN
NGORONGORO
LAMU
ARUSHA
Kilimanjaro
MOSHI
MALINDI
UJIJI
Lake Tanganyika
UVINZA
TABORA
MOMBASA
TANGA
DODOMA
TANZANIA
BAGAMOYO
DAR ES SALAAM
MBALA
MBEYA
KILWA
CHITIPA
MISUKA
KARONGA
LIVINGSTONIA
MPIKA
MUFULIRA
NKHATA
CHITAMBO
NDOLA
Lake Malawi
MALAWI
CHIPATA
ZAMBIA
LILONGWE
LUSAKA
DEDZA
ZOMBA
KARIBA
BLANTYRE
Lake Kariba
MULANJE
CHIROMO
SINOIA
SALISBURY

CHAPTER 13
SERENGETI

Through one of Beryl's many contacts she had been invited to join a group for a tour of the game parks, including Serengeti and whilst there she had stayed at the Seronera lodge. The organisers of the group knew the manager and as a tenuous result of this I was invited to stop over should I visit the park. It had always been my plans to see both the Serengeti and the neighbouring Ngorongoro Parks and whilst no incentive was required this was an opportunity too good to miss.

Armed with my letter of introduction I set out via Lake Manyara and one hundred and ten miles later reached the outer edge of the Ngorongoro Park. I was able to crash out overnight at a control post and started a new day testing my prospects of hitching my way down into the crater.

The crater at Ngorongoro and the surrounding conservation area were originally part of the Serengeti Park but were separated in the 1950's. It is reputed that the crater plays host to some twenty-five thousand animals mainly ungulates, gazelles, wildebeest, zebra and eland along with a high density of lions and a good number of black rhinos and hippos, a natural one hundred square mile volcanic amphitheatre for wildlife.

I was fortunate to be given the opportunity to ride along with a group on a day trip and we set off down the twisting track of what appeared to be the sheer side of the crater, dropping onto the vast grasslands 2,000 feet below. In the centre of the crater lies the salt lake which varies in size depending on whether it is the wet or dry season and in addition to the lake there is also a couple of natural springs, the largest in the east section where a large swampy area exists and that in turn is ideal habitat for the local hippo population.

The grassland and occasional clump of acacia trees afford a surprising amount of cover to the untrained eye but we were still able to catch sight of lots of plains game as well as lions, rhinos and elephant, the latter three being among the big five on everyone's 'must see' list. The leopards and buffalos would have to wait for another day.

With an excellent day's safari behind us we once more took to the twisting track and four-wheel drove up to the crater's edge and onto the park's boundary where another night beneath the African skies was passed, next stop was Serengeti.

Having spent a couple of nights at the control I had been able to chat to the guards and with their assistance managed to secure a lift with some ministry officials who were passing through Serengeti on their way to Musoma a town on the Tanzanian shore of Lake Victoria.

We skirted round the southern edge of the crater once more giving me the opportunity to take in the magnificent scenery and then dropped down through the yellowed grasslands towards the Olduvai Gorge.

This is the site known as 'the cradle of mankind', following excavations started in 1931 by Louis Leakey and his wife which provided the most continuous record of human evolution over the past two million years. Unfortunately I was not in a position to ask my companions if they would like to stop and view the site in more detail; however one got a strange feeling being at the very spot where our existence was believed to have begun.

On reaching the flat plains below we made steady progress and once through the formalities of entrance to the park we continued to the lodge at Seronera where I made myself known to Babu the manager, handing him my letter of introduction. One never knows what reaction one will receive in such circumstances where kind offers of help have been volunteered by, or to, third parties, but any fears were quickly dispelled as I was given a very warm welcome.

The lodge at Seronera housed the dining and social rooms but the bulk of the accommodation was under canvas though definitely one up on the usual camping experience with the luxury of sprung beds, mattresses and linen along with a rudimentary but effective shower. I was allocated one of these tents for my use during my stay and so commenced what turned out to be an unforgettable three weeks in Africa's finest game reserve.

Like all tourists my main aim was to see the wildlife and tick off the aforementioned big five, and my first opportunity came on my first morning when a large group who were resident at the lodge were making a trip out and I got invited along. Suitably armed with my camera at the ready, we set off in anticipation, but unfortunately all the big game had a different agenda and stayed well tucked out of sight, not the most exhilarating start, but all was about to change.

Being the guest of the manager and dining with him and his family opened many doors as I was introduced to both members of the research institute and game wardens along with organisers of the many tours that used the lodge as their base.

Having had one such introduction an offer to accompany one of the research team on his rounds was quickly accepted and despite the early crack of dawn start the results were staggering. With a very complete knowledge of the habitat of the animals being studied, we were soon in close proximity to a pride of lions and shortly afterwards a cheetah with four, three month old cubs. More lions, including a mating pair, and several more cheetah families followed. The researcher had christened all the animals in question, along with many more we were to see during the next couple of hours. He identified them by noting markings on their face or body, and was tracking who was mating with whom, along with their movements and that of their offspring. Hearing that I was actually looking at Tom, one of Harry and Mary's kids put a new light on the viewing experience.

As the days progressed and the daily safari trips unfolded I slowly warmed to the conservators' view which was somewhat at odds with that of the tourist department. Understandably the tourist side wanted to promote more visitors and were in the throws of constructing a brand new non-camping lodge complete with all the trimmings required by those on a package tour, whilst the other side wanted to restrict visitors and retain the natural habitat for the animals.

I had initially been as keen as anyone to simply snap away at anything that moved though if asked later what it really looked like and how it fitted into its surroundings I would have been at a loss to explain. As time passed by my camera got used less and less and what I was seeing became far more important than simply obtaining a few good wildlife pictures, and those camera free images are the ones that remain indelibly printed on my mind.

On another occasion I was introduced to Valerie the manager of the sister lodge at Fort Ikoma situated just outside the park. Not to be outdone I was invited to visit her establishment and spend a couple of days as her guest at the old German Fort. How could I refuse? The outcome of this was a most enjoyable few days spent in the relative luxury of a private rondavel, the standard accommodation at the lodge and somewhat more secure than the canvas I'd become used to, though the latter certainly delivers the true African night experience.

This area was one used by hunters and the lodge had several hunting parties staying there, and game meat was frequently on the menu. In addition to shooting with guns, photographic safaris were also starting to emerge where all the skills of the hunter were still required to stalk the prey but instead of a carcass, a picture was the client's trophy, arguably more rewarding, certainly more environmentally friendly and every bit as dangerous for the thrill seekers.

Feeding Lisa the orphaned cheetah cub.

A casualty of some local poachers was a cheetah cub which had been given the name Lisa. One of the hunting parties had perversely rescued it when they found her next to her mutilated mother. Much in the same mould as Elsa, the lion cub made famous in the film Born Free, this little lady was being hand reared with a view to releasing her back into the wild once she was mature enough. I couldn't resist the chance to give her one of her bottle feeds and though only a few months old and very playful I bore a few superficial marks from the encounter. The other lasting memory was how rough her tongue was as she licked my arms and legs, more like a sheet of sandpaper than a tongue.

I duly returned to Seronera and got back into the daily routine of game runs with either the research team, Babu himself or one of the touring parties that were passing through. One such group, which were doing it in style, rolled up in a large Mercedes bus with an equally large trailer attached which quickly transformed into sleeping accommodation and a fully fitted kitchen, they weren't exactly roughing it, but had no doubt paid handsomely for the privilege.

One evening David the chief game warden was discussing the damage that errant elephants cause to the trees and bemoaning the presence of a group of four bulls who had encroached within the proscribed radius they try to keep around the camp. They planned to move them out which sounded quite exciting and I cheekily asked if I could go along with them. It was pointed out that the exercise would not be without its dangers but that just made it sound even better and exonerating him from any responsibility towards me it was agreed that I could join them.

The following day the party was assembled, three Land Rovers with a motley crew of local game wardens under the supervision of David with whom I was riding. The crew were armed with guns, thunder flashes and noise producing equipment, for which read empty tin cans, and once the morning Safaris had finished and everyone else was back having lunch we set out to do battle with our pachydermal foes.

On reaching our targets the vehicles split up and we skirted round behind the group and with surprising ease managed to get them moving out of the acacia trees and bushes where they were browsing and onto the open plain. It was now a matter of keeping up a supervised level of noise and keeping them running. On the way we came to another strip of heavy vegetation and needless to say the elephants decided to give up their lunchtime work out and took cover. In the course of flushing them out into the open again, using various flanking tactics and thunder flashes, we disturbed several groups of animals, amongst them three rhinos, the first I'd seen in Serengeti.

Eventually they were on the move again and being heralded out of harm's way and all seemed to be going to plan until one of them decided not to play our little game and turned round and started to head back towards us. The following half hour was spent vainly trying to change his direction, and despite some daring positioning, much shouting and banging and several speedy chases over the rough virgin terrain all our efforts were to no avail. Towards the end it was obvious that the lone bull was becoming agitated, and on several occassions charged towards our vehicles, which, whilst good for photography did nothing for the blood pressure.

At around 2.00 pm David called it a day not wishing our activities to be seen by any tour groups who may well have been none too pleased at us moving animals beyond their reach, but there had been a good reason behind it all and moving three out of four was deemed to be a satisfactory result.

Further outings during my stay involved visits to the hippo pool and an hour long session watching four lionesses with eleven cubs when even an unexpected thunderstorm couldn't diminish our enjoyment of their antics.

Elephant damage to a Baobab tree.

With the constant change of visitors, socialising was part of the scene, and in addition to partaking of a few beers now and again, and again, and again, there was also a dartboard on hand. A bit like being down the local but with the added spice of the background murmurings which only the African bush can provide.

Such murmurings took on a ferocious level one evening while a group of us were sat around the campfire. A kill had taken place only a couple of hundred yards away and Babu took us over towards it in his Land Rover. By the lights of the vehicle we could see a group of lions scrambling over the freshly killed zebra carcass, ripping off chunks of meat for all they were worth, an absolutely incredible scene though somewhat gory, a point emphasised by one lioness when she raised her head to display her blood covered face.

The growling and roaring was brought to a higher pitch by the arrival of a male who obviously wanted his share of the feast, though that seemed to be much to the annoyance of the girls who had done all the work. We retrenched back to the fire but the feeding frenzy continued and in the morning there was little trace of the unfortunate zebra, the hyenas and jackals had done an excellent job of clearing up the remains overnight.

It seemed a fitting end to another fantastic adventure. I had spent three weeks in Africa's premier game park and through the many contacts I'd made, had encountered enough animals to last me a lifetime, the big five included. Chasing the elephants and the lion kill had been experiences money just couldn't buy, only the annual migration of the wildebeest herds had escaped me, but all good things have to come to an end and there was still a lot of Africa to explore.

With a heavy heart I said my farewells and trekked back to Arusha.

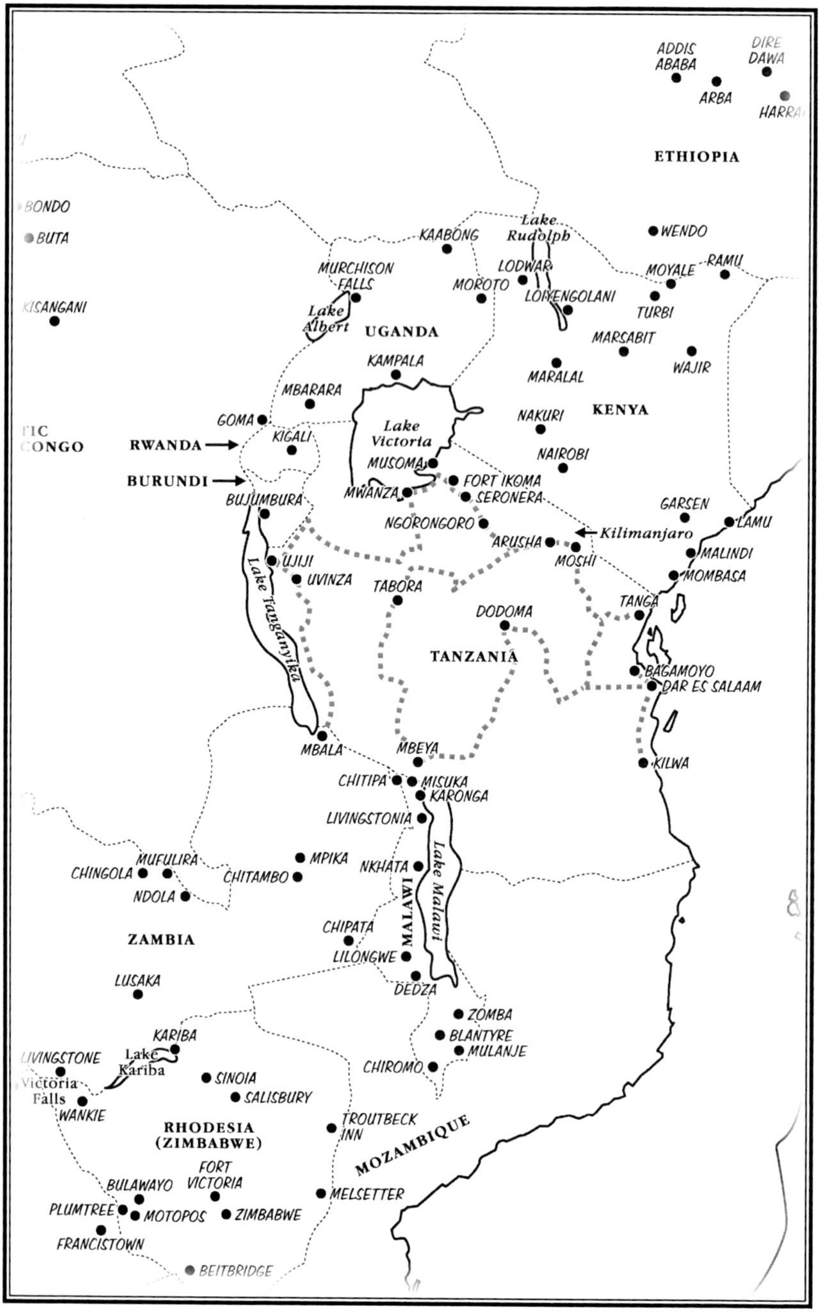
ADDIS ABABA
DIRE DAWA
ARBA
HARRA
ETHIOPIA
BONDO
BUTA
KISANGANI
WENDO
KAABONG
Lake Rudolph
MURCHISON FALLS
LODWAR
MOYALE
RAMU
MOROTO
LOIYENGOLANI
TURBI
Lake Albert
UGANDA
MARSABIT
KAMPALA
MARALAL
WAJIR
MBARARA
NAKURI
KENYA
GOMA
Lake Victoria
KIGALI
NAIROBI
RWANDA
CONGO
MUSOMA
BURUNDI
MWANZA
FORT IKOMA
SERONERA
BUJUMBURA
GARSEN
NGORONGORO
LAMU
ARUSHA
Kilimanjaro
MALINDI
UJIJI
MOSHI
MOMBASA
UVINZA
TABORA
Lake Tanganyika
TANGA
DODOMA
TANZANIA
BAGAMOYO
DAR ES SALAAM
MBALA
MBEYA
KILWA
CHITIPA
MISUKA
KARONGA
LIVINGSTONIA
MPIKA
MUFULIRA
CHINGOLA
CHITAMBO
NKHATA
Lake Malawi
NDOLA
ZAMBIA
CHIPATA
MALAWI
LILONGWE
DEDZA
LUSAKA
ZOMBA
KARIBA
BLANTYRE
LIVINGSTONE
Lake Kariba
MULANJE
SINOIA
CHIROMO
Victoria Falls
SALISBURY
WANKIE
TROUTBECK INN
RHODESIA (ZIMBABWE)
MOZAMBIQUE
FORT VICTORIA
BULAWAYO
MELSETTER
PLUMTREE
MOTOPOS
ZIMBABWE
FRANCISTOWN
BEITBRIDGE

CHAPTER 14
JAMBO

I had now fulfilled my aim of climbing Kilimanjaro and safariing in the Serengeti but as both of these lie near the northern border with Kenya there was still a vast amount of Tanzania to explore.

I had the good fortune of having been invited to several homes for Christmas and whilst Arusha seemed to make most sense rather than trekking back north to Nairobi, the big day was a month away. Not wishing to kick my heels for a few weeks I decided to take in the coastal and central regions of the country in a large circular tour that would see me back in time for the 25th.

Heading for the coast took me along the Pare Mountains with the massive Masai steppe plains stretching off to the southwest. The journey passed through mixed bush land and large sisal plantations the latter being one of the countries big exports. Houses were rectangular in shape built from the common combination of wood, mud and thatch these materials being pretty universal throughout the inland non-nomadic villages, though shapes varied between round and rectangular depending upon location and country.

The aim was to make for Dar es Salaam another of Africa's magic sounding names but on the way I detoured off to the coastal town of Tanga, a very popular location for shell collecting along its coral reef.

The town, like many on this eastern coastline had Arab influences but away from the seafront it spread outwards in a wave of Asian homes then on the outer edge African settlements. Walking around, it was easy to be enticed into sampling the local refreshments being touted about with fruit juices, among them my favourite mango, and young coconut milk high on the list.

This coastal belt is also home to the Makonde carvers, and I found it fascinating to see how these bits of tree branch or even flotsam were so skilfully transformed into the intricate carvings which abound in this region. Another possibly lesser skill was actively employed by a smaller group of entrepreneurs who were taking empty cans and with a fair amount of snipping and hammering, turning them into oil burning lamps which were widely used as a source of light.

The local medicine man also appeared to be a popular calling point and the assortment of potions and artefacts he had at his disposal were mind boggling with 'dolls' made from a veritable pile of rubbish, beads, radio valves, bits of mirror, a babies dummy and a binocular eyepiece among the assembled components, but the finished article no doubt held some mystical healing powers, for those who believed.

After Tanga I slowly continued my journey to Dar es Salaam; slowly, as traffic was not plentiful but on the bright side there were mango trees everywhere along the route so I was quite happy to put up with my leisurely pace of progress.

The final part of this journey was in the company of a German couple and their young six year old daughter. They all spoke very good English a point that the little chatterbox made abundantly clear and it transpired that she also conversed with her local school friends in their local language. This phenomenon was not uncommon in my travels where we Brits are pretty poor at learning languages but the children take to it like ducks to water, and on many occasions the kids were called over to act as interpreter between parents and locals.

For my part I had always tried to learn the basic greetings and pleasantries of whatever country I was in, and having spent quite some time in East Africa I had grasped the basics in Kiswahili. This language is widely used throughout the region in addition to local dialects and of course English which is the medium for administration purposes.

Not unlike our own greetings where we hail each other and ask after our respective healths, though not really expecting to be greeted with

JAMBO

tales of woe, Kiswahili follows a strict series of questions and answers as detailed below.

1st Party	*Jambo* (Hello)
Respondee	*Jambo Bwana* (Hello sir)
1st Party	*Habari yako?* (What news have you got?)
Respondee	*Mzuri sana* (Good news)
1st Party	*Unakwenda wapi?* (Where are you going?)
Respondee	*Mimi nakwenda Nairobi* (I am going to Nairobi)
1st Party	*Unatoka wapi?* (Where have you come from?)
Respondee	*Mimi natoka Mombasa* (I have come from Mombasa)

Armed with this information and by judging the point at which one became engaged with a passing stranger I was able to hold what appeared to be a flowing conversation with them. The trick was to have walked far enough past them before the next unanswerable question was fired in my direction thus giving the impression that it was not ignorance that prevented me from replying, purely the fact that I hadn't heard the question. This ploy was put to good use on many an occasion whilst out on the rural roads.

During one of my stays in Arusha I had been introduced to Tec an English guy working in Dar, and had been invited to look him up on my arrival which I duly did, and was lavishly accommodated in his idyllic beach front home while in the city. The old hangover from the colonial club still existed in the form of the gymkhana and yacht clubs both of which had a vibrant social side and a most enjoyable few days were spent taking advantage of the sea location with sailing and water skiing high on the agenda.

Dar itself was not so impressive, smaller and not as modern as its northerly neighbour Nairobi, and sadly left little impression on me.

One impression I had picked up from my movement around Tanzania so far was that tribal divisions were less apparent, with the obvious exception of the Masai, who still went about their nomadic way of life pretty well regardless of governmental influences.

President Julius Nyerere had definite left-leaning tendencies in his political philosophy and gave more than a passing nod to the plight of the freedom fighters actively involved in struggles in Angola, Rhodesia and Mozambique, with posters and signs promoting their activities dotted around the city.

Another sign of his left allegiance was the close connection he had nurtured with the Chinese who were actively building the Tan–Zam rail link connecting land locked Zambia with the coastal ports of Tanzania thus opening up a line of export for their copper which had previously simply flowed south through the now pariah state of Rhodesia.

To the north and south of Dar lay a couple of places worthy of a visit and Bagamoyo to the north was first on my list. The relatively short journey up the coast took me past more mango and cashew growing areas and this was the season when the fruit of the latter was out, giving a fresh scent to the air and providing the ingredients required for one of the local brews.

Bagamoyo had been the colonial capital during the German occupation prior to British rule in 1918. The town had a chequered history having been one of the main collection points where slaves were gathered prior to being shipped the short twenty-two miles across to the Omani Arab run island of Zanzibar before onward shipment across the globe. On a more humanitarian point it was also the site of the first Roman Catholic mission in East Africa which was set up circa 1870, and was the starting point for explorations undertaken by Burton, Speke and Grant.

The southern ruins at Kilwa were next on my list and the true interest lay on the island of Kilwa Kisiwani, another old stamping ground of the Arabs, along with the Persians and Portuguese all of whom left their architectural stamp on the landscape in the form of ruined forts and mosques. Unfortunately with the start of the rainy season the road conditions deteriorated and though I was able to reach Kilwa through the black quagmire masquerading as a road it became impassable whilst I was down there. Spending the festive season marooned among ancient ruins wasn't on my plans and one window of opportunity offered itself up when I came across a small 6-seater Cherokee aircraft. It had arrived with some Agip oil chaps and after a bit of persuading I secured the final empty seat and so was back in Dar a lot sooner than I had expected.

The south of the country was pretty much out of bounds as it bordered Mozambique and the Frelimo fighters were active in the area. Even a visit to Mbeya, which was on my proposed circular route, required governmental permission, though this was granted without too much hassle and so I moved away from the coast, the luxurious comfort of Tec's beachfront home, and headed due west inland to Dodoma.

JAMBO

My movements west started on a good tarred road but it was one still under construction and soon the original dirt track took over, frustratingly following the unfinished new section where all efforts were focused, thus the old track was left unmaintained resulting in a rough old ride.

The journey west over the plains took me to the location of the ill-fated groundnut scheme. In 1946 Clement Attlee attempted to establish in what was then Tanganyika, a massive groundnut cultivation programme to provide for the production of vegetable oil. Sadly it was doomed from the start with a catalogue of disasters and ill-founded judgements not least that the area suffered from drought whilst the crop required annual rainfall of twenty inches. It was finally abandoned in 1951 at considerable cost to the British taxpayer.

From Dodoma the road plunged south and up a long escarpment that forms part of the lower eastern side of the Rift Valley, climbing to 5,500 feet. The route on to Mbeya closely followed the escarpment and one of the lifts I secured was with a Greek gentleman, one of the few remaining private plantation owners. His crops were tobacco and maize but he informed me that most of his fellow sisal growers had been forced out or simply upped sticks and gone rather than put up with all the hassles they faced from the authorities.

After encountering the under construction Chinese railway I eventually reached Mbeya which is situated near the point where the west and east sides of the Rift Valley join together. While down in that area I came across a small fleet of Mercedes lorries each carrying some sixty personnel who I soon found out were in fact Angolan guerrillas undergoing training, another sign of the benevolent manner in which such groups were entertained by the local regime.

This being the southernmost point of my circle it was then north through some of the most beautiful mountain scenery I had come across on the continent before dropping down to the plain below. The area had previously not been settled due to the presence of tsetse flies which cause havoc to animal herds and give us more than an annoying bite as they cause human sleeping sickness. Much work had been carried out to eradicate and control their presence and on several occassions I had been in vehicles which were subject to a thorough spraying with chemicals aimed at preventing any of the little beggars being moved to non-infected areas.

The route north passed by several 'Ujamma' projects. These were collective farms set up by Nyerere's government under his social and economic development plans, but were generally not welcomed by the indigenous people who were frequently forced off their homelands and relocated to these co-operative based farms. In addition to the main collectively cultivated area each resident was allocated a plot for their home, which would be built on a self-help basis, and an area to grow their own subsistence level crops. Despite the best efforts to establish the policy, the name of which comes from the Kiswahili for extended family, it was doomed to fail; I just think the Africans were not ready to give up their independence to follow a Mao style philosophy.

Many of the lifts I acquired were on the back of lorries and whilst I was heading back towards Arusha I seemed to pick an interesting selection of them as my transport.

It was not uncommon for the locals to be accompanied by vast amounts of belongings when moving around the country and one family took it to the ultimate level when we pulled up outside a typical wood/mud house. First, several trips were made in and out of the home emptying it of its content then the man of the house commenced to remove the wooden windows, door and door frame, all whilst I and several other passengers looked on in amazement. The content, windows, doors and all were then loaded up and our journey progressed once more.

Another couple of lifts resulted in me having what could hardly be described as a fragrant smell. I had been walking along the road hoping something would shortly come by when the heavens opened and the most horrendous torrential rainstorm saw me soaked to the skin and wearing boats in place of shoes. I plodded on regardless as there was no shelter available and eventually reached a small village and in true fashion, so often displayed by the local folk, pity was taken on me and I was sat down in front of a fire to dry out.

The hut typically had no chimney and the smoke from the fire lingered in the air and soon tainted my apparel but at least I was dryish and the rain had stopped. Once back on the road the grateful sight of a lorry appeared and responded to my outstretched thumb and I clambered aboard among the cargo of goats and a liberal layer of muck which despite my best efforts got all over my shoes, but I was heading in the right direction. After the saga with the goats my next and final lift of the day saw me bouncing along the rough dirt road surrounded by large bags of charcoal each of which dispersed a fine black cloud into the air each time the vehicle hit a bump and boy did we hit a lot of bumps. The end result saw me emerge at the end of the day looking like one of the natives and spreading 'L'Air du Chevre' perfume to anyone within striking distance of me. A cafe was the immediate focus of my attention from which I emerged white and somewhat cleaner but still leaving much to be desired and so I remained until I was directed to the Catholic mission and at last was able get myself and my attire cleaned up.

As I progressed further north and nearer to the final loop of my circular trip we left the tsetse fly area and herds of cattle and goats once more became part of the scenery on the plains which the recent rains had turned into a lush green colour. Having once more climbed up the eastern Rift escarpment with its wooded slopes giving a fine view of the plains stretching out below, I joined the previously travelled final seventy miles of tarred road into Arusha. It was now 4.30 pm on the 24th December, I'd made it by the skin of my teeth.

On one of my previous stopovers in Arusha I had been introduced to the manager of the local meerschaum pipe company, who turned out to be a fellow citizen of Malvern. His son Mike was over for the festive season and I was invited to spend Christmas day with them and a very enjoyable time was had by all drinking, nibbling, chatting and finally gorging ourselves on a full traditional Christmas dinner, though the equatorial temperature seemed an odd accompaniment to the seasonal fare.

Understandably I was interested to hear about the products that Les's company were involved in, this area being one of the few sources of the raw material. The mine supplying his factory was situated just over the border at Lake Amboseli in Kenya, whilst on a worldwide scale Turkey was the major commercial producer. The pipes created from meerschaum are intricately carved and designed and demand a high price. Many older pieces are highly sought after by collectors not only for their craftsmanship but also as they do deliver the finest smoking experience for the dedicated pipe smoker. Over time and constant use the original white colour will turn incremental shades of yellow, orange and red adding to the beauty of these carved masterpieces. Sadly as a non-smoker I wasn't in the market to undertake a product test but could appreciate the finished articles for their aesthetic value at least.

Having now covered the north, coastal and central regions of the country it was time to move off and head for Zambia and my chosen route was via the country's natural western border, Lake Tanganyika. Before once more heading into the bundu there was a small matter of seeing in a new year to contend with. This was done in fine style at the club in the company of the many friends I had been lucky enough to have met over my frequent visits to the town and around 5.00 am we decided to call it a day and so year three of my six month trip through Africa commenced.

Initially I headed round the southeast corner of Lake Victoria and then crossed over to the Burundi border which I followed down to the lakeside port of Ujiji. Traffic in the border area was sparse and progress slow through the wooded landscape, though there was a fair number of villages and I came across several groups catching the seasonal delicacy of flying ants. These are normally fried in oil though many of the eager harvesters showed a ferocious appetite for them and were happy to simply eat them raw, I, however, was not among them.

Being only across the lake from Burundi it was hardly surprising that the people of this area had links with their neighbours. The housing in particular followed the Rundi style where the wooden dome shaped

Memorial to Stanley and Livingstone meeting at Ujiji 1871.

frame was covered in a 'shaggy dog' look thatch from top to bottom with only one doorway and no windows accessing the outside.

Ujiji is the site of the Livingstone memorial marking the location of the mango tree under which Livingstone and Stanley famously met on 10th November 1871. There is also a tribute to mark the presence of the earlier explorers Burton and Speke who were in the village in 1858 whilst exploring the lake. At the time of their visits the Arab run slave trade was in full swing with the area south of Ujiji and across the lake in the Congo being the main source of their chattels, and after assembly at the lakeside town their captives were force marched across the country to the previously mentioned coastal port of Bagamoyo and thence onto Zanzibar. Needless to say mortality and sickness was rife throughout the harsh journey that could take many months to complete.

I had hoped to travel down the lake by boat but no regular service existed and I was strongly advised against using the local network of water taxis. Instead I headed slightly inland initially on a chaotic train journey to Uvinza, then slowly by dirt track to the higher mountain region at the south east end of the lake from where the views over the vast waters below were enhanced by some fine sunsets. The lake is the largest in the Rift valley being four hundred and twenty miles in length and a relatively narrow thirty-two miles in width and is also the second deepest in the world at 4800 feet.

After a long slow journey entailing much walking and many heavy rainstorms I finally reached the border and crossed over into the copper rich country of Zambia previously known as Northern Rhodesia prior to being granted independence on 24th October 1964.

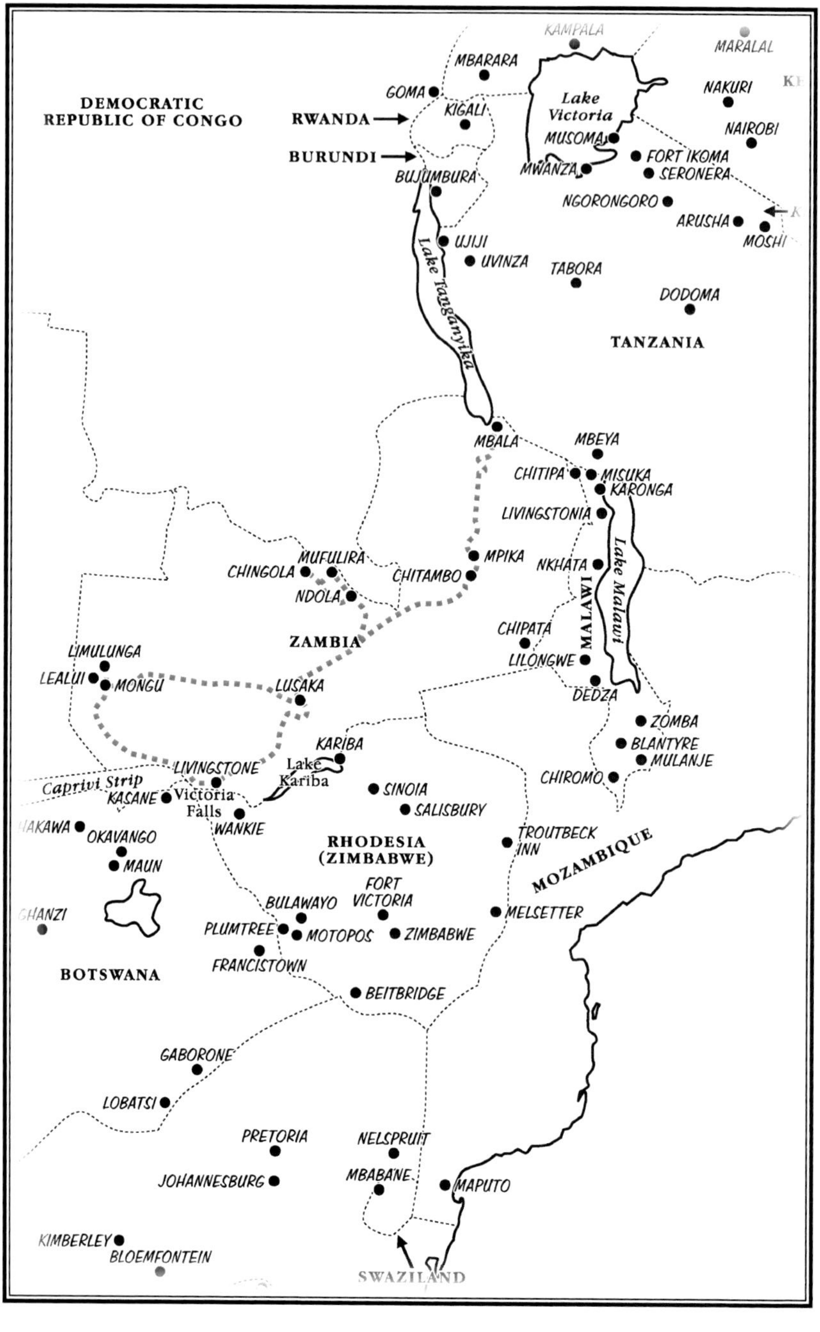

KAMPALA
MARALAL
MBARARA
NAKURI
GOMA
DEMOCRATIC REPUBLIC OF CONGO
RWANDA
KIGALI
Lake Victoria
NAIROBI
BURUNDI
MUSOMA
FORT IKOMA
MWANZA
SERONERA
BUJUMBURA
NGORONGORO
ARUSHA
MOSHI
UJIJI
UVINZA
TABORA
Lake Tanganyika
DODOMA
TANZANIA
MBALA
MBEYA
CHITIPA
MISUKA
KARONGA
LIVINGSTONIA
MPIKA
MUFULIRA
NKHATA
CHINGOLA
CHITAMBO
Lake Malawi
NDOLA
MALAWI
CHIPATA
ZAMBIA
LIMULUNGA
LILONGWE
LEALUI
MONGU
LUSAKA
DEDZA
ZOMBA
KARIBA
BLANTYRE
MULANJE
Lake Kariba
LIVINGSTONE
CHIROMO
Caprivi Strip
SINOIA
KASANE
Victoria Falls
SALISBURY
WANKIE
OKAVANGO
TROUTBECK INN
RHODESIA (ZIMBABWE)
MAUN
MOZAMBIQUE
FORT VICTORIA
BULAWAYO
MELSETTER
PLUMTREE
MOTOPOS
ZIMBABWE
FRANCISTOWN
BOTSWANA
BEITBRIDGE
GABORONE
LOBATSI
PRETORIA
NELSPRUIT
JOHANNESBURG
MBABANE
MAPUTO
KIMBERLEY
BLOEMFONTEIN
SWAZILAND

CHAPTER 15

MOSI-OA-TUNYA (THE FALLS)

I crossed the border and walked for a fair distance through the green wooded hills and having been unsuccessful in getting mobile was directed to an American mission who kindly allowed me to shelter for the night. Whilst I thoroughly commend the work ethics of all the many missionaries I had met most did enjoy a reasonable level of comfort, however as an exception to the rule this establishment was run on a shoestring, though I was still very grateful for the bowl of water I was given to freshen myself up with and so by the light of my torch, no flicking of a switch here, I got myself settled down for the night.

The main border control was in the first town of Mbala, which like so many had been renamed losing its colonial nomenclature of Abercorn, though somehow the results didn't conjure up the same magic, Kabwe replacing Broken Hill being just one such example.

The border control proved no problem as I was travelling south but controls had been tightened up for north bound travellers. They would often make a detour to Malawi and obtain a new passport thereby erasing any reference to their stay in either of the southern 'enemy' regimes of Rhodesia and South Africa. The guards had got wise to this and now wanted sight of original documents as well, resulting in many frustrated journeys. Just another sign of how the white colonialists in the south were viewed.

The town seemed to be well stocked with shops and it was a relief to be away from the pervading eyes of the Tanzanian TANU party personnel who would regularly stop and ask for travel documents without any reason other than that, they could. Another change from across the border was the emergence once again of liberal European style clothing, which was frowned upon in its northerly neighbour, where miniskirts were banned and even shorts were not welcomed.

On the reverse side of things the tribal identity of Zambians was still exercised and in keeping with most other countries one tribe, not necessarily the largest, was more prominent in the governing of the country. Location would often play its part with reference to which tribe this was with those geographically close to the old colonial centres often being recruited to help in admin roles and thus given further education and ultimately the ability to take over the reigns of power. This tribal division was something that Julius Nyerere in Tanzania had strived to replace with a unified nation through his many social programmes.

I moved on further south and reached Mpika where I joined the Great North road also known as the 'hell run', this being the route linking Zambia's copper mines with the port of Dar es Salaam and a notorious route for accidents. Many of these were no doubt caused through exhaustion and lack of sleep as the endless convoys relentlessly plied their goods across half the width of the African continent, though the intake of the mild narcotic qat (the Yemeni name) probably played its part.

At least from here road conditions improved a bit and traffic was more plentiful as I moved on towards Lusaka over another of the Rift Valley escarpments which gave fantastic views over the Luangwa river valley stretching out below to the east. I passed nearby Chitambo, the final resting place of Dr. Livingstone or to be more precise his heart. He died there on 1st May 1873 and his heart was buried under a tree whilst his faithful servants carried his disembowelled corpse, preserved in a cocktail of salt and brandy, back to Bagamoyo in a bark coffin.

Once into Lusaka I did the rounds of the Embassy and Poste Restante to catch up with news from home. The city had quite a vibrant commercial sector separating the centre of government on one side and the industrial area on the other and through various contacts I had made I spent several days in the capital before heading up to the copper belt in the north.

MOSI-OA-TUNYA (THE FALLS)

I had no sooner reached the first main town of Ndola when a news article caught my eye and this resulted in a six hundred mile trip off to the remote far western town of Mongu situated on the edge of the Zambezi flood plain and near the site of one of the rare remaining tribal traditions, the Kuomboka.

The chief or 'Litunga' of the Lozi tribe, who live around the river, moves his court from its dry season location at Lealui near the banks of the river out to the edge of the flood plain at Limulunga, returning once the flood waters recede. The movement out to higher ground is the main spectacle and this is what I wanted to witness. Fortunately, though remote, the road out west was good and having allowed several days for my journey I arrived in time. The already swollen river had transformed the area with its mixture of green grass and shimmering water into a patchwork lake stretching out some thirty miles across and one hundred and ten miles from north to south.

My travels were not complete on reaching the town, as the starting location of this ancient ceremony was eleven miles away over the water. On meeting one of the resident Irish priests this problem was solved as I was assigned the duty of helping to keep an eye on a party of school children they were taking by boat, so everything was in place for the main event the following day.

An early start saw me down to the departure enclosure and past the control post then with the assembled school party on board we set off on a three and a half hour trip to Lealui. In conversation with one of the kids I was informed that someone had come all the way from Scotland to witness the spectacle, and though I couldn't be absolutely sure, I had a feeling that person was little old me, as the priest had given that impression to some government officials earlier in the day.

On reaching the noisy, crowded starting point we were greeted with the sight of the assembled barges being ceremoniously loaded with the chief's possessions and once all was on board he appeared dressed in his traditional departure outfit of top hat and tails. The costume, which had obviously evolved over the years, was totally at odds with the leopard skin loincloths and lion's mane headdresses of the paddlers.

The chief's barge, or Nalikwanda, was some sixty feet long and painted with thick black and white vertical stripes on the outside. In the middle was a white wicker canopy (nowadays adorned with a replica of a huge black elephant) under which the chief was located. Apart from the one hundred paddlers the Nalikwanda also housed the musicians who drum up an infectious and mesmerising rhythm to drive the man-powered vessel onwards. There was also a fire on board, the smoke telling the assembled crowds that their chief was alive and well.

In addition to the main vessel there were further boats, carrying his wife, and other dignitaries. The boats were preceded by two white painted five-man dugouts which acted as lookouts and once the all clear had been given, and with an almighty effort on behalf of the standing paddlers, the procession groaned its first few feet forward on the ensuing six hour journey to their higher destination. It is said that in days gone by any paddler who showed signs of fatigue was cast overboard to the crocodiles; whether true or not, that fate no longer awaits the oarsmen who take great pride in having been chosen as one of the royal party.

Kuomboka barges.

The colourful procession passed right in front of our boat and with the accompaniment of the hypnotic drumming it really was a fantastic sight that sent a shiver down my spine.

With the procession on its way it was now a frantic dash to get back to our starting point and up to the arrival location at Limulunga. With the currents now in our favour we took only two hours to return, and once back on land our party was driven across to the finishing point

MOSI-OA-TUNYA (THE FALLS)

and with a bit of cajoling we once again secured ourselves a waterside position and awaited the pageant.

The sound of distant drumming heralded its imminent arrival. First on the scene were the two white scout dugouts checking all was clear and even then the main vessel did not simply sail in and land. It charged fiercely at the bank, retreated, repeated the charge, retreated and only at the third attempt, once any enemies had been expelled, did the craft plough up onto the bank, followed by the other boats in the procession.

A vast boisterous crowd had assembled to greet their chief and welcome him to his seasonal palace with displays of singing, dancing and drumming filling the air, and setting the scene for several days of festivities. As if the departure outfit of top hat and tails was not incongruous enough, during the trip the chief changed into his arrival outfit, that of a British navy admiral in which he looked quite resplendent but wholly at odds with his native surroundings. The outfit was apparently given to one of his ancestors by a member of our own royal family during colonial times.

This visit really had been worth all the rushing around and hassles involved with getting across the country in record time. The ceremony which has its roots in the practical problem of escaping the rising waters is held with great symbolism and importance by the Lozi inhabitants of the flood plain and it was gratifying to see such tradition still attracting its full pomp and glory in modern times.

Although I had been in the copper belt prior to the visit and did intend returning there, I decided to take advantage of my rural location and follow the Zambezi River south to the Victoria Falls. To this end I was given a massive helping hand by the series of Catholic missions that were dotted along the remote road that mirrors the river's course southwards. Not only did the missions extend a welcoming hand and lots of interesting local information, but they also provided my transport, as I joined priests or simply goods being ferried from one location to another, and over the course of the next week I inched my way towards the world famous Falls.

The latter part of this journey ran parallel to the Caprivi Strip, a wild finger of South West African land which lies between Angola and Botswana and which was widely regarded as dangerous guerrilla territory. Fortunately nothing untoward befell us and I safely reached my destination of Livingstone.

UNDER AN AFRICAN SUN

The town of Livingstone was the previous capital of Northern Rhodesia prior to the establishment of Lusaka back in 1935. The main street was a wide tree lined avenue which continued on into the countryside and became the main road covering the five miles down to the Falls.

The local name of Mosi-oa-Tunya translates to 'the Smoke that Thunders' and although the thunder was not audible in the town, the smoke, in the guise of the fine white mist which rises one thousand three hundred feet into the air, was clearly visible and made a very inviting and impressive sight.

As we were in the rainy season the falls were in full flow, disgorging a mind-boggling ten thousand tons per second across its five thousand six hundred foot width. One down side of this was that the spray being so intense made it impossible to see to the bottom of the falls some three hundred and sixty feet below. In order to get the best views across the wall of roaring, foaming water it was necessary to snake down a small pathway which, whilst affording a great vantage point, was well and truly under the constant canopy of spray. With only a shirt and my trousers for protection it was only a matter of seconds before I was drenched to the skin.

At the Victoria Falls.

MOSI-OA-TUNYA (THE FALLS)

Having spent an hour or so just soaking up the awesome spectacle from my vantage point I made my way down to the river gorge below, beneath the rail bridge. This took me down a narrow, muddy path, through thick jungle style vegetation and finally saw me clambering over boulders, but the rewards were well worth the effort. Looking up at the exit path of the river on to the face of the falls, there were rare occasions when the cloud of mist parted and the full magnificence of the cascading wall of water became visible.

The gorge into which the water drops is not that wide and the torrent is then funnelled out through a relatively narrow exit for some five hundred feet before entering a series of zig-zagging gorges as it continues its journey which eventually sees it reach the Indian Ocean at the Mozambique town of Chinde.

Although political relations with Zambia and what was then Rhodesia were allegedly non existent and trade had officially ceased, the rail bridge, built back in the early 1900s, was still covertly used, with carriages shunted on at one end and shunted off at the other. Thus whilst no direct train steamed over the bridge goods still found a discreet way across.

With the smoke and thunder well and truly explored I headed back to the Copper Belt to continue my previously aborted visit, and started where I had left off at Ndola. In addition to the mining activities of the town, Ndola also had a Dunlop tyre factory and a Land Rover assembly plant. Whilst I had already been round the UK headquarters of the latter I had no idea what went into tyre production, a point that was easily rectified by a most interesting morning being shown round by one of the many ex-pat workers at the plant, and in the process another flake joined the ever increasing snowball of contacts I had to look up on my continuing travels.

Next up the road was Mufulira, another clean and spaciously laid out town which was about to play host to the Zambian Open golf tournament. The chap who gave me a lift there was a member of the club so I got all the low-down on it first hand and was invited to join him in the evening for a special club event.

To spice up the proceedings the club held a raffle, with the prizes being the chance to win a golfer's name, and should that party go on to win the tournament, substantial money was up for grabs, two thousand pounds to be precise. Understandably several syndicates had been formed and an exciting atmosphere hung over the evening's proceedings.

The tournament was due to start on the Thursday and I was invited to stay over and though not a golfer myself it seemed like a good idea, and as I wanted to visit some of the mines it all fell into place very nicely.

Many of the golf club members worked at the mines and it proved very easy to arrange a visit as some of the professional golfers were due to have a tour and I was simply added to their party, and so with crash hat in place we set off on a tour of the 'top' mine production plant.

This dealt with the ore once it had come up to the surface and we were taken through the complete process from the arrival of the raw ore to the final casting into pure copper ingots, with all the crushing, sorting, filtering, smelting and chemical procedures involved all fully explained. At each stage recycling was evident in order to eke out the maximum yield and with only a small amount of the original rock containing processible copper ore, every extra morsel available was gratefully received.

With the 'top' visit over we were then taken down to the bowels of the mine, two thousand five hundred feet below at its lowest point. We stopped at around fifteen hundred feet and then entered a maze of well-lit, white washed tunnels and made our way to the hoist room, nicknamed the cathedral, which operated three large lifts. It was difficult to believe that we were in fact underground as the vast fluorescent lit white washed room hewn from the original rock face almost had a surgical feel about it and gave no sensation of being so far underground.

From here we were taken down further via a network of wide passages which we shared with a constant flow of large and small machinery and trucks, up to the face and the true reality of a miner's work, the area being far from well lit and movement unsure underfoot due to standing muddy water. The ore mined from the various faces was then dropped down to a series of crushers at the base of the mine from where it was hoisted up to the 'top' area we had visited earlier in the day. The whole experience was fantastic and I was pleased that I felt no claustrophobic apprehension at all despite being a couple of thousand feet below.

Back on the golf front the second phase of the earlier raffle took the form of an auction. With two rounds completed the player's form was starting to show, and everyone with a golfer's name ticket had the option of putting it up for auction. Needless to say there was considerable interest in those on the current leader board, in particular the tournament favourite, the young Australian Jack Newton. Jack went on to enjoy a sparkling career throughout the 1970s and early 1980s before having the most horrendous near fatal accident when he walked into the spinning propeller of a light aircraft he was about to board and lost his right arm and eye and sustained severe abdominal injuries.

Once the auction formalities were over a party ensued which included an 'open mike' session where accompaniment was provided by the evening's quartet. I was coerced into doing a spot, though in truth I didn't need my arm twisting very far, and an interesting swing version of a couple of good old folk standards followed. Something must have been alright as I was given a VIP pass for the remaining two days, complimentary entrance to the sponsor's tent for refreshments, lunch etc., and an invitation to the official cocktail party on the final day, not bad for the rendition of a couple of songs.

And so for the next couple of days I made the most of my new found status and even enjoyed the golf which was won by Christy O'Connor junior, the junior tag being in deference to his uncle another well established golfer. The final evening party was another great knees up with more singing, including several numbers from the Celtic clan comprising myself, Christy and a certain young Scot named Sam Torrance who incidentally went on to win the tournament the following year.

Before bidding farewell to the copper belt I went up to the vast open cast mine at Chingola, which covered three square miles, another visit arranged by the Mufulira mafia. The statistics here were mind blowing as a fleet of two hundred ton juggernauts hauled the ore from the open mine face in a relentless convoy moving two hundred and forty thousand tons of the stuff every day. The ratio of the various materials broke down into seven hundred tons of mined rock yielding fifty tons of copper ore which in turn yielded one ton of finished copper. At the time of my visit, the mine was already down to a depth of eight hundred feet and they believed it was feasible to continue down to a depth of fifteen hundred feet. So there was a lot more digging to be done.

Having well and truly slaked my thirst for all things copper related and having enjoyed to the full the unexpected twists my stay in the Copper Belt threw up, it was back to reality, no more VIP status just the hot dusty road to Malawi, my next scheduled stop.

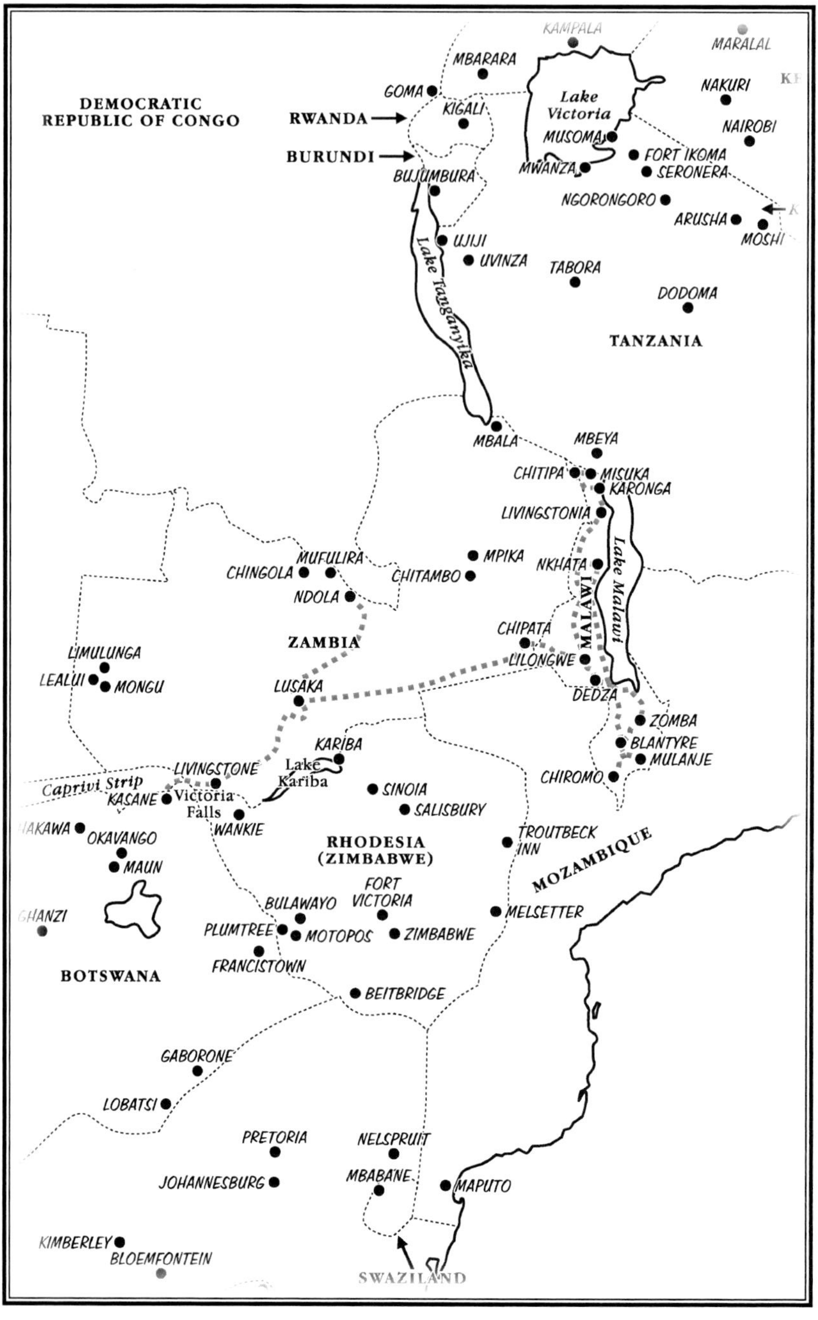

CHAPTER 16

NYASALAND

With the Copper Belt behind me I made my way back to Lusaka then headed out East on the main road connecting Zambia with Malawi. This took me over the long plateau that forms most of the eastern region of the country, with the flat profile broken by the snaking Luangwa River which we had to cross just north of the Mozambique border, an area which was still regarded as unsafe due to the activities of the Frelimo fighters stationed there. Their long-standing guerrilla war against their Portuguese colonialists being equally disruptive as their fellow fighters regaling against the same power in Angola.

Once over the river the road closely followed the Mozambique border then broke off heading slightly north up to the Malawian border at Chipata formerly Fort Jameson. I arrived too late to cross over as the Zambian control post closed at 6.00 pm although their Malawian counterparts operated a twenty-four hour control, a somewhat ridiculous situation as either way one could not progress once the Zambian side packed up for the day, and so it was out with the sleeping bag to make the most of the overnight delay.

Once normal border crossing routines were re-established in the morning I was quickly on my way to the transition town of Lilongwe. At that time the town was going through a regeneration programme that would transform it into the new capital city with government buildings strategically positioned on yes, Capital Hill. The whole area was a building site but the original town some three miles away was still vibrant with the usual market stalls selling a well stocked selection of the local fruit and vegetables, and the ever present 'witch doctors' stalls with the usual eclectic mix of charms and potions at their disposal. Throughout Malawi the markets normally had a presence from 'Admarc' the Malawian co-op through which much of the local produce was bought and sold, and here was no exception.

Dr. Banda and his government still maintained links with many of the regimes alien to their neighbours and movement of goods from Mozambique, Rhodesia and South Africa was not restricted and they even had contact with Israel which was generally not the case throughout the continent. The maintenance of diplomatic relations with the southern states did bring its rewards as many Malawians worked in the south, mainly in the mines, and brought important foreign currency into the government's coffers.

Despite this liberal trading position the country was, as most, a one party state, and membership of the party was the expected norm with several high profile cases of groups such as Jehovah Witnesses falling foul of this ruling and paying the price. Another less liberal view existed on clothing where again mini skirts were banned and even trousers were not allowed to be worn by women. For men, flared trousers were a no-no, and a short back and sides policy was policed with some vigour, fortunately my flowing locks fell within the accepted parameters. A further insight into the government's philosophy was the banning of George Orwell's *Animal Farm,* and the heavy censorship of foreign newspapers, initially by cutting out offending copy, then later by using marker pens to obliterate unwanted text.

From Lilongwe I moved on south towards the commercial capital of Blantyre named after the birthplace of Dr. Livingstone, one of several Scottish connections I was to encounter whilst in Malawi. Just beyond the town of Dedza the road followed the Mozambique border once again to the extent that it was Malawian on one side and Portuguese (Mozambique) on the other, making a mockery of border controls as one shopped in one country on one side of the street then crossed over to a different country on the opposite side, a strange situation but one got the chance to sample the 1 litre bottles of cerveza freely on sale.

Housing was once again of a rectangular, wood and mud construction topped off with thatch, though one difference here was the extended roof line held up with wooden supports forming a wide veranda to the front. One particular example I passed stood out as it was freshly painted with a glass panel door and a neat garden laid out to the front, such features rarely found in societies where the house is purely a shelter and little care is afforded to such design detail.

The old town of Blantyre showed its roots in the old colonial regime with the majority of the buildings being from that period and having more than a passing resemblance to many a town back home. This being the commercial centre it hosted many shops and industries the textile trade being particularly prominent and whilst in the town I took the chance to tour round one of the processing plants, thus adding it to my experiences in the copper mines and tyre factory. As was so often the case a spin off from the visit was an invitation to stay over for a couple of days and a list of further contacts to meet as I continue my journey south.

During the resulting stop over I made a trip north to the Zomba Plateau, a high lush wooded area dotted with valleys and clear streams and affording spectacular views over Lake Malawi to the north and the massif which is Mount Mulanje to the south. Below this plateau stood the current capital city of Zomba which would shortly be losing its status to the new city of Lilongwe.

The spectacular 9,855 foot Mt Mulanje had a hypnotic effect on me and that was my next destination. Progress was slow and the final run in took a total of six separate lifts just to cover a mere forty-five wet miles, but little did I know the rewards that awaited me.

On arriving in the town, the day had all but passed when I saw the signs for the town club, which as throughout virtually all Africa had its roots in colonial times. I popped in and was welcomed by the barman and a couple of social drinkers and it turned out that a folk night was taking place that evening and that was the catalyst which saw me becoming a temporary resident of the community over the next few weeks, being royally looked after at the barman's mansion. In reality far from being a barman Alex was the manager of the tea plantation, but in his role as a member of the club committee, he took his turn at bar duties, it's a hard task but somebody has to do it!

The folk night proved very enjoyable and with a concert on the horizon an invitation to stay over had been extended by Alex and his wife Marge. Their home was situated on the edge of the tea plantation and the lush green carpet of the crop with the backdrop of the mountain was a wonderful sight, especially when viewed from the comfort of the veranda with a cool gin and tonic in hand. The property had originally been the guesthouse of Henry Brown who back in the late nineteenth century started propagating tea in Malawi from seeds obtained from the Edinburgh botanical gardens, and how the crop had blossomed. The house was a fine building of generous proportions but due to its age needed a constant bit of T.L.C., though this was definitely worth any hassles to secure not only a home but also a view to die for.

The view from the verandah over the tea plantation to Mount Mulanje.

From my new found base I made a sortie on further south to Chiromo from where the final finger of Malawi extends like an arrowhead into Mozambique and where the Rift Valley finishes and the final plains of the Zambezi river take over down to the Indian Ocean. The area further south of Chiromo was once again deemed to be bandit country, so I settled for the fine view then took a short cut into the bundu. I was accompanied by an English speaking local, though I started to question the short cut element as we crashed through bush and woodland seemingly getting deeper and deeper into the rolling hills, however all worked out fine in the end.

On the way we stopped at a little hamlet where a local still was in full flow making the illicit local brew 'Kachaso'. Simple as it was it proved very effective. The main ingredients of the brew, a mixture of water, maize and sugar, had been left standing for a few days and were now being boiled up in a large earthenware pot over a wood fire. Inserting another smaller pot into the opening and sealing it with grass proved surprisingly successful in creating a watertight container. From the top of the mixing vessel, a length of thin metal pipe ran at a downward angle through a water filled dug out tree branch. This acted as the condensing chamber and at the other end of that pipe there was a straw down which the resultant liquid ran into the neck of a waiting bottle. It was only polite to try some but I doubt that it would find its way onto many bar menus, taste apart, I dread to think just what type of alcohol the spirit contained after its crude production, but it was obviously very popular with the assembled crowd.

The crude illicit still near Chiromo.

The visit to the pub over, I crashed on back to the main road which then ran through a development area where a vast mixture of crops were under cultivation, various grains, rice and cotton among them. A little further on I went through a sugar plantation where I was given a tour of the operation. Whilst down in this rural corner of the country I met some European nursing staff attached to a mission who were going off on their weekly dispensing surgery and I spent an interesting morning in their company.

One treatment that did surprise me involved the treatment for snakebites where it wasn't serum that was used but a 'black stone' obtained from the fathers in Holland. I had previously come across a reference to the healing qualities of the stones but had put it down to mumbo jumbo however here we had professionals swearing by it. I remain mystified as to how it works but by applying the stone to the opened wound the poison is drawn out, though no visible signs appear on the stone. After each treatment the stone was soaked in water then milk then once more in water and so was ready to be used again.

I was back in Mulanje in time for the concert which again proved to be a great evening, and during the proceedings one of the crowd suggested that we should climb the mountain. Initially there was a group

Flimsy bridge over a gorge on Mount Mulanje.

of six of us but on the day this had been whittled down to Geoff, who had a mountaineering background, and myself so I felt in good hands.

Being at the tail end of the rainy season the weather could be hit or miss and for the upward journey we hit a 'miss' day. Initially we trekked through long grass and scrub which gave our legs a good soaking and when a fine drizzle started to fall our uncomfortable drenching was complete. We crossed to the base of the climb over a river by means of a skimpy wood and wire bridge which I for one was relieved to get off, then it was a steady climb up to the top. This was not without a couple of wrong turnings which necessitated an impromptu lesson in the practice of chimneying ourselves vertically up a narrow gap between two rock faces, skills which I doubt I will ever require again.

At last we reached the welcome sight of the overnight hut that was manned by a watchman and with copious amounts of crystal clear mountain water, a cooker and heater we were set for the night perched at nearly 10,000 feet. The weather was kinder for our return trip though ignorance had proven to be bliss on the way up, as around half way down we came to a section of sheer rock face along which ran a small shelf with heavy vegetation clinging to the slope below. I froze, as I could not see how we could cross such a narrow strip with a sheer drop awaiting any slip of the foot, but Geoff pointed out that in the misty conditions of the previous day I had gaily walked across the exact spot without any trepidation. In the end he took my pack and I crawled across it on my stomach, staring into the rock face by my side all the way over and proving beyond doubt that serious mountaineering would definitely not be for me. From there on it was relatively plain sailing, though the slippery conditions under foot had us on our backsides on a regular basis, but finally we reached the bottom, bumped, bruised, scratched, wet and filthy but all was soon forgotten when faced with a cold beer.

One of the favourite pastimes with the ex-pat community in Mulanje was to make the short trip over the border into Mozambique and avail themselves of the excellent beer and food offered in the neighbouring town, a speciality being fresh prawns shipped up daily from the coast. The formalities of border control were suspended, one simply crossed over leaving one's passport at the Mozambique control and as long as one returned before they closed at 6.00 pm no stamps, visas, etc. were required, a thoroughly civilised way to deal with the issue.

Tours of the plantation and processing plant along with a visit to the local fruit canning factory helped to fill my days but firm in the knowledge that all good things must come to an end, and with a heavy heart I eventually moved on to head up along Lake Malawi and into the striking mountain scenery at the northern tip of the country.

My route led me from the very southern tip of the lake winding up the road which was never far from the lakeside. On several occasions, a short detour saw me sleeping out under a moonlit sky beneath a panoply of stars on a bed of soft sand, with the sound of water gently lapping the shore to accompany my slumbers, and a magnificent sunrise acting as my alarm clock. One such evening brought an added bonus of seeing the local fishermen at their evening task of laying their nets in a circle, then, with the aid of lights fixed to the boats to attract their catch to the surface, they ensnared them in a pincer motion. Judging by the fruits of their efforts it was a good evening's work.

Approximately half way up the lake, at the small port of Nkhata, the road north stopped and I headed inland over the rolling hills climbing up to the very picturesque Vipya plateau. I made several trips around and over it in different directions to take in all the glorious woodland scenery and views of the lake below, which was sometimes shrouded beneath a white sea of rolling mist.

Pushing further north took me to the Rumpi gorge then a long climb high into the green wooded mountains on a bumpy rough road to the mission at Livingstonia, which was more like a town than a mission. The route had offered up some magnificent views over the lake and across to the mountains on the far Tanzanian side of the lake.

Livingstonia as the name suggests was set up by the Scottish Free Church to continue the work of Dr. Livingstone and this site was the third and final location of the mission. It was founded by an Aberdonian doctor Robert Law who also had a background in building which was obviously put to good use in constructing the site. In addition to the expected church there is also a post office, school, administration offices and a clock tower all constructed from red brick and resembling many a town back home. There was an exception to the red brick buildings in the guise of his own home which used locally quarried stone, possibly a throwback to his Granite City origins.

The church has a fine stained glass window depicting Dr. Livingstone with a backdrop of the lake, though this however embodies a touch of poetic licence, as the great explorer never actually visited this sight on his travels.

Though the climb up to the mission had been very scenic the descent, via the escarpment edge on which it sits, was even more awesome. This was added to by the seemingly sheer two thousand foot drop the tiny mountain track follows via a series of twenty hairpins to the lakeside below, reminiscent of the roads to Lalibela and Hajjah. The eleven mile route took over one hour to cover and looking up from the lakeside it was difficult to believe that any road could exist on the wall of rock before us.

At this point the road once more followed the lakeside up to Karonga. The surrounding area had been the scene of several battles during the First World War between the British, based in Nyasaland (the old name for Malawi) and the Germans over the border in Tanzania, which they controlled up until 1918.

The area was very fertile with lots of maize grown some of which found its way directly into the production of the local beer, and no doubt the illicit brew I had stumbled upon in the south. Traffic however was not so fertile with very little movement and having walked on up the road away from the town I was yet again grateful for the hospitality offered by a local family when night began to fall. I took up residence for the night in the simple surroundings of their thatched, wood and mud constructed home, waking in the morning to the hypnotic rhythm of the women pounding the grain with traditional pestle and mortars. This was the first stage in the preparation of another meal of their staple maize porridge diet, locally known as Nsima but elsewhere more commonly referred to as Posho, which, coupled with a sauce of some description had been my evening meal on many occasions.

My final push north took me inland past Chitipa and slowly onto the tiny village of Misuka perched high up on the Malawi/Tanzania border overlooking the Songwe River valley and the intense folds of mountains sweeping away to the north. From this breathtaking vantage point I could look out in all directions and choose mountains, lakes or open plains an area that must rank in the top natural vistas of my whole journey and worth every bit of hardship and time it took to reach it.

My exploration of 'Nyasaland' was now complete and it only remained to head back south, but I couldn't resist a reverse trip up the sheer escarpment from the lakeside to Livingstonia. Although it delayed progress a little, as so often had been the case, it was well worth it and with any itinerary I originally set myself well and truly consigned to the bin, a few days here or there was of little consequence.

The long narrow strip of land that runs parallel to the lake forming the country had thrown up some spectacular scenery especially in the north and south but I was now leaving the Rift Valley, which had been a constant feature of my travels from Ethiopia southwards and heading west.

Retracing my steps into the central belt, then out to the border with Zambia, was fairly straightforward and three months after arriving I stuck my thumb up and headed back over the eastern plains of Zambia.

I couldn't believe my luck when an English doctor and a colleague stopped and picked me up. They were heading for the copper belt via Lusaka and I settled in for what I thought would be a long but speedy journey, however divine intervention was once again destined to scupper such thoughts.

The two of them quite obviously enjoyed lining their throats on a regular basis and appeared to have contacts dotted all along the road who were visited and their health celebrated in true arm raising fashion with regular monotony. The end result being that we finished up staying at a friend's hotel for the evening having covered only a fraction of the three hundred and fifty miles expected, however there was always tomorrow, and there was a TV in the room. Zambia unlike Malawi, Tanzania and South Africa did have a TV network.

Tomorrow duly arrived to a frantic commotion all around the hotel and it transpired that one of the locals had murdered his young wife during the night and somehow Ian, being a doctor, got embroiled in the proceedings. Initially this involved helping the police on the scene then later undertaking the post-mortem, a fairly gruesome affair, and needless to say one I would have preferred not to be so close to, but even my assistance was called on, and the day ended with us spending another night at the hotel. As if any excuse was needed much drowning of the sorrows was high up on my travelling companions' list before the evening was over.

We did at last strike out for the capital and having taken my leave of them I headed south, once more past the Falls, and onto the border crossing with Botswana.

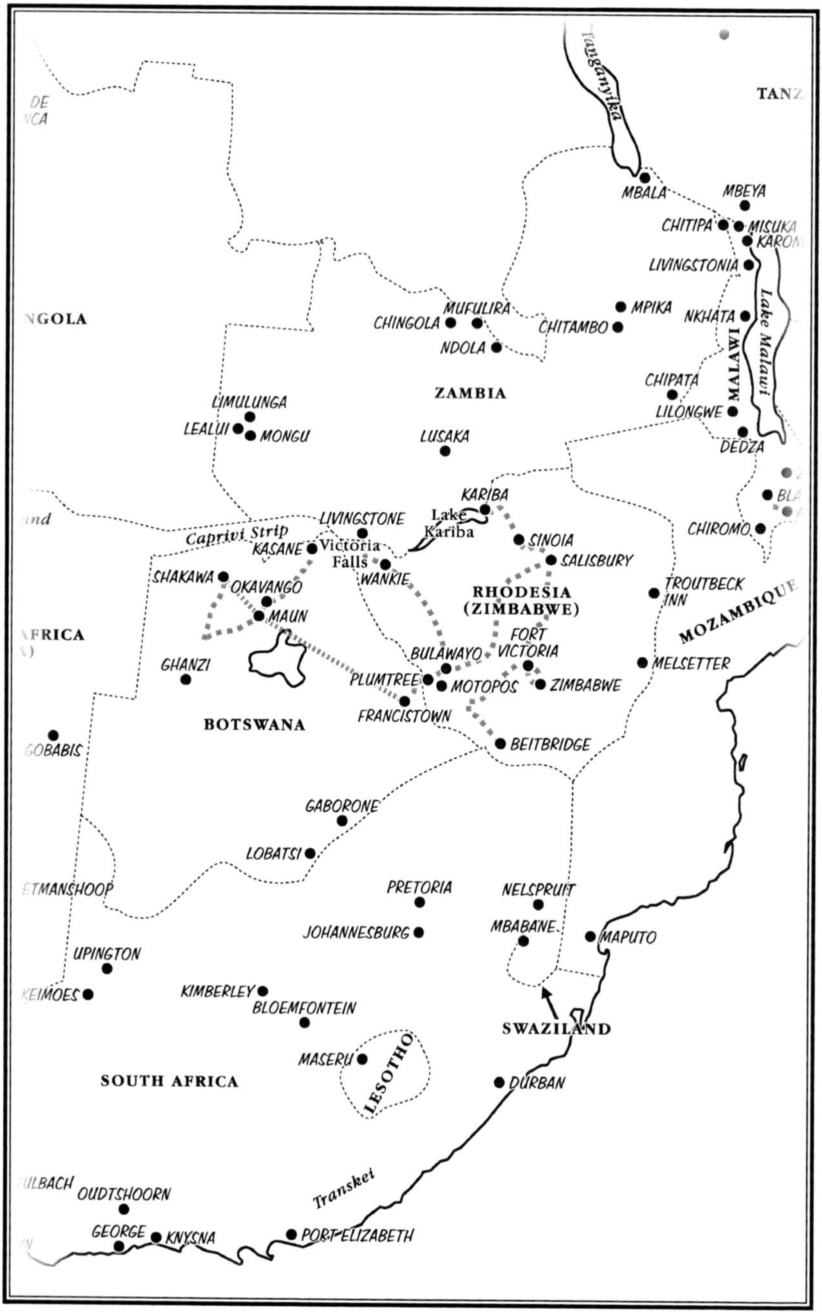
TANZ
Tanganyika
DE
NCA
NGOLA
MBALA
MBEYA
CHITIPA
MISUKA
KARON
LIVINGSTONIA
MUFULIRA
MPIKA
NKHATA
Lake Malawi
CHINGOLA
CHITAMBO
NDOLA
MALAWI
ZAMBIA
CHIPATA
LIMULUNGA
LILONGWE
LEALUI
MONGU
LUSAKA
DEDZA
KARIBA
BLA
and
LIVINGSTONE
Lake Kariba
CHIROMO
Caprivi Strip
KASANE
Victoria Falls
SINOIA
SALISBURY
SHAKAWA
WANKIE
TROUTBECK INN
OKAVANGO
RHODESIA (ZIMBABWE)
MOZAMBIQUE
MAUN
FRICA
FORT VICTORIA
BULAWAYO
MELSETTER
GHANZI
PLUMTREE
MOTOPOS
ZIMBABWE
FRANCISTOWN
BOTSWANA
BEITBRIDGE
GOBABIS
GABORONE
LOBATSI
ETMANSHOOP
PRETORIA
NELSPRUIT
JOHANNESBURG
MBABANE
MAPUTO
UPINGTON
KEIMOES
KIMBERLEY
BLOEMFONTEIN
SWAZILAND
MASERU
LESOTHO
SOUTH AFRICA
DURBAN
ULBACH
OUDTSHOORN
Transkei
GEORGE
KNYSNA
PORT ELIZABETH

CHAPTER 17
OKAVANGO – CROCODILE COUNTRY

I crossed over the Zambezi River and into northern Botswana then walked the nine miles to Kasane, a remote spot at the tip of the politically unstable Caprivi Strip. My aim was to head south to the Okavango swamps which among other things were famed as a centre for crocodile hunting. The small town of Maun on the edge of the swamps was not well connected and after enquiring about transport at the border I was informed that there might be a government vehicle leaving in six days, but other than that traffic was very limited.

Having resigned myself to another lengthy game of hunt the driver, I was pleasantly surprised when I met a Caterpillar plant mechanic. He was doing a round trip servicing and repairing such machinery and his next port of call was Maun but not by any direct route. His appointments were scheduled to take him into a couple of game parks and well off the beaten track, which sounded great to me, and it was not long before we were entering the Chobe game reserve.

Botswana generally was a flat sparsely populated country roughly the size of France but with a population of only seven hundred thousand. Under the leadership of their President Seretse Khama a four party political system existed along with a second parliamentary chamber made up of tribal chiefs. They had also maintained good relationships with their colonial neighbours, Rhodesia, South and South West Africa and shared the same currency as the latter two, and unlike so many countries on the continent, they didn't have any civil unrest to contend with.

Our servicing trip took us over three hundred miles of often virgin bush land as on several occasions the track was either flooded or blocked by trees pushed over by elephants and we were forced to forge our own way through the surrounding undergrowth. The large 4WD Ford pick-up proved to be well up to the job, though we did get well and truly bogged down in some very loose black soil which involved a lot of hacking and manoeuvring before it set us free.

The second smaller reserve at Meroni was interesting, as it had been established in 1961 by the local Batawana tribe. In a most unlikely and far sighted manner, they had realised that the game needed protection and had gone about setting up their homeland area as a reserve which they maintained and administered with some help forthcoming from the nearby Chobe personnel as required. During our trip we slept in the pick up and encountered a good cross section of wild life but after my experience at Serengeti any park would struggle to impress, and the big cats were conspicuous by their absence, unfortunately the tsetse flies weren't.

Throughout the journey down to the swamps, over a mixture of acacia and virgin bush land, there had been very little signs of habitation, but as we approached the town, homesteads started to pop up. These consisted of several round huts connected into a circular formation by way of reed fencing. The huts themselves were constructed using a tight circle of wooden posts, some reinforced with mud and topped off with a thatch roof, the raw materials being plentiful in the adjoining swamp lands. Donkeys were the preferred means of transport and many were seen pulling sledges or water filled fifty-gallon oil drums behind them.

Okavango is the world's largest inland delta and is a triangular area covering ten thousand square miles of very flat swampland where the slope of the land is a mere 1:5000. The area is fed from the north by water from the Angolan highlands, and due to its virtually flat landscape and high temperatures, drainage is very poor and evaporation extremely high. The dual effect of this being a mass of water which has no outlet, and simply dissipates across the ever-widening delta.

Throughout the swamp there runs a series of navigable water routes though the relatively shallow nature of the water and the dense underwater plant life makes progress by powerboat difficult and the native dugout canoe or mokoro is the normal mode of transport. The locals punt these vessels deep into the swamps to cut the copious reeds that are then piled high onto their craft and somehow punted back to terra firma, from where they are sold as house building material among other things.

The idea of getting deep into the delta appealed to me and through some contacts I was able to secure the services of a local lad to take me into the delta for a few days to experience the solitude and aura of this unique area.

Stocked up with the necessary food supplies and using some borrowed cooking equipment we set out into the vast water network and were soon punting through high sedge grass and white fluffy topped reeds. Now and again we came out into open pools of clear mirror calm water with pink and purple water lilies abounding and the massed underwater roots and grasses clearly on display. The whole area plays host to a vast array of bird life, and insects, often found balancing on the flat lily leaves swaying on the top of the water.

Punting through the Okavango Swamps in a mokoro.

Freeman, my guide, made the whole process look effortless but I am sure that if I had been in charge of the narrow, flat bottomed, straight sided, twelve foot long craft our progress would have been negligible, but we punted on through the day before establishing camp on one of the many small islands dotted throughout the area. There was some welcome shade from the fierce sun which a few hours later provided us with a glorious deep red sunset and heralded the invasion of mosquitoes. After rustling up our evening meal from the assortment of tins I'd taken with us, it was a matter of crashing out for the night, and not for the first time the decision had to be made to either get into my sleeping bag and boil, or sleep on top of it in the relative cool and get ferociously bitten. Fortunately the temperature did drop and to the music of the surrounding Okavango bush I eventually dropped off.

The next day saw us once more peacefully punting deeper into the delta repeating the scenery and surroundings of the previous day. Late in the afternoon we reached a most idyllic small island, with a canopy of trees and thick bush, where we established camp number two. Freeman once again cast his fishing net and unlike the previous day came up trumps, with several fish, though what they were I have no idea, but with the aid of a quickly arranged fire, a veritable feast was soon dished up.

It was an early sunrise start to the final day which saw us assisted by what little tide there was making progress easier and after a most enjoyable three days lost in the surroundings of the swamps we returned to dry land.

One of the main claims to fame of the area was its connection with crocodile hunting which was now restricted to an annual cull of five hundred, that number spread over the year at thirty per month between April and September, the balance to be taken up by November, giving some protection to the once highly hunted beasts.

I was introduced to Eileen, the daughter of Bob Wilmot who had established the Crocodile Camp situated at the swamp edge. It was still fully operational, with a wealthy clientele of would be hunters paying handsomely for the privilege to stalk down their prey. Having made myself useful helping with some maintenance around the camp I was rewarded with the offer to stay. In the evening I was one of the small assembled crowd of guinea pigs used to try out a new recipe. Curried crocodile tail had been conjured up and very good it was too, tasting something like an exotic chicken, and having been awarded the thumbs up it was likely to become a regular feature on the menu which already sported several game dishes, kudu, reed buck and wildebeest among them.

One of the other local characters was Lloyd, a second-generation crocodile hunter who ran a small tented camp deep in the delta to which he commuted by a small two-seater plane. I was given the opportunity to fly out to it with him and giving little regard for how I would get back, grabbed the chance. The small aircraft was a great way to see the area from a new perspective and as we headed north towards the top apex of the triangular shaped swamp the jigsaw of waterways, dense vegetation and islands covering the landscape made a spectacular view.

On the way Lloyd was looking out for a colleague; this resulted in even more time than usual being spent on a reconnaissance mission which suited me just fine. The camp was situated on Xaxaba island which didn't support an airstrip but after a hairy bit of buzzing the camp and some fancy aeronautical displays to firstly summon up a mokoro and secondly to clear the simple rough airstrip on the neighbouring island of a herd of animals, we landed safely and were soon being punted over to his base.

The camp consisted of six tents and was rudimentary with no running water or electricity, and featured mainly game meat on its menu, but that didn't deter his wealthy hunter guests. I settled in for a couple of days spent in true crocodile hunter terrain, but at ease in the knowledge that a professional was close at hand should any unwelcome visitor come ashore. We went out on a couple of evening sorties and though we didn't bag anything the adrenaline was certainly pumping and every noise or movement around us simply added to the night time excitement.

I had noticed that Lloyd had a fork tipped walking cane and had thought nothing of it until we were walking through the bush and came face to face with a python, one of the few times I had come across a snake in my entire journey. I was told to stand still and before my eyes, using the forked end of the cane he pinned it down just behind its head. With equally swift reactions he grabbed the tail and in a second had swung it round in a large arc smashing the head on the ground and taking that particular python off the predator's list.

One of the other guests, a Swiss banker wouldn't you know, had chartered a small plane to head up to Shakawa at the swamp's northern edge where he had a reservation in a quite exclusive lodge. Once again adapting the 'don't ask don't get' philosophy, I asked if it would be possible to ride along with him and a positive response was received with a seat soon secured. Lloyd had a further piece of land near to the said lodge and told me I could use it as a base until I could find some transport back, so with everything in place I climbed on board the small Piper Cherokee and we were shortly up in the air once more taking in the swampy vista below, which progressively narrowed as we reached the northern apex of the triangular delta.

Nearby were the Tsodilo hills in Bushman country, where early rock paintings by their ancestors could be found, though not by us, until one of the locals took us on a bit of a hike and soon we were casting our eyes over the red hunting scenes painted on the rocks. Not having any knowledge of this art form it was impossible to ascertain their authenticity, but for the sake of the argument we all agreed that they were worthy of the effort spent in reaching them. My companions on that trip were all staying at the posh lodge and after the viewing exercise they laid out their picnic lunch that resembled a five star buffet including smoked Kudu fillet. Somehow it all seemed so out of place especially as nearby there was a small Bushman encampment where the virtually naked inhabitants were sheltering in their small 'beehive' shaped, wooden

The rudimentary dwellings of Bushmen.

framed, partially grass covered nomadic homes, with only the barest of essentials, skins, gourds, etc., strewn about them.

The town of Shakawa was hosting a political rally and one of the ministers, along with several regional dignitaries, was there to whip up interest in the forthcoming elections. It turned out that they were then heading back to Maun via a series of small villages where the hustings would be repeated and as transport was as rare as rocking horse droppings, I played all my cards and got permission to ride along with the convoy. This proved fascinating seeing the reaction of the assembled crowds, many of whom would be more influenced by their local chief than some distant politician. In the evenings we were accommodated in the encircled homesteads of the local headman and I was often brought into conversation with the minister to discuss news items, and so over the coarse of a couple of days we bounced and bumped our way round the delta's edge and I finally arrived back at Crocodile Camp.

On the unwritten agreement that in lieu of me giving a general hand around the place my accommodation would be found, I settled once more into camp life and met an interesting cross section of guests. One such crowd had come to do some aerial photography of the region and had a bit of a set back when some tanked up local was caught astride the tail of their DC3 with a book containing aircraft numbers, radio codes and frequencies. Though the apparent damage was minimal, for safety's sake they were returning to Francistown, and once again an opportunity too good to be missed came my way.

The sight of a very low flying DC3 buzzing farewells to the camp below must have been something to behold and once on our way I was invited into the cockpit and provided with earphones making the whole experience one to remember. Being in the middle of nowhere and whether right or not we were able to fly low enough to take in the wildlife roaming below, often in quite large herds, and half way across we flew over the massive Makarikari saltpan.

Shortly after touching down at Francistown the chance of a lift up to the Rhodesian border transpired. The dirt road was being treated to a grading process which very simply involved dragging a large bush behind a tractor. The jury is still out on just how much benefit was gained from this but one by-product was a heavy cloud of dust that reduced our visibility to virtually nil and made safe overtaking impossible, but such are the pleasures of a drive in the country in these parts.

I was through the border control at Plumtree without any of the attendant hassles I had been warned of and was swiftly heading for Bulawayo, Rhodesia's second city. I had set my first stopping point as the capital Salisbury, now Harare, and with the pleasure of good roads and a steady flow of traffic, the three hundred miles were effortlessly covered. After nearly three years on the continent it was strange to once again be served by white people in the shops and everywhere seemed so much more like home.

Despite all the sanctions imposed on Ian Smith's regime the shops were well stocked and the country had become self sufficient in many commodities, the one big exception being oil which had led to a fuel voucher system being in operation. The country had one of the biggest coal reserves at Wankie and research projects were well advanced to process the solid black stuff and turn it into the liquid black stuff so badly needed.

The capital was a blaze of colour with the lilac and purples of the jacaranda trees abounding, and a trip to the top floor of the highest hotel gave a great view over the busy city below. I did my tour round to collect mail and dropped in on several contacts to pass on 'Jambos' from friends and families I had met on the way.

Salisbury, being situated at the centre of the country, became a base from which I set out to visit the Victoria Falls, for the third time, the Kariba dam and the ruins at Zimbabwe from which the country took its name after gaining independence in 1980.

Although the falls were six hundred miles away, the roads and ease of getting lifts, made moving about very simple, and on several occasions cars pulled up and asked me if I wanted a lift without any thumb action required. The hospitality of the white folk was amazing and lifts were often followed by offers of accommodation and further contacts to look up on my future travels.

It was interesting to view the falls from a different perspective though being later in the season the floodwaters had receded and the spectacle was somewhat less impressive. The road took me past the aforementioned Wankie coalmine and I ventured in to pay it a visit but tours were not on the agenda, something I became increasingly aware of throughout Rhodesia, where security around any production plant prevented any visits.

OKAVANGO – CROCODILE COUNTRY

The four hundred and seventy-five mile journey from Wankie back to Salisbury was accomplished in one day with the same ease as before, and from there, Kariba was next on my list to see.

On my way I stopped over at the limestone caves at Sinoia, which drop to one hundred and fifty feet below the surface and have the most incredible clear, cobalt blue pools of water that are over three hundred feet in depth. Understandably they were very popular with the diving community, but that is one pastime I'm afraid I do not share an interest in.

The route up to the northern border and Lake Kariba went through farming country then over the final twenty-five miles slowly dropped three thousand feet off the central plateau down the escarpment to the lake. The view onto the face of the dam shows the mass of its two thousand foot wide, four hundred foot high structure to its full extent. Looking over the lake, then downstream, as the Zambezi continues its journey to the coast, it is difficult to believe that the vast man-made water mass was once simply part of the same watercourse.

The scheme was originally designed to accommodate two hydro systems, one in Rhodesia and one on the Zambian side. The latter however was never commissioned but with the threat of power being cut off by its enemy to the south, the Zambian one was now under construction, fifteen years after completion of the dam.

From the dam I headed once more to the hub of my Rhodesian travels the capital, then moved out south on the final push to South Africa. The oldest town in the country, Fort Victoria, was on my route. The old tradition of pealing the clock tower bell at 9.00 pm to signal the start of the curfew when the indigenous inhabitants had to be off the streets, still rings out daily, though the curfew has long become a thing of the past.

Nearby, next to the man made Lake Kyle was one of the few game reserves to play host to the white rhino, though the animal is no more white than its more numerous relation the black rhino. The name is in fact derived from the Afrikaner word 'weit' meaning wide and refers to the shape of the animal's upper lip. Whatever the origins it was one species I had not encountered in East Africa, a situation quickly resolved when I was able to accompany a small group touring round the park.

The lake area had one more wonder to offer up, the mystifying ruins at Zimbabwe. The origins of these dry stone built ruins have been accredited to various groups from early Shona tribesmen to Portuguese and Arab traders and they appear to date back to the fourteenth century. They cover a considerable area and contain several very well preserved buildings some of which appear to rise straight from the solid granite boulders and are unique in their architectural style adding to the mystery that surrounds them.

A two hundred and fifty mile trek to my final destination of South Africa lay ahead once I left the ruins behind, and this journey took in a mixture of European and Tribal Trust Lands, the former well laid out and where ranching was practised, well fenced, whilst the latter sadly reflected the poor state of indigenous farming, a patchwork quilt effect over the landscape with clumps of varying crops dotted over the area.

Part of the mysterious Zimbabwe ruins.

As I continued south I dropped through the southern hills of the central plateau, an old gold mining region where small mines could still be found amongst the predominantly cattle breeding countryside, and so I reached my final border crossing at Beitbridge, or, to be more precise, what should have been my final border crossing. Somehow the prospect of bringing my trans-Africa journey to its conclusion by crossing over didn't sit comfortably, I wasn't ready to call it a day.

Apart from the reputedly beautiful Eastern Highlands region of Rhodesia which I hadn't visited there had recently been the change of power in Portugal. The new regime had different political aspirations towards its former colonies and things had improved in both Mozambique and Angola which would make travel to these countries less hazardous, now that the freedom fighters had all but achieved their goal. I consulted my trusty map and concluded that a few more hours of footslogging were still required before making that final crossing, so

I about turned, and headed east towards the very productive low veld region of the country. I also decided that by crossing the Kalahari Desert and subsequently turning right I could be up in Angola to see what that embryonic state had to offer.

It was now mid-September and I set myself a target of reaching South Africa by the end of the year.

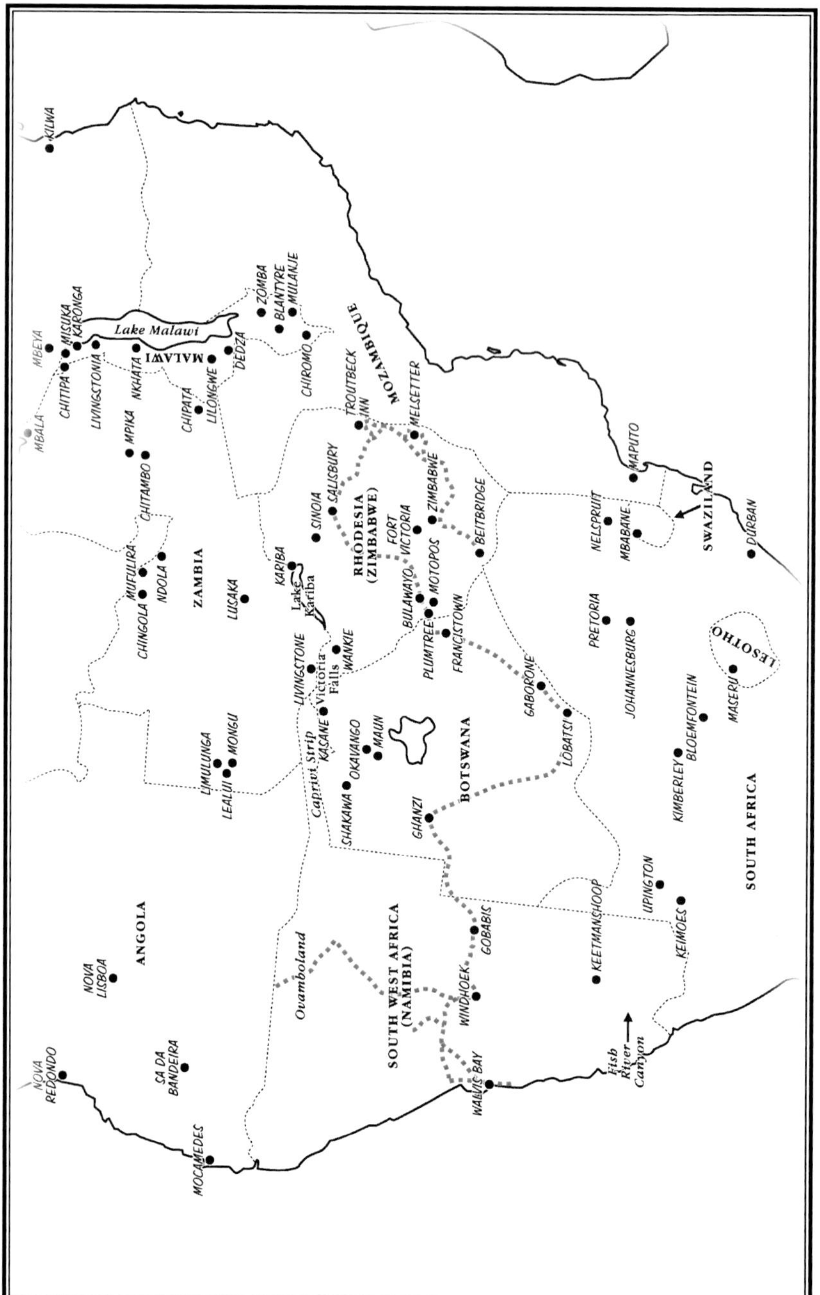
KILWA
MBEYA
MISUKA
KARONGA
Lake Malawi
ZOMBA
BLANTYRE
MULANJE
CHITIPA
LIVINGSTONIA
NKHATA
MALAWI
LILONGWE
DEDZA
CHIROMO
MOZAMBIQUE
TROUTBECK INN
MELSETTER
MBALA
MPIKA
CHITAMBO
CHIPATA
SALISBURY
SINOIA
RHODESIA (ZIMBABWE)
FORT VICTORIA
ZIMBABWE
BEITBRIDGE
MAPUTO
SWAZILAND
NELSPRUIT
MBABANE
DURBAN
ZAMBIA
MUFULIRA
NDOLA
CHINGOLA
LUSAKA
KARIBA
Lake Kariba
BULAWAYO
MOTOPOS
PLUMTREE
FRANCISTOWN
PRETORIA
JOHANNESBURG
LESOTHO
MASERU
LIVINGSTONE
Victoria Falls
WANKIE
KASANE
Caprivi Strip
OKAVANGO
MAUN
GABORONE
LOBATSI
BLOEMFONTEIN
KIMBERLEY
LIMULUNGA
MONGU
LEALUI
SHAKAWA
BOTSWANA
GHANZI
SOUTH AFRICA
ANGOLA
UPINGTON
KEIMOES
KEETMANSHOOP
GOBABIS
SOUTH WEST AFRICA (NAMIBIA)
Ovamboland
WINDHOEK
NOVA LISBOA
SA DA BANDEIRA
NOVA REDONDO
WALVIS BAY
Fish River Canyon
MOCAMEDES

CHAPTER 18

THE KALAHARI

To the east of Rhodesia lay the high mountains that act as a natural boundary with neighbouring Mozambique but despite the air of political change sweeping over these Portuguese colonies, the area was still somewhat unstable. Many remote farmers, along this beautiful part of the country, ran the risk of attack from the militants backed by their freedom fighting brothers over the border. The scenery however was apparently stunning and I decided it must be worth a visit.

To reach the mountains the road at first climbed back up onto the central plateau then dropped into the eastern low veld, a highly productive agricultural area where irrigation schemes had been very successfully introduced. Rivers had been dammed and through a series of canals and pumping stations the once bush land had been transformed into the country's richest farmlands. These now fertile acres produced crops of sugar, wheat and cotton and the intensity of the farming aimed to achieve two yields per year, with a crop of wheat then cotton often taken from the same acreage. The contrast with the indigenous areas was once again highlighted.

I was able to arrange a tour around a couple of these vast complexes but in keeping with the rest of the country visits to the resultant production plants were forbidden. One of them also boasted a large cattle herd where up to two thousand head were contained in pen type constructions and fed a rich diet, partly made from the waste materials left over from the sugar and cotton production plants. Whilst the animals appeared to be in good shape and produced excellent meat it did seem to be a first step towards battery farming of livestock that didn't sit comfortably in my mind.

Shortly after leaving the lush fertile low veld I crossed through another area of Tribal Trust land and as previously stated the contrast was very striking, though more like true Africa with the inhabitants once more using wood and mud to construct their round homes with the raised grain stores adjoining them.

The southern end of the border mountains was next to get my attention and I made a couple of trips up the slopes and around the lower wooded sections where the landscape was broken by coffee and tea plantations, the latter as always providing a lush carpet of green, contrasting with the backdrop of the grey granite mountains. This area also had a small section of indigenous forest, with huge one hundred and fifty feet tall mahogany trees reputedly up to one thousand years old. Another striking feature was the Bridal Veil Falls, near the town of Melsetter and whilst on my way there I came across one particular

An example of a vast 'upside down' Baobab tree.

example of the Baobab or 'upside down' tree that sported a massive girth of one hundred and ten feet.

Moving further north, I once again made several detours into the granite mountains which rewarded me with fantastic views from Worlds View over waterfalls, river valleys and the sheer majesty of the peaks. Fortunately throughout my excursions along this border area the militants and rebels showed no signs of their presence, though on one of the trips in the company of a white farmer it was emphasised that the area was far from trouble free.

Among the many contacts I had made during my stays in Salisbury was Tim, who had told me to look up his family should I reach the far eastern borderlands and Major McIlwaine, his grandfather, greeted me. What I hadn't realised, as Tim had not made an issue of it, was that this very gentleman had founded the beautiful Troutbeck Inn, a very select lake side establishment set among the rolling green hills with Rhodesia's highest peak Mount Inyanga looming high above it. With the combination of white staff and the stunning scenery it felt more like Scotland than Africa.

As a bonus Tim and some colleagues were staying at the family home over the weekend and what a fantastic weekend it turned out to be. The country home was situated on the shores of one of the lakes enjoying the same spectacular scenery as the Inn, and a combination of hill walking and water sports, interspersed with excellent food and the odd beer, soon saw the time fly past. The final cherry on the cake was that Tim and company were heading back to Salisbury on the Sunday evening so even my transport was taken care of.

Having managed to safely navigate my way round nearly every corner of the country, a return visit to Botswana and the Kalahari Desert awaited and this entailed yet another trip down the Salisbury to Bulawayo road. This time I finished up driving, when my benefactor suggested I took the wheel while he caught up with some sleep, as he had started off well up country in the early hours. I obliged but couldn't get over the trust shown.

I had one more call to make to look up a family who were farming in the Motopos hills just south of the second city. This was also the area containing the final resting place of Cecil Rhodes which I had intended visiting anyway. Dave and Julia were in charge of farming the family acres and were yet another contact resulting from my days in the Copper

Belt. It was a cattle ranch and they had been dogged with the feeding habits of a local leopard. It had already killed two of his calves, so he was out to set a trap for the beast, but unfortunately by the time I left a couple of days later, the predator was still on the loose.

Sadly, animals were not the only problem posed to the farming community in this area with an ever-increasing militancy arising among the locals. This had pushed Dave and his wife into extreme measures of security, one being that he had armed them both with F.N. rifles and these were put to regular use on their private practise range. Only the passing of time would prove how founded those fears were.

Following a visit to the round topped, solid granite grave of the country's founder which is perched on a rock outcrop among the hills, I was given a lift back into Bulawayo. The trip on down to the border was straightforward, and once across it I was soon back in the real Africa as one imagines it, after my brief sortie into the European lifestyle in which Rhodesian society was run.

I was under no illusion that the route ahead across the Kalahari Desert would be easy, but first I had to move south to the capital Gaberones from where the trans-desert road began. The road south followed the railway line and for the three hundred mile journey the terrain was as expected, uninspiring flat bush and yellowed grass, with barely any signs of inhabitants or farming until nearing the capital itself.

Gaberones was a small newish town being developed to accommodate the government buildings of the country, which under its Bechuanaland name whilst being British, had been administered from Mafeking over the border in South Africa.

The last bit of civilisation before the Kalahari was the town of Lobatsi some forty miles further south and that was where the hunt for trans-desert traffic began. I drew a blank at some of the usual suspects, local government, police, etc., but was put in touch with a very entrepreneurial woman who had business interests in the town as well as Ghanzi, at the other side of the desert. It was most unusual to meet an African businesswomen and she was obviously very successful, and had a couple of vehicles making the crossing the following day and agreed to let me ride along with her.

In keeping with many such events in the past the timetable proved to be fluid, literally so in this case, as it was caused by one of the drivers having a bit too much of the local 'Pombe' fluid, resulting in a further

THE KALAHARI

twenty-four hour delay. However beggars can't be choosers and the prospect of reaching SWA in virtually one lift was worth any small rescheduling, so another evening sharing local hospitality was on the cards at the home of one of the crew.

Our convoy did eventually head out, at first through some small hills but quickly it became flat, flat, flat with the familiar sparse covering of bush and yellow grass interspersed with the occasional small acacia bush.

Approximately one hundred miles into the desert, one of the vehicles got a rear puncture and unbelievably neither carried a spare. The faulty tyre was despatched back to Lobatsi in one vehicle, while we struck camp for the night using bits of tarpaulin, rope and anything else deemed useful, and so passed away the clear, moonlit night, in the magic tranquillity only a desert location can provide.

The new day saw the surprisingly early arrival of the others. With everything back to normal we set off for what was to prove to be my longest journey of my whole trip, which would see the sun set and rise again before we reached our destination.

Progress became slower as we pushed deeper into the Kalahari and the sandy soil became looser, though it was still able to support a covering of bush and rough grass, so at least in the vegetation sense, the area was not in fact deserted. A further blow awaited us when the only fuel station turned out to be empty, however a detour off to a hunting camp did resolve that matter. On we plodded, coping with a couple of minor mechanical breakdowns, into the moonlit night and out of it again, with the dawning of another new day upon us before the distant outline of Ghanzi broke the horizon.

With four hundred miles of desert covered, a further two hundred lay ahead before reaching the relative civilisation of the South West African (SWA) town of Gobabis, situated near the western edge of the desert. My luck was in, as after a mere two day delay I secured a ride in a Land Rover. Despite being designed to cope with just this sort of loose sandy terrain, progress was still slow averaging twenty-five m.p.h. but at last the Kalahari was behind me.

I encountered no problem getting through the border controls and pushed on up to the five thousand five hundred foot high plateau on which the main town of Windhoek stands. The plateau forms a backbone down the central and southern regions of the country separating the desert and coastal areas.

Windhoek showed all the trappings of its former German occupants, with many fine Teutonic style buildings topped with their distinctive red roofs, a marked contrast to the modern flats and office blocks that could exist anywhere. One thing that couldn't exist anywhere was the local black population, as even more so than in Rhodesia, segregation was rife for this permit carrying majority, with separate park benches, post office counters, public transport and in some cases shops.

The German influence resulted from their occupation of the country from 1884 up until the end of World War 1 after which the League of Nations mandated administration to South Africa, where it was regarded as the fifth state of that country. Unfortunately, like so many of its neighbours, there was a strong anti-colonialist freedom movement SWAPO causing unrest within its boundaries.

One of the many contacts I had gathered throughout my trip was based in the coastal town of Walvis Bay and I travelled down there in the company of a chap who was in a hurry. Due to fuel shortages, an official fifty m.p.h. speed restriction applied throughout South and South West Africa, but we bombed along the tarred road and covered the two hundred and fifty miles in less than three hours.

I was made very welcome by Dave and Di. They showed me around the small town, and over the ensuing weekend we took a trip down the coast into the sandy Namibian Desert and Dave being a keen fisherman cast his rod into the Atlantic Ocean to see if he could bag dinner. Though nothing edible resulted from his efforts he did hook up a small shark which was duly returned to its rightful place and we just hoped it remembers our kind gesture should we ever meet again.

Movement on this southern coast line was very restricted due to its mineral wealth, in particular diamonds, and the restriction not only covered the coast but stretched inland up to one hundred miles in places, so our little fishing trip was as much as I saw before once more heading back to the town.

Walvis Bay was in a pretty remote part of the country and although fishing and processing the catch was its main business there were no local communities to draw on for labour. All the workers were from up country and in keeping with the apartheid rules had there own compounds where they lived, away from the European district. The town roads were constructed from a mix of salt and gravel which provided a sound hard surface but must have played havoc with any vehicle exposed to the area for any length of time.

THE KALAHARI

Before leaving I was kindly invited to attend a party being held by Di's mum back in Windhoek at the weekend which allowed me a couple of days to amble back taking in more of the country at my leisure.

Initially I moved up the coast, passing a large salt reclamation plant where seawater was pumped into vast shallow reservoirs. It was then left to evaporate under the strong sun and over an eighteen-month period transformed into unpurified salt crystals, a process I was later to encounter again much further up the Atlantic coast. From the coast I headed once more inland, away from the desert, towards the high central plateau. I made a diversion to look up another contact, this time however I knew the people concerned, as Beryl's neighbours Fred and Brigitta from Arusha had left and returned here to their native land and were running their family farm.

The farm in question was a massive thirty-five thousand acre ranch supporting cattle and Karakul sheep, a very lucrative strain whose lamb pelts were very sought after in the fashion industry. Game also ran wild and was hunted for food, not trophy reasons, with Kudu being particularly popular and featuring regularly on their dinner table. In addition to the ranching side of their business, the land also had deposits of amethyst that were being evaluated to see if they were sufficient in quantity and quality to justify a commercial enterprise. My only fear was that with the growing unrest in the country their move back home might not offer them the peaceful life they hoped for.

I was back in Windhoek for the party and was again made very welcome and invited to drop back on my return from my next excursion to the far north and over the border into Angola. To travel I needed permission to transit through the northern Bantustan an area designated for indigenous people. The long term view of the South African state was to set up a series of such self governing territories for the main tribal groups and this one, Ovamboland, had been earmarked to be among the first to be developed. Others such as Zululand in the south would follow. These small enclaves within the main country's boundaries would still be heavily dependent on their hosts, and the solution was a far cry from the majority rule independence movement that was ever growing in strength.

With permission granted I took to one of the few roads which headed north and was picked up by a very plucky elderly woman. She had lived in the northern area all her life and made it clear that she had no intention of going anywhere no matter what the future held for the country, showing characteristics of her 'voortrekker' ancestors who migrated north many years before.

One condition of the transit permit prohibited stopping in the Bantustan, however my lift dropped me some fifty miles from the Angolan border and left me no option other than to illegally move off on foot, but all was resolved later in the day and the border was reached without incident. Ovamboland had started with little signs of habitation but as I progressed north the vegetation changed from bush to grass with palm trees dotted over the landscape and homestead kraals became more frequent, the road however changed from tar to dirt.

Between lifts I had come across one village where a butter maker was in full swing, the latter being the precise movement involved in the production. The liquid had been poured into a large gourd which was encased in straw netting with a straw handle. This was suspended from a crude wooden frame comprising two fork ended stakes driven into the ground supporting a cross member. The suspended gourd and its contents were then swung repetitively back and forward by the seated operative, in time producing the somewhat rancid butter as an end product.

Having safely negotiated the Bantustan, it was now time to see what the nascent Angolan state over the border had on offer.

A butter maker in full swing.

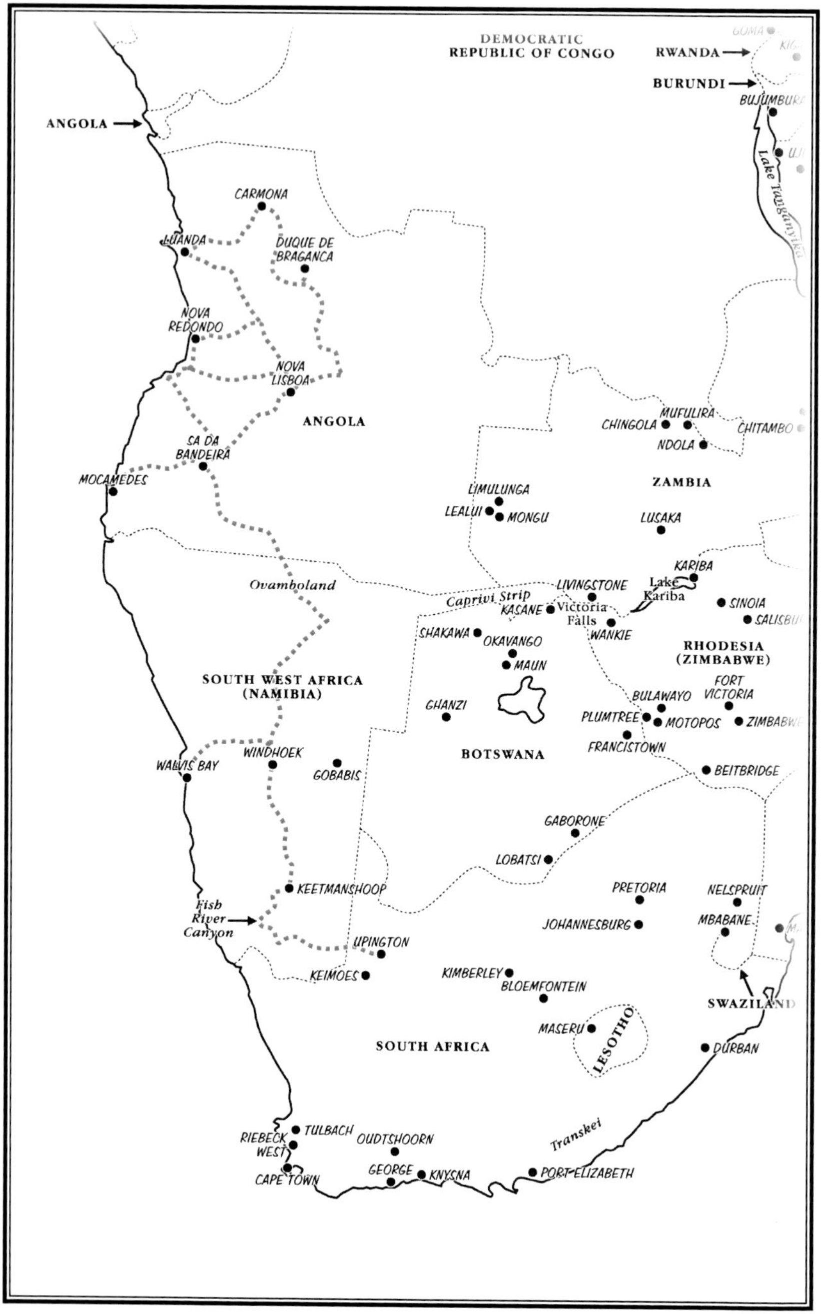
DEMOCRATIC REPUBLIC OF CONGO
RWANDA
BURUNDI
BUJUMBURA
Lake Tanganyika
ANGOLA
CARMONA
LUANDA
DUQUE DE BRAGANCA
NOVA REDONDO
NOVA LISBOA
ANGOLA
SA DA BANDEIRA
MOCAMEDES
CHINGOLA
MUFULIRA
CHITAMBO
NDOLA
ZAMBIA
LIMULUNGA
LEALUI
MONGU
LUSAKA
KARIBA
Lake Kariba
LIVINGSTONE
Ovamboland
Caprivi Strip
KASANE
Victoria Falls
WANKIE
SINOIA
SHAKAWA
OKAVANGO
MAUN
RHODESIA (ZIMBABWE)
SOUTH WEST AFRICA (NAMIBIA)
GHANZI
BULAWAYO
FORT VICTORIA
PLUMTREE
MOTOPOS
FRANCISTOWN
BOTSWANA
WALVIS BAY
WINDHOEK
GOBABIS
BEITBRIDGE
GABORONE
LOBATSI
KEETMANSHOOP
PRETORIA
NELSPRUIT
Fish River Canyon
JOHANNESBURG
MBABANE
UPINGTON
KEIMOES
KIMBERLEY
BLOEMFONTEIN
SWAZILAND
MASERU
LESOTHO
SOUTH AFRICA
DURBAN
Transkei
TULBACH
RIEBECK WEST
OUDTSHOORN
CAPE TOWN
GEORGE
KNYSNA
PORT ELIZABETH

CHAPTER 19

TOWARDS THE EQUATOR AGAIN

Entering Angola posed no problem and for the first two hundred and fifty miles the road followed much the same flat bush and grass countryside as I'd encountered on the southern side of the border. This took me through the tribal lands of the Cuanyama who dressed in much the same way as the rural Karamojong and Turkana tribes I had seen in and around Lake Rudolph in East Africa but these people were typical Bantu in features unlike their tall northern brothers.

Masai apart, the East Africans who still followed their tribal customs were living in the relatively remote wilds of their countries, these people however, were more in contact with the European influences. Despite this they had still maintained their dress traditions with the bare breasted women wearing leather skins around their rears with modesty aprons, and lots of bead and shell necklaces, metal bracelets and anklets. Hair was commonly shaven on the crown then plaited into pigtails adorned with bone decorations.

The kraals consisted of several round huts constructed from upright wooden poles with thatch roofing and a similar pole construction was used to create the circular perimeter fence.

My first encounter with an Angolan town was Sa da Bandeira situated at the southern tip of the mountains which follow the spine of

UNDER AN AFRICAN SUN

Local Cuanyama girls in Southern Angola.

the country north. There was a definite Latin feel to the town and no obvious segregation, society here was split more by economic factors than racial ones and my first impressions were that the Portuguese seemed to have lower social expectations than their white southern neighbours.

The recent change of government in Portugal had led to a tentative cease-fire on behalf of the various guerrilla groups but an undercurrent of unrest had replaced this, with each group jockeying for position, in readiness for imminent self-rule. Different parts of the country tied their allegiance to different factions who in turn often had outside backing, with the MPLA sharing communist ideals, the FNLA having American backing and UNITA being a more home grown party.

Before pushing north I took a detour down to the coast, exchanging the mountains for the bleak grey coloured earth through which a few rivers wove their paths to the coast supporting a slither of bush vegetation slicing across the otherwise dry countryside like a snake shaped oasis. One form of plant that could eke out an existence in this arid soil was the Welwitschia a ground-hugging shrub more common to the southern Namibian desert.

From the coast I retraced my steps back up the mountains and moved north to the country's second city Nova Lisboa, passing more signs of agriculture among them sisal, pineapples and sugar. I popped into a wine maker about which our trading standards people may well have had a view; not a single grape came near the production line, rather a mixture of pineapple, sugar and water fermented and filtered to create the Vinho Verde with some chemical additions required to change it to Vinho Tinto.

Moving on northwards I got the feeling that the Portuguese had never made the most of the agricultural potential of the country, preferring to take the role of traders and merchants and a couple of large scale projects I did come across were run by non-nationals, with an American running a large cattle ranch and in the same area an English chap in charge of a massive chicken farm. George the American invited me to see round the operation and we rounded off the tour down in one of the local bars where an eclectic mix of the community was gathered. Unfortunately a few of them had been there a little too long and a tense argumentative situation had developed which we kept well out of, however our attention was somewhat focused when one of the party produced a double barrel shotgun and started threatening all and sundry; time, we felt, to make a discreet exit.

The Duque de Braganca waterfall was also in this area, however so were some of the more militant followers of the FNLA, which posed a small problem, as despite hostilities having officially ceased a month earlier, sporadic attacks were still occurring. This problem was resolved when I met the district military governor who happened to have his sister staying and was due to make a visit to the falls and I was invited to join them. As he had arranged a small well armed guard to accompany them I felt in good hands and the visit was very rewarding. Though not on the scale of the majestic Victoria Falls the half-mile wide, horseshoe shaped wall of white crashing down some three hundred feet contrasted with the green surrounds to create quite a spectacle.

Released from my military bodyguard I moved further north to a point a mere five hundred miles south of the equator before about turning in the knowledge that from here on it was all south bound. The area around Carmona was the centre of the country's number one export, coffee, which grew amongst the forested hills. These forests were often on extremely steep slopes and with the addition of the damp weather, tending them became a seriously difficult operation. Even getting around the narrow mountain tracks of the coffee estates was often a heart in mouth experience. I found this out first hand when taken on a tour by a somewhat exuberant manager who didn't share the fear the awaiting sheer drop off the muddy track offered a misjudged manoeuvre.

The forest and coffee clad steep coast-bound mountain road eventually gave way to the hot lowlands as I made my way down to the capital city Luanda, a journey which until recently had only been undertaken in armed convoys.

Unlike Rhodesia, where I had many contacts and of course the language was no problem, Angola found me once again relying on my limited French which some of the Portuguese also spoke, but that didn't prevent communication. Even here I was often given shelter for the night, or directed to the local police station where an unlocked cell became my lodgings. When such options failed it was out beneath the stars as many a night had previously been spent.

Luanda was to prove the exception to this rule as Stuart the chicken farmer had arranged for me to meet his colleague Mike in the capital and he and his wife Jean took me under their control over the next few days. The city was a bit of a concrete jungle but the sea front was very pleasant with a long spit of land forming a sheltered area and the old seventeenth century Fort Sao Miguel in the older section overlooking the bay. It also has its 'snobs corner' on the cliffs overlooking the harbour and beaches, contrasting with the nearby shanty town.

The weekend saw us pairing up with some other friends and setting up camp on nearby Mussulo Island, which was famed for its magnificent tropical beaches. It was a very popular venue for water sports and a fantastic weekend of sailing, skiing and sunbathing in this idyllic location soon flashed by. One of the assembled crowd thought it would be a good idea if I could do an interview for the local rag and that sparked the idea that I should give a talk about my travels to another's school assembly. Having briefly recounted my experiences for the paper, it was pretty plain sailing to reiterate them for the school. I was quite surprised at how attentive the pupils were and, judging by the questions raised, how much they had taken in and I found the whole thing surprisingly enjoyable.

Another of the weekend crowd ran a holiday camp much further down the coast at Novo Redondo and I was soon winging my way with them back up to the central highland area before once more dropping down through more coffee plantations to the crashing Atlantic waves next to which their camp was situated.

Nearby were the Sumbe caves, a large grotto complex with fine examples of stalactites that added to the underground atmosphere along with the bats and the resultant dank foul smell. The main cave, which we reached after descending into the surrounding gorge, was over six hundred yards long and rose up to two hundred feet in places. Having picked our way by torchlight through the muck and slippery under foot conditions we reached the river which detours from the gorge outside, weaving its way underground for the next part of its journey. As we were returning towards the entrance I had my second encounter with a monitor lizard having previously come face to face with one of these three-foot giants out in open countryside in Tanzania. On that occasion I at least had the open terrain to aid my escape, here things were much more confined. Which of us was the most scared I didn't intend hanging about to establish, and had a sigh of relief when we were back out in the open air, only to be confronted with one of its pals a few feet away from the entrance. Fortunately it slithered away into the undergrowth and no further sightings occurred.

I was now eight hundred and fifty miles away from the southern border and had either one or three days of my visa left depending on one's interpretation of a month and needless to say mine was the latter. It was a matter of retracing my tracks once more up onto the higher ground, then down through the colourful southern lands of the Cuanyama. I reached the border, where no visa issues were raised, indeed the border guards seemed happy to have some company, and I finished up spending my final Angolan night as their guest.

Once safely over into SWA a further five hundred miles lay between me and a rendezvous with Mrs. Price and family at Windhoek but my movement ground to a halt, and by the day's end I had progressed the grand total of a few hundred yards from one border post to the other. This time it was the SWA guards who turned hosts. During the evening a couple of border patrols could be seen passing by as this was a SWAPO stronghold, and one of their leading sympathisers was known to be in the area.

As I couldn't stop over in Ovamboland I was pleasantly surprised when I was able to hitch a direct ride through to Windhoek and as the sunset around 7.30 pm we arrived after a long journey through the sparsely inhabited countryside, and the offer of a roof over my head was warmly welcomed.

Refreshed from the previous day's trek I looked up Leslie and her mum and with Christmas just round the corner arrangements were quickly put in place for me to join them to celebrate the day down at Dave and Di's in Walvis Bay.

A frantic spell of rushing around followed, sorting out the customary bout of Christmas shopping, and on Christmas Eve, we set off for the coast. By sharing the driving we made excellent progress and arrived at lunchtime, following our two hundred and fifty mile trip.

Being mid-summer, and at a low coastal location, the weather was far from the snow covered image we conjure up back in UK but it didn't deter us from having a thoroughly enjoyable celebration with the full turkey dinner and trimmings, all washed down with copious amounts of wine. What a great day.

My host's work commitments necessitated returning to Windhoek the following day and as on the way down the driving was shared and a similar good time was achieved. With only a few days of 1974 remaining my plan to reach South Africa by the end of it meant covering a further six hundred miles, and there was one detour I planned on the way, to see the Fish River Canyon.

TOWARDS THE EQUATOR AGAIN

After another round of fond farewells I raised my thumb and was fairly soon crossing the flat dry Karakul sheep rearing countryside down to Keetmanshoop, where the road to the canyon split from the main road south.

Having crashed out at the local train station I took to the road with very little success, however the railway followed the road, or visa versa, so I considered the option of a train journey. Although no passenger trains were due in, the station staff soon had me on my way as part of the next departing goods train. This took care of the next seventy-five miles of my journey, but dropped me five miles away from the canyon road, you win some and you lose some.

Having plodded on and endured the dry heat of the day I reached the road. A long, long time passed before a vehicle eventually appeared on the horizon, a Rhodesian registered Land Rover with a Belgian couple on board and so the final leg of this trek was covered in style. Sadly by the time we arrived at the canyon the sun was already pretty low, making photography nigh impossible, but as the like-minded couple had little regard for itineraries, a decision to camp out overnight was soon mutually agreed.

The Fish River Canyon.

By the time the full moon had replaced the dying light of the day in a cloudless sky we had a warm fire crackling away and a cowboy style meal being rustled up, then with the aid of a couple of make shift wind shields I settled down for another night beneath the stars, though the stony terrain would have been better suited to an Indian Fakir.

With the first light of day we were all up and ready to absorb the views over the world's second largest natural canyon which had been scooped out over a period of three hundred and fifty million years by the Fish River. As with the previous night's sun problem we had to wait a couple of hours before the gorge below us felt the warm ray's effects and offered itself up to its true stunning magnificence. The gigantic ravine runs for approximately one hundred miles, snaking its way through the arid, flat, surrounding plateau at a depth of eighteen hundred feet, and although the river flows in the late summer, for most of the year it is simply a series of narrow ponds.

We were able to access only some twelve miles of its total length but were all duly impressed, and when it turned out that they were also heading for the South African town of Upington, my day just got better and better.

We took a different route out, heading down the canyon to the hot springs at Ai Ais, followed by a rather uninteresting final two hundred and fifty miles through more flat dry lands, though the occasional sight of a quiver tree broke the monotony. These members of the Aloe family have a series of fibrous branches which the Bushmen used to hollow out to make quivers for their arrows. They also played host to some of the communal weaver nests though these birds had also adapted to the lack of trees by building their large nests on the telephone poles.

And so on the 29th of December I finally crossed into my twenty-second African country though it was a low key event much like moving from Scotland to England as South West Africa was deemed to be part of South Africa for border control reasons.

The six-month schedule Roger and I had set for the trans-continental journey had proved to be somewhat inadequate and with the vast swathe of South Africa still to explore my journey was by no means at an end yet.

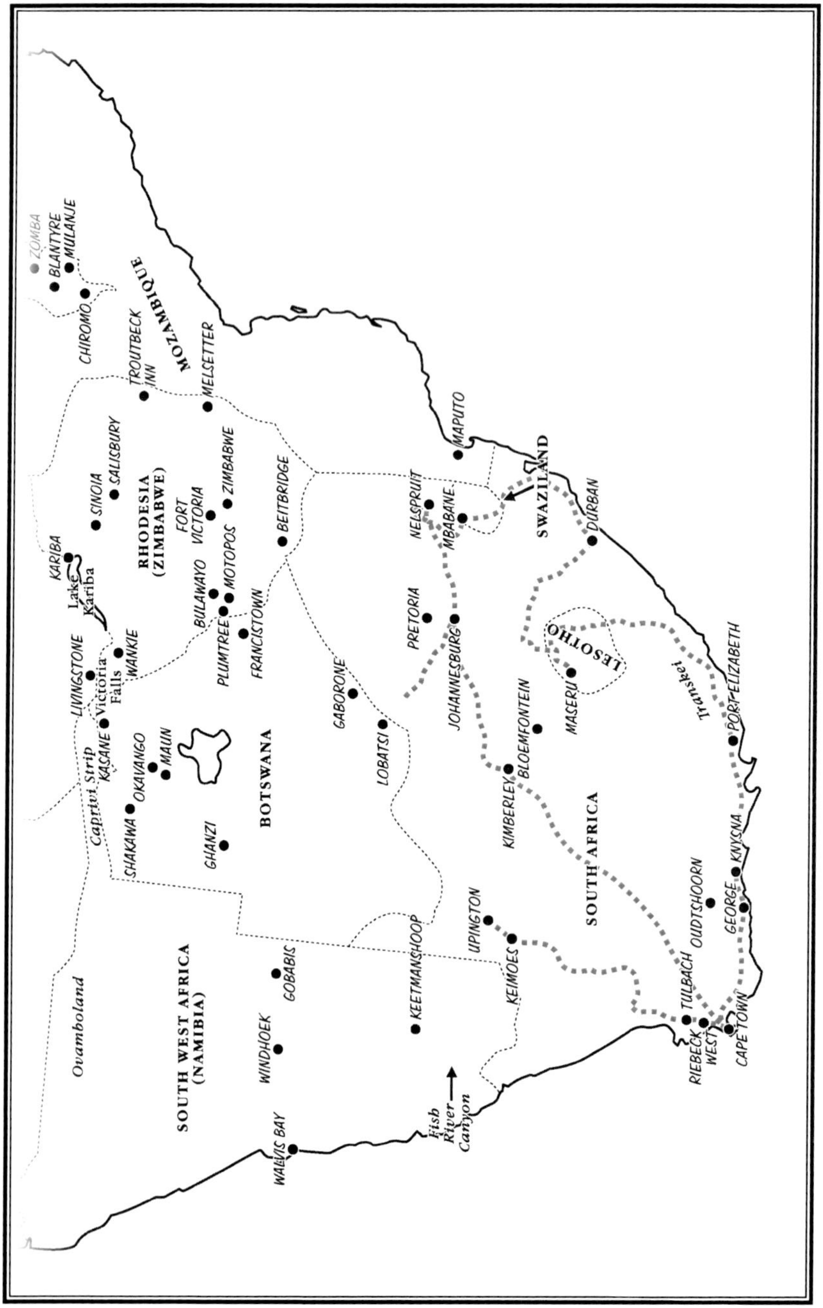

ZOMBA
BLANTYRE
MULANJE
CHIROMO
MOZAMBIQUE
TROUTBECK INN
MELSETTER
MAPUTO
SALISBURY
SINOIA
RHODESIA (ZIMBABWE)
FORT VICTORIA
ZIMBABWE
KARIBA
Lake Kariba
BULAWAYO
MOTOPOS
BEITBRIDGE
PLUMTREE
FRANCISTOWN
LIVINGSTONE
Victoria Falls
WANKIE
KASANE
Caprivi Strip
OKAVANGO
MAUN
SHAKAWA
GHANZI
BOTSWANA
GABORONE
LOBATSI
NELSPRUIT
MBABANE
SWAZILAND
DURBAN
PRETORIA
JOHANNESBURG
LESOTHO
MASERU
BLOEMFONTEIN
KIMBERLEY
Transkei
PORT ELIZABETH
SOUTH AFRICA
KNYSNA
GEORGE
OUDTSHOORN
UPINGTON
KEIMOES
TULBACH
RIEBECK WEST
CAPE TOWN
Ovamboland
SOUTH WEST AFRICA (NAMIBIA)
GOBABIS
WINDHOEK
KEETMANSHOOP
WALVIS BAY
Fish River Canyon

CHAPTER 20

SOUTH AFRICA AT LAST

I had spent my first night in South Africa in the small town of Keimoes on the banks of the Orange River, courtesy of the one-man local police station. With the distant hope of Cape Town on the horizon, I was up bright and early and in pole position at the end of the town. Nearby was an old water wheel which had once irrigated the surrounding fields but was now a monument to the past, with electricity rather than water providing the power as it aimlessly rotated, round and round, with no purpose other than its ornamental value.

The morning came and went but unfortunately the same could not be said for the traffic that simply never came at all, and prospects of any progress began to wane, however the sight of a pick-up truck looming on the horizon perked me up. Just how that moment was to influence the next few months of my life was to unfold when the driver pulled up bound for the Cape area and struck a pact, I look out for the police cameras and he would do his best to have us in the Cape by nightfall, five hundred miles down the flat semi-desert road ahead. We fairly sped through the mainly sheep rearing countryside where vast tracts of land are required to sustain the equally vast herds, many acres per head needed due to the poor grazing available.

True to his word, and without the unwelcome interference from the traffic cops, we reached the small town of Riebeck West having dropped off the mountains down to the Olifants River valley with its irrigated orchards and vineyards. It was well into the evening hours when we reached Alwyn's farm and I was invited to stay over, the start of a long association I was to have with the wine growing industry.

It was suggested that I should stay over for a couple of days and see a bit more of the area and as part of his farming activities involved a vineyard he had some contacts with the local co-operative. With the harvest just round the corner the possibility of short term work was mentioned and as it had always been my intention to work here to raise some funds for whatever my next move was to be, this prospect seemed well worthy of investigation.

The day, indeed the year end soon flew by as I accompanied him on his rounds of the farm, a mixture of both livestock and arable, wheat being the other major crop assigned to his acreage, and so in the most civilised and sober state, I saw out the old and welcomed in the new 1975 in the comfort of the family farm house with the most amazing plumped up down filled pillows I have ever rested my head on.

The prospect of even short term work raised the issue of work permits etc. and not wishing to fall foul of the authorities at the first hurdle, I took advantage of an offer of a lift into Cape Town to get the ball rolling and also to look up the uncle of an old friend from back in Edinburgh.

On the legal side the options were to simply apply, and hopefully get, a temporary work permit, though this was not guaranteed, or apply for permanent residency. The latter involved masses of red tape and a mountain of paperwork and could take six months to be processed but had the advantage of virtually guaranteeing legality until the final decision was reached, and so I gathered the necessary documents together and got the process underway, and in doing so cleared the way for the all important work permit.

Jim's uncle Dave was then tracked down and a very warm welcome awaited me at their Tamboerskloof home in the suburbs that was to become my weekend lodgings throughout my stay in the beautiful Cape region.

Back at the farm I was introduced to the manager of the wine co-op through which Alwyn processed his grapes and my first spell of gainful employment was arranged to commence later in the month when the harvest started, and with the requisite documentation in place, I returned to explore the attractions of the big city.

Dave and Gertrude took me on a couple of sight-seeing trips around and about the scenic peninsula and I ventured up onto Table Mountain, the magnificent backdrop to the city. Though I had set out in good conditions the 'table cloth' descended over the mountain, and my reasonable sense of direction was severely called into play before I found my way back to the cable car and out once more into the clear blue skies which everywhere but the mountain top had been enjoying, a phenomenon that can often occur. At least I had spent a couple of hours before the mist rolled in, gaining a great perspective of the city and the surrounding mountains and bays, including the enforced abode of Nelson Mandela, Robben Island.

One annual event that was taking place was the setting up of the Government's summer home in the city. The complete government along with many embassies and peripheral operations move from the capital Pretoria down to the Cape in early January returning six months later. The mass exodus is largely undertaken by train which had been christened by the locals 'the zoo train', an indication of the high regard in which politicians were generally held.

I made enquiries about the folk music scene in the city and was put in touch with George who ran a music shop, and also did quite a bit of entertaining. The upshot of this chance encounter saw me joining forces with him for his cabaret spot at a very popular bistro, The Spanish Gardens, something that was to become a regular Saturday spot over the ensuing couple of months.

Work at the wine cellar started with me being given an overview of the operation and it was then all hands to the pump to get everything ready for the first deliveries of grapes that commenced towards the end of January and ran through until the end of March, peaking at a daily rate of eight hundred tons.

The deliveries were weighed, stripped from their stalks, crushed then processed through a centrifuge system where the juice was separated from the skin and flesh. A complex network of pipes, pumps and storage vessels then saw it moved into large fermentation tanks before further filtration saw the final product ready for the market. The bulk of the output from this co-op went to merchants for blending though a small amount was bottled on site mainly for the benefit of the co-op members.

Needless to say I was able to sample the results of our labour, purely for professional reasons of course, to ensure the quality was being maintained. Nothing was wasted and whilst only the first pressings went into making the wine which bore the grape's name, additional pressings took place with the initial resultant juices going into blended wines and the final pressings plus the residue being processed through a still, to produce a highly controlled liquor with a ninety percent alcohol level.

A few days into the season I was assigned to centrifuge duties which was one of the first and last sequences in the production process, and though there were three such machines in the cellar, there were never more than two fully working, turning this into a round the clock operation, and a shift pattern emerged. As I had no other commitments and was staying on site, I had the afternoon shift starting at 2.00 pm and finishing when the entire product had been processed. This soon settled into a regular seventeen-hour pattern with me handing over to the others at 7.00 am, crashing out, and then starting the cycle all over again. Despite the long hours, time simply flew by and our small crew were never without one incident or another to contend with. Burst pipes seemed to be a favourite, and the complex network, connecting the various tanks to machines, required meticulous oversight to ensure the valuable liquid found its way to the correct destination, and wasn't simply spewed out onto the cellar floor.

Helping out were a number of contracted black Africans who came in from the various homelands on strict rules, whereby their movements were limited to the area of employment and a trip into Cape Town for them was not on the cards. They all received wages and rations, along with accommodation, thus their everyday needs were met but the second class status they were tagged with was obviously never going to continue *ad infinitum*. With all the surrounding countries already well on the way to majority rule it could only be a matter of time before a more equitable society replaced the current minority rule.

The Cape area was designated 'coloured', a classification which itself had several sub-divisions from Asian communities to mixed race. The latter in itself was a vast mix of white and black, white and coloured. etc., too numerous to cover all the possible options, but 'coloured' they were in the eyes of the apartheid government. They were often artisans and tended to enjoy a status somewhat above the indigenous black people but once out of the Cape region, they too were prone to restrictions.

SOUTH AFRICA AT LAST

Alwyn, like most of the farmers in the area, was an Afrikaner and had strong ties to the Dutch Reform Church which still held a lot of sway in the community, and any social occasion on a Saturday had to be concluded by midnight on the dot, no revelries allowed on the Sabbath. One offshoot of this was that no work occurred on the Sabbath either and so as soon as I had finished on a Saturday morning it was off into Cape Town, a few hours sleep, then cabaret time with George at the bistro, where a circle of regulars built up and long standing friendships developed. By taking different routes back and forward I was able to see most of the beautiful Cape countryside with its high mountains, fertile valleys and fine Dutch style architecture which was shown to its full effect in many of the older established towns like Tulbagh.

Dutch style architecture at Tulbagh.

So I passed the first couple of months in the Cape, then, once the fruit dried up and the co-op's duties were concluded for another year, I made moves to follow the coastal route in the direction of Durban.

The road through to George and Knysna covered the Garden Route, a very scenic area with patches of indigenous forest and fine seascapes of the white rollers piling in from the Indian Ocean. On the way I detoured inland towards Oudtshoorn visiting the Cango caves, another fine example of underground limestone formations, with stalactites and stalagmites and many other features open to individual interpretation. Unfortunately more than a touch of commercialism had crept in with concrete paths and stairways and even a Son et Lumiere display at one point. Despite all that it was worth the visit and as it lay near to one of the large ostrich farms, I was able to combine two very different visits in one area.

The farm was going through a renaissance having seen a recent resurgence in demand for the feathers that were the main source of income. The animals were pruned for some fifteen years then culled but even then an income stream was generated, with the skin being used for leather products, the meat for steaks and biltong, bones for fertiliser and the feet for ornamental lamp stands, the latter being quite revolting but there's no accounting for some people's taste. We were also given a display of ostrich riding, a most ungainly race with the jockeys hanging on for dear life. It was alleged that ostrich eggs could withstand a pressure of two hundred and fifty pounds laid on their side and five hundred pounds if standing on their end, but I have no idea how much credence should be attached to this bit of trivia.

I made several trips in different directions around the Garden Route, taking in the fine mountains and coastal views coupled with farms nestling in the many green river valleys winding down to the sea. Having well and truly explored the area, I then pushed on along the coast to the town of Port Elizabeth, where my next session of gainful employment was to occur.

Initially the folk scene had been my port of call and through this connection, not unlike Cape Town, an evening job singing in one of the busier pubs took care of my evenings. One particular crowd of Scots became regulars while they were docked in the harbour and I was invited on board to join them for lunch. During the visit I was played a tape of an up-and-coming Scot who's uncle was part of the crew, the lad concerned went on to do quite well for himself being none other than Billy Connolly.

Through one of the lads in the folk club, I got fixed up with a temporary day job doing cost analysis at the Firestone tyre factory, one of the many car related firms operating in South Africa. Assembly of foreign vehicles was rife, though an ever increasing importance was being placed on self sufficiency, as the long term future of the economy could not rely on tie ups with potentially unwilling trading partners.

With the temporary work at an end, I moved on further along the coast into the Ciskei, another of the homelands being developed with an element of self-governance, which along with its neighbouring Transkei, was home to the Xhosa people. Once again various detours took me up, over and around the area sandwiched between the coast and the backdrop of the Drakensberg Mountains. On this part of my travels it was once more the Africa of round mud huts and thatched roofs, though many of the dwellings were adorned with white geometric patterns, brightening up the otherwise dull brown constructions.

Whilst walking through one remote area I came face to face with a young man covered from head to toe in white, wearing only a hessian loincloth and armed with a stick. I was later to find out that this was part of the Umkhwetha circumcision ritual still practised by some sectors of the Xhosa tribe. Another ritual, not now so widespread, involved cutting off the last joint of the small finger to ward off illness, bad enough but when the resultant wound was bandaged in cow dung and leaves, one wonders how any of them lived to ward off any illness at all.

Before venturing into Durban I headed inland to the independent mountain kingdom of Lesotho, one of two such land locked countries which lie within South Africa, the other, which I was to visit later, being Swaziland, though this did share a section of its border with Mozambique.

Having left the rather over grazed landscape of the Transkei behind and travelled through flattish cattle country, I reached the Sani Pass, the southern entry point up to the kingdom. The South African control point was at the foot of the pass while the Lesotho one was at the top, the bit in between seemed to be no man's land and the dirt road, a term I use loosely, appeared to bear this out. Only 4WD vehicles were allowed to use it and the surface left much to be desired as it snaked its way up to 10,000 feet.

The small country is largely covered by the vast complex of bare mountains and valleys and with few roads, indigenous travel was mainly by horse or donkey. Temperatures understandably could get on the chilly side, and the blanket clad Basotho people built their thatch roofed round homes from the readily available stone found in the riverbeds. The unusual sight of chimneys adorn many of the homes, which were somewhat more substantial than those built by their plains living brothers below.

Sturdy stone built home high up in remote Lesotho.

On reaching the northern outer rim of the mountains I had another clammy hands descent through a long series of hairpins before dropping to the flat countryside below. Here I crossed over the Caledon River back to SA and wound my way down through orchards, then cattle country, to the city of Durban.

As if like a broken record, the folk scene was once again to prove a great connection as I had been invited to stay with a group I had become acquainted with in Port Elizabeth, and so found my way out to the salubrious suburb of Cowies Hill, the home of the most hospitable Scott family.

There were several issues I had to sort out, mainly hassles over my permanent residency which had got bogged down in bureaucracy with some of the documents going astray. I was also aware that some of my funds had been acquired on a cash basis, and with strict currency controls in place, I investigated alternatives in the form of Krugerrands, and after some discreet enquiries I managed to secure a direct line of purchase.

Although I had been very grateful to get the previous couple of short-term jobs, I really wanted to secure something more permanent and made several fruitless journeys into the city following up potential leads. On one such hitch a very well spoken German chap, who ran the local branch of a construction company, picked me up.

Witch construction had been started in Johannesburg by an English chap called Cliff, and it specialised in creating home extensions using a hardwood modular form of construction with lots of glass, akin to an up market conservatory. The operation had recently been expanded to Durban and in order to drum up some business a stand had been booked at the forthcoming Ideal Homes Exhibition, however manpower was thin on the ground. Though not the long term opportunity I was seeking, I was offered the chance to help out on the stand for the ten day duration of the show, and after a crash course about the product I was engaging the Durban public in the delights of being the proud owner of a 'Witch Room'.

My knowledge, or more precisely my lack of it, came to the fore when asked by one interested party if it could be built with a pitch roof. Sadly pitch was not a term I had come across and went off rambling about the special long lasting impregnated material we used on our flat roofs and understandably was met with a polite blank look. The gent in question returned later and spoke to Eric, one of the construction team who had arrived on the stand, and having firstly put the customer on the right track he proceeded to do the same to me, after which I at least knew the difference between a flat and a pointed roof, and wouldn't be looking quite so stupid next time round.

The show was a great success and our stand even won the Gold award, much down to the labours of Dave the company's design boffin. This called for a small celebration which would normally have been a simple matter of popping into a restaurant, however Wolf in his forward thinking manner had employed a tall striking young lady as his very efficient secretary, the only problem was that Angela was black. Because of this she would not have been allowed to join us due to the rules of the segregated society, so instead it was all back to his house where a couple of celebratory bottles of champagne were dispatched.

With the show over, Wolf asked if I would like to accompany him following up some of the leads I had generated, and with little else to occupy my time I agreed, and was soon lending a hopefully helpful hand with the tasks of measuring up and calculating prices. Several successful calls later Wolf suggested that I should take the lead roll and only then did I realise how much I didn't know. A very sharp learning curve followed with the help of all the other members of staff and the outcome of it all saw me spending the next two years of my life as a 'Witch Room' sales consultant.

Full time employment required a larger wardrobe than I had become accustomed to over the previous three and a half years and with that taken care of, and lodgings sorted out, I settled into the job at hand. I had no sooner started to get to grips with things when my application for permanent residency was refused, however after confirming my new found employment situation, backed up with some self-penned character references, that bomb shell was rectified, and the Witch machine was soon in overdrive.

The whole construction industry closed for a three-week break over Christmas and I decided to use the time seeing parts of the country as yet unexplored and lost no time getting back into traveller mode as soon as the holiday arrived.

My new found wealth had been partly blown on a set of wheels, an Apache, a South African special based on the Austin 1100 but with the addition of a boot, and I was soon heading through the sugar plantations to the north of Durban, crossing Zululand and winding my way up into Swaziland.

Though there was no tribal conflict here the schism between old and new cultures was apparent. The traditional folk still wore their loincloths and were adorned with animal manes and tails, worn as headgear and armlets. A variation of this male dress saw colourful, mainly orange, printed cloth replacing skin for the loincloth with a matching toga, all accompanied by their arms of battle, spears, shields and sticks. Ladies also sported colourful togas over their hide skirts and as throughout Africa, beads were a popular form of neck jewellery and were often also fashioned into a square amulet. The younger element on the other hand had endorsed the European dress of their neighbours.

The dress sense was not the only outside influence they had adopted. Swaziland, despite its king still embracing the traditional way of life, had seen the potential financial benefits of having a casino. While this was firmly aimed at attracting the South Africans, where gambling, other than on horses, was banned, many local inhabitants had sadly fallen under its addictive spell. Another big attraction to their neighbours was their open society, where mingling with the natives was allowed, and the ladies of the night took full advantage of that state of affairs.

The countryside was a scenic mixture with the central agricultural basin surrounded by forest-clad mountains but by no means as high or imposing as those of its land locked partner Lesotho. Having woven my way to the western border I was once more back in SA and headed north to the very beautiful Eastern Highlands region around Nelspruit. The Longton pass over Mt Anderson was particularly breathtaking with stunning views over the forested hills and valleys dropping away to the Sabie River, Kruger Park and the distant flat lands of Mozambique.

By contrast the drive up to Johannesburg was less interesting though the rains had at least given a pleasing green cover to the flat maize growing surroundings. Once into the metropolis I contacted Cliff where a Christmas invitation had been extended and a luxurious couple of days followed.

The trappings of Cliff's success with the Witch brand were evident in the driveway, where a Rolls Royce Silver Shadow took pride of place, one of only a handful in SA, and a means of transport that I was to enjoy the luxury of over my brief stay. I was given a quick tour of the city, which was enhanced by climbing the Strijdom (Telkom) tower which gave a bird's eye view, but I'm afraid the concrete jungle below didn't impress me.

Cliff's African maid Anna was off for the Christmas break and he had arranged to take her back to her rural home out near the Botswana border and I went along for the ride. The road was flat and deteriorated as we progressed further west, but the Rolls ironed out the bumps and the reception on arrival at her village was one to behold. The chance of the average South African catching a glimpse of one of these majestic motors was rare enough, but seeing one in the bundu was a real one off. Everyone turned out to inspect the massive metal carriage in which she had been transported from door to door and I can only imagine that her credibility status within the village would have been given a substantial boost.

As with the previous couple of years the warm sunny weather made appreciating Christmas day a bit more difficult, however appreciating the fine fare was not a problem and a most enjoyable time was had by all. Another of Cliff's trappings of success was a TV. These had only recently been introduced to SA, and it was a common sight to see crowds assembled around the TV shop windows soaking up this new entertainment media, though the local schedule didn't quite match up to a typical Christmas evening Morecambe and Wise special.

The next leg of my journey was a mammoth eight hundred and fifty mile trip down to Cape Town and after an early start I made good progress over the flat rather uninspiring landscape. I broke my journey some three hundred miles down the road at Kimberley, the home of the 'Big Hole' which resulted from the open cast diamond mining that took place there between 1871 and 1914. Having duly peered over the edge and inspected the remnants, it was back to the monotonously straight south bound road and having covered half the distance I called it a day.

The second half of the trip crossed the semi-desert Karroo region before I eventually started to rise into the first foothills of the glorious mountainous Cape region and all its attendant vine clad valleys where I somehow felt at home, almost exactly one year after first encountering it.

So another New Year was shown the way in, spent down at my old haunt, The Spanish Gardens, with George and the old crowd and it seemed as if I'd never been away. Having the car, I was able to once more tour round the beautiful wine-growing valleys and further investigate the peninsula, which confirmed my opinion that this really was the gem of this vast country. Whilst I had warmed to my hometown of Durban it was no match for the Cape.

All too soon it was time to head home, and I broke the long journey at Port Elizabeth where another round of reunions saw me back at another old haunt, the Stage Door for a typically boisterous Saturday night, before the final push on to Durban, completed my two thousand mile round trip.

Throughout my two year stay in Durban the music scene was always a large part of my social life, regularly attending the folk club and becoming great friends with a professional group The Silver Creek Mountain Band, who had a regular spot at one of the top hotels. Work commitments allowing, I could normally be found in their company and enjoyed an almost fifth man status with them, often thrashing out many a folk classic with their incredible multi-instrumental musical backing lifting the roof off.

Having settled back into a working routine, an opportunity arose for me to be able to conjure up a visit from my family as adjoining my accommodation there was a self contained flat and I was able to secure the use of it and so in the summer of 1976 a reunion/introduction was arranged as along with my mother, sister and her husband I was introduced to my new nephews. I had received the news that I was an uncle whilst in Zambia and Kieran's arrival had been quickly followed by that of his brother Neil, still a babe in arms at the time of their visit. Obviously having nearly five years of tales and news to exchange and arranging sight-seeing trips made the short visit flash by in no time and all too soon they were on their way back home which for my mother who had never flown anywhere in her life was the second leg of her maiden experience.

Unfortunately, as time progressed and the political situation over the border in Rhodesia deteriorated, life in SA also became more difficult. Selling the 'Witch' product was not a problem, however arranging finance was, and we started to see more sales aborted due to bonds (mortgages) not coming to fruition.

I had never gone to South Africa to settle, indeed it was just stage one of my proposed world trip, but having now been away for five and a half years, I decided to return to UK before planning any onward travel. Not wishing to cause any undue hassles I gave as much advance warning as possible to my Witch colleagues and after a series of farewell parties with the many friends I had been lucky enough to meet, I found myself once more going through tearful goodbyes at an airport, but this time it was me who was boarding the homeward bound plane.